Complementarian Spirituality

WEST Theological Monograph Series

Wales Evangelical School of Theology (WEST) has produced a stream of successful PhD candidates over the years, whose work has consistently challenged the boundaries of traditional understanding in both systematic and biblical theology. Now, for the first time, this series makes significant examples of this ground-breaking research accessible to a wider readership.

Complementarian Spirituality

Reformed Women and Union with Christ

NATALIE BRAND

WIPF & STOCK · Eugene, Oregon

COMPLEMENTARIAN SPIRITUALITY
Reformed Women and Union with Christ

WEST Theological Monograph Series

Copyright © 2013 Natalie Brand. All rights reserved. Except for brief quotations in critical publications or reviews, no part of this book may be reproduced in any manner without prior written permission from the publisher. Write: Permissions, Wipf and Stock Publishers, 199 W. 8th Ave., Suite 3, Eugene, OR 97401.

Wipf & Stock
An imprint of Wipf and Stock Publishers
199 W. 8th Ave., Suite 3
Eugene, OR 97401

www.wipfandstock.com

ISBN 13: 978-1-62564-000-0

Manufactured in the U.S.A.

*For my husband Thomas,
who loves, nourishes, and sanctifies, like Christ*

Contents

Abbreviations / ix
Acknowledgments / xi
Foreword / xiii

1 **Introduction / 1**
　　Aims
　　Where We Are Heading
　　Contemporary Spirituality
　　Reformed Spirituality/Spiritualities

2 **Union with Christ: A Reformed Legacy / 32**
　　A Historical Method
　　Terminology
　　Pre-Reformation Influence: Incarnation and Theōsis
　　The Reformation
　　The Beginnings of Reformed Orthodoxy
　　Puritans
　　A Downgrade
　　Twentieth Century to the Present
　　Conclusion

3 **Possessing Christ: Union with Christ in Contemporary Reformed Thought / 67**
　　Introducing Union with Christ in Scripture
　　Method
　　Crucial Theological Suppositions
　　Union with Christ and Conversion
　　The Nature of Union with Christ
　　Communion: The Fruit of Union
　　Ecclesiastical Significances
　　Conclusion

4   **Jesus Christ the Bridegroom / 90**
    Methodology
    A Feminine Reformed Theological Understanding
        and Expression of Union with Christ
    Conclusion

5   **The Church the Bride of Christ / 110**
    The Covenant Bride in Scripture
    The Corporate Imperative
    The Bride's Submission to Her Loving Husband
    The Bride's Loving Respect for Her Husband
    The Bride's Purity
    The Eucharistic Union of the Bride and Groom by the Spirit
    Conclusion

6   **Women in the Reformed Tradition / 143**
    Where We Are Heading: Spirituality and Pastoral Theology
    Women in the Reformed Tradition: Self-critical Observations
    A Ministerial Use of the Reformed Female Community
    Pastoral Implications of a Reformed Feminine Spirituality
        of Marital Union
    Conclusion

7   **A Reformed Feminine Spirituality / 169**
    A Reformed Feminine Contribution
    A Sample of Contemporary Characteristics
    Conclusion

Bibliography / 197

Abbreviations

ALH	*American Literary History*
CD	*Karl Barth's Church Dogmatics*
CH	*Church History*
CTQ	*Concordia Theological Quarterly*
JAAR	*Journal of the American Academy of Religion*
JETS	*Journal of the Evangelical Theological Society*
JRE	*Journal of Religious Ethics*
JR	*Journal of Religion*
NDCEPT	*New Dictionary of Christian Ethics and Pastoral Theology*, edited by David J. Atkinson and David H. Field (Downers Grove, IL: InterVarsity, 1995)
NDT	*New Dictionary of Theology*, edited by Sinclair B. Ferguson and David F. Wright (Downers Grove, IL: InterVarsity, 1998)
NIBC	New International Biblical Commentary
NPNF[1]	*Nicene and Post-Nicene Fathers*, series 1, edited by Philip Schaff, 14 vols. (New York: Christian Literature Co., 1886–90)
NWDCS	*The New Westminster Dictionary of Christian Spirituality*, edited by Philip Sheldrake (Louisville: Westminster John Knox, 2005)
RAR	*Reformation and Revival*
RRelRes	*Review of Religious Research*
RO	Reformed Orthodoxy
TynBul	*Tyndale Bulletin*

Abbreviations

NICNT	The New International Commentary on the New Testament
TNTC	Tyndale New Testament Commentaries
TSCJ	*The Sixteenth Century Journal*
WCF	Westminster Confession of Faith
WDCS	*Westminster Dictionary of Christian Spirituality*, edited by Gordon S. Wakefield (Philadelphia: Westminster, 1983)
WLC	Westminster Larger Catechism
WSC	Westminster Shorter Catechism
WTJ	*Westminster Theological Journal*

Acknowledgments

I WOULD FIRST LIKE to give my profound thanks to my parents, Peter and Hazel Tunbridge, who lovingly and most generously supported me throughout my theological study. Their partnership in this gospel work has been self-sacrificial and a great gift to me.

I am indebted to my doctoral supervisor, Dr. D. Eryl Davies, who initially encouraged me to undertake my research and who has guided, pruned, and inspired me throughout it. I am grateful for his experience in the pastoral ministry and for bearing patiently with my idealistic ways and pastoral naivety. Thanks goes to Dr. Robert Letham, who has helped me grasp a little more of our Great Trinity and kindly provided a foreword. In addition, my appreciation goes to Rev. Dr. David Cornick, who was a gracious and stimulating examiner and who has kindly reviewed this work for publication.

Lastly, I owe my deepest gratitude to my husband, Thomas, who supported me throughout my doctoral study and modeled Christ in his patience. It is a privilege to display this glorious doctrine in my covenant with you. Like the dear church, I am undeserving, thankful, and joyful in this union.

Natalie Brand
Soli Deo Gloria

Foreword

I KNOW OF NO book quite like this. In its overall scope, Dr. Brand covers ground rarely, if ever, traversed before. She investigates the doctrine of union with Christ and its implications for Reformed feminine spirituality, and does so from a position that heartily respects the text of Scripture and the tradition of interpretation within which she works.

Dr. Brand's grasp of the doctrine of union with Christ in Reformed thought is thorough. She explores the strong Trinitarian focus of Reformed spirituality and its pneumatic-christological construction of the *unio mystica*. A strong point in this argument is her awareness of the patristic background to classic Reformed thought on these matters, particularly seen in her treatment of *theōsis* in Athanasius, Cyril, and others, and the current debates on its impact on Luther and Calvin. She is fully aware of the range of discussion on spirituality in Reformed theology.

The icing on the cake is Dr. Brand's treatment of feminine spirituality from a Reformed complementarian perspective. This is where the groundbreaking nature of her work is particularly evident. Feminine spirituality is an area extensively developed by feminists of various kinds. Many of these have dismissed much of the Christian tradition, including the biblical text, as incorrigibly patriarchal. Consequently they frequently employ a hermeneutic of imaginative reconstrual. On the other hand, conservative Reformed scholars, and the churches they represent, have largely ignored the matter, despite its being a pressing question in today's postmodern culture. In contrast, Dr. Brand presents a highly effective blend of doctrinal theology and spirituality that is biblical, contemporary, historical, and pastoral. She relates her claims to a range of issues from a feminine perspective, issues largely neglected in Reformed churches, relating to church life, pastoral concerns, and involvement in the family and the public arena.

Foreword

This is not a book of interest only to women. The argument it presents—biblical, historical, theological, pastoral—should be read widely. A work of major academic integrity, it will also have far-reaching impact on a wider stage.

Robert Letham, PhD
Senior Lecturer in Systematic and Historical Theology
Wales Evangelical School of Theology

1

Introduction

It has been said that contributions on Reformed spirituality "are as rare as hen's teeth."[1] In a similar tone, Reformed theologian Joel Beeke laments a dearth in Reformed spirituality: "we confront the problem of dry Reformed orthodoxy, which has correct doctrinal teaching but lacks emphasis on vibrant, godly living. The result is that people bow before the doctrine of God without a vital, spiritual union with the God of doctrine."[2] Conservative theologian J. I. Packer also appeals for further work in the subject of spirituality.[3] In noting the countless number of Evangelical works on Christian living lining the shelves of Christian bookshops, it is probable that Cornick and Beeke are calling for contributions that are distinctively *Reformed* as well as pastorally effective, that is, material grounded in the theological and spiritual legacy of the Reformed tradition throughout the centuries, undiluted by the individualism and conversionism of Evangelical spirituality.

It seems, therefore, that the Reformed tradition has some work to do; at a time when spirituality is high on the agenda of today's popular culture, from "Hollywood to politics,"[4] the Reformed tradition should not fail to respond in line with its rich spiritual heritage. Therefore, there remains a need to examine contemporary Reformed spirituality and its unique theological contribution to spiritual formation; to test whether it is truly effective to Reformed believers under its wing as they seek to know, glorify, and enjoy

---

1. Cornick, *Letting God*, 11.
2. Beeke, *Puritan*, viii.
3. Packer, "Evangelical Foundations."
4. Stetzer, *Postmodern*, 137.

the triune God in contemporary life, and to contribute new articulations accordingly.

As we unpack this book's central features by highlighting our aims, we will also consider the structure of the work and introduce the terms basic to this discussion. This will give the reader necessary background for our later exploration into a complementarian spirituality. In this chapter we will also look briefly at the contemporary movement in spirituality, its impact on Christian and Evangelical spirituality, and attempt to characterize Reformed Spirituality in its contemporary mode.

AIMS

This work is an exploration into an approach to Reformed spirituality that is anchored in the believer's union with Christ. We will achieve this by investigating the posture and theological nature of the doctrine of "union with Christ" in the Reformed tradition, then presenting a particularly *feminine* articulation of its significance and relevance for a contemporary Reformed spirituality, in both corporate and personal spiritual formation.

The need for the subject of spirituality to be addressed is evident in the declaration of a "crisis" time in Evangelical spirituality, wherein some forms have been labeled "modern Gnosticism."[5] Pentecostalism and general Evangelical spirituality have been characterized, together with contemporary American religion as a whole, as "inward, and deeply distrustful of institutions, mediated grace, the intellect, theology, creeds, and the demand to look outside of oneself for salvation."[6] This of course can be devastating to the spiritual lives of the Reformed since many possess an Evangelical expression of spirituality, for it is vital to acknowledge cross-fertilization between traditions and denominations. This cross-fertilization, which has seemingly contributed to the weak contemporary representation of Reformed spirituality, is exemplified in the noticeable influence of Evangelical individualism upon Reformed spirituality. Howard Hageman comments on this in his affirmation for a renewal in American corporate worship in line with Calvinistic spirituality.[7]

This unfortunate shaping of Reformed modes of worship by unbiblical or *extra*-biblical Evangelical ideals proves the dynamic nature of spirituality in culture. Thus, the study of spirituality cannot be subject to a

5. Peterson, *Spirituality*, 4; Horton, *Face*, 22.
6. Horton, *Face*, 22.
7. Hageman, "Reformed."

Introduction

denominational vacuum or one specific context of historical Christendom. Yet some delineation of a contemporary biblical spirituality is paramount for the continuing life of the Reformed tradition specifically and Protestant churches in general.

Similar to the above assertions that the subject of Reformed spirituality has undergone neglect in scholarly theology and church life, it is held by some that the doctrine of union with Christ, though labeled as "most important" and "most profound," has also suffered in this manner.[8] Tudur Jones hails union with Christ as "an integral stage" in the order of salvation. He writes, "it is therefore all the more surprising that while justification and sanctification have had their share of theological consideration there has been a deep and prolonged silence about union with Christ."[9] This is the case in both popular and academic Reformed and conservative Evangelical works on the Christian life, demonstrated in the author's undertaking of a literature review.[10] At this point one might interject that the *unio mystica*'s usual treatment as a soteriological category in Reformed theology might have restricted the doctrine from any wider application in spirituality. Indeed, this disregard might be owing to the brevity of Protestant spiritual writings, which Don Carson contrasts to Catholicism's reams and the legacy from the Catholic mystics of other centuries emphasizing perfection and mystical union.[11] Consequently, it seems Protestants may have tended to avoid this doctrine and its spiritual applications due to heavy reliance on it in Catholic mysticism.

In light of this unfortunate neglect, our first aim is to reassert this doctrine and reflect on how it can stimulate the Reformed tradition to an appreciation of Christian spirituality that is more in line with its historical-theological heritage, particularly Calvinism. For, "the heart of Calvin's theology and spirituality is the mystical union between Christ and the believer."[12] Mark Garcia notes, "it has long been appreciated that the Calvin corpus contains numerous passages in which the theological, ecclesiological, and

---

8. Pink, *Spiritual Union*, 7; Donnelly, *Life*, 11; Jones, "Existential Nerve."

9. Jones, "Existential Nerve," 189.

10. This literature review has not been included in this work due to its length, in kindness to the reader. However, its findings have been summarized at the end of the current chapter and the beginning of chapter 4.

11. Carson, *Gagging*, 557.

12. Cornick, *Letting God*, 33.

practical significance of union with Christ is prominent."[13] The legacy of Puritanism to the Reformed tradition also calls for contemporary appreciation of this doctrine, which has been designated "the existential nerve of Puritan piety."[14]

This realigning of the tradition with a doctrine it is well at home with will automatically reaffirm the requirement for theology-based spirituality. This presupposes and attests to the belief that "spirituality is inseparable from theology," affirming with Donald Bloesch that a restatement of spirituality will include a restatement of *theology* or gospel fundamentals.[15] In this study, this comes in the form of recentralizing the doctrine of union with Christ in Reformed spirituality in order to recover the core of Calvinistic spirituality.[16]

The need for a greater *Reformed* spiritual expression in church life, as opposed to an Evangelical mode, is further exemplified in another of Hageman's observations regarding American Reformed spirituality, which he claims has shifted from its original high view of the sacrament of baptism. Such downgrading is equally distinguishable in the contemporary observance of the Lord's Supper.[17] For Calvin, says Hageman, spirituality was grounded in salvation in Christ, signed and sealed in the sacraments. "[Yet] for a large number in the Reformed Churches today, it is the sign of the decision of the converted person. That shift has had all kinds of consequences for understanding church and sacraments and is fundamental for the concept of the Christian life."[18] These factors are imperative to understanding a truly Reformed spirituality, as we will see in later chapters.

This moves with some fluidity to the second aim of this study, namely, to explore the possibility of unique feminine contributions and insights to a Reformed theological expression of union with Christ.

Recent flourishing in feminist and women's spiritualities has ensured a female perspective on spirituality to be of growing interest. This awareness of the feminine has shaped contemporary spiritualities to be more "holistic," moving away from the traditional "disembodied" spirituality that perceived both matter (therefore the body) and the feminine to be problematic

---

13. Garcia, *Life in Christ*, 15.
14. Jones, "Existential Nerve," 186.
15. Bloesch, *Spirituality*, 13.
16. Lane, "Calvinist Spirituality"; Hageman, "Reformed," 142–43.
17. Letham, *Supper*, 1.
18. Hageman, "Reformed," 143.

or unholy.[19] Prior gender bias has left a great chasm in theological female scholarship; Sheldrake notes, "to say that women's religious experience was caged within a male theology is more than to note that theological teaching was for so long dominated by men. Although, theoretically, theology was a priori, in practice the categories and tones expressed a male mentality."[20] In recent decades, it has been the responsibility of each theological tradition to counteract this prevailing male voice. Scholars such as Elizabeth Schüssler Fiorenza and Mary Grey, both Catholic scholars, and Elizabeth Moltmann-Wendel, wife of the renowned liberal theologian Jürgen Moltmann, and neo-Evangelical Virginia Ramey Mollenkott, are but a few names of women theologians who are changing the male-dominated landscape of theological writings. With these women influencing their own denominational frameworks, the Reformed tradition cannot allow itself to be negligent any longer. Owing to the fact that the Reformed possess a traditionally conservative, although continually challenged, regard for gender roles in church life and leadership, the result has been a theological arena generally monopolized by male contributors. This dearth of female Reformed theologians is a serious shortcoming to the tradition and to "complementarianism" as a belief system. Consequently, this study will endeavor to contribute a contemporary feminine Reformed articulation of the doctrine, and its significance in enjoying an experiential knowledge of Christ.

In applying the above, our third aim seeks to suggest ways in which our research outcomes may be relevant to pastoral church life, especially to women. By utilizing tools from pastoral theology, we will consider our findings in relation to pastoral concerns, so that suggestions might be made for an increased measure of care and discipleship that takes into account a Reformed feminine spirituality. Packer concurs, "competence in the field of spirituality is always important as a basis for pastoral care and direction . . . *Pastors need insight into spirituality in order to teach and advise for the furthering of spiritual health.*"[21] Thus there is the hope that this book may appropriately inform church life and practice. Practical doctrinal application is essential to counteracting the concerns that we have noted and responding to the stereotype that the Reformed tradition is overly cerebral and not associated with spirituality. For where the Catholic tradition has enjoyed a flourishing of spiritual theology, "Reformed theology has long

---

19. Sheldrake, "Spirituality"; Tacey, *Revolution*, 4.
20. Sheldrake, "Spirituality," 38.
21. Packer, "Evangelical," 232 (emphasis added).

played Martha to Catholicism's Mary."[22] In short, this third aim involves the contribution of a unique feminine Reformed spirituality that might be valuable and germane to women in Reformed churches and perhaps the wider Evangelical community.

WHERE WE ARE HEADING

The structure of this work seeks to realize progressively the three aims outlined above by means of seven chapters. The first three chapters give the relevant background so that the explorative discussions of the next four chapters can take place.

The rest of this initial chapter continues to set the scene for our study, introducing and characterizing the contemporary spirituality movement in the UK and US, in all its diversity, and then briefly suggesting what a distinctly *Reformed* spirituality looks like. This is done by highlighting some apparent themes and trends.

Looking at the nature and significance of the doctrine of union with Christ in contemporary Reformed thought, chapters 2 and 3 systematically outline its development since the time of the Reformation, yet focusing on its place in contemporary theology since 1950.

The following four chapters explore a uniquely feminine Reformed articulation of the doctrine of union with Christ in relation to the believer's Christian life. Chapters 4 and 5 consider the Christ-union in a theological and corporate church context, and chapters 6 and 7, whilst underlining potential pastoral implications raised by the study, look at a personal expression of the *unio mystica* in Reformed feminine spirituality.

Methodology

The approach used in this study is historical-theological, conducted within a Reformed systematic theological framework in order to arrive at an essentially *Reformed* spirituality. We may account for this exclusivity towards the Reformed tradition by utilizing the apt words of Alister McGrath in a similar work: this focus is not for the sake of preoccupation with "sectarian perspectives. Nor is it to develop an unhealthy interest in a divisive period of Christian history.... Rather, it is to allow a major formative and creative

---

22. Cornick, *Letting God*, 17.

Introduction

period in the history of the Western Christian church to impinge upon our present-day thinking."[23]

The employment of this systematic theological approach allows us to restate and possibly develop a specific Christian doctrine in order to explore its further application in the realm of spirituality. Consequently, this places our study into the category designated by David Perrin as the "doctrinal approach," in which doctrine is the necessary data. "The first step in this use of theology as a research method is to determine which categories or doctrines of theology, that is, the known or positive data, are to be used for the study."[24] Thus, the doctrine of union with Christ is our positive data, which we attempt to apply to contemporary Reformed spirituality using a feminine approach.

The work also uses other disciplinary approaches in order to achieve its aims. The outline of our doctrine from pre-Reformation thought to the present day in chapter 2 will employ a strong historical method. In addition, in order to achieve our third aim, pastoral theology will be woven into the study in the consideration of pastoral implications towards the end of the book.

The methodology in this work is also *feminine* as it incorporates female insights and expressions in Reformed and Evangelical spirituality in the hope of tracing a rudimentary outline of a Reformed christocentric spirituality that may be relevant to Christian women. Below we will look in further detail at the meaning of the term "feminine" as it is used in this study.

Definitions

We will now define some key terms that bear significantly on this work. Most of these terms, particularly "Reformed," "Evangelical," "spirituality," and "feminine," have somewhat fluid meanings and are loaded with historio-cultural connotations. This is especially true of the term "mystical," which although not present in our title possesses a particular historical relationship with Christian spirituality that demands some attention.

Reformed

Unlike many other contemporary scholarly works on Christian spirituality that are strongly ecumenical in approach, this contribution operates from

23. McGrath, *Roots*, 20.
24. Perrin, *Studying*, 36.

within a Reformed theological framework whilst engaging in dialogue with Reformed and wider conservative Evangelical writings. Due to the urgency of proper identification of such categories we will offer a careful working definition for our particular use of the term "Reformed." This will create a clear line of distinction between that which is "Reformed" and that understood to be "Evangelical," which is crucial when one notes the mutual bearing between them.

The designation "Reformed" in the contemporary setting has a whole host of potential meanings. One might be "Reformed" because of an expressed loyalty to the theological and ecclesiastical tradition that finds its roots in the sixteenth-century Reformation, or due to a particular model of church government that originates from the Reformers' contest against Rome's ecclesiastical structure. Additionally, one might name oneself "Reformed" in upholding Calvinistic theology or covenantal theology, or simply in taking on the maxim *Semper reformanda* ("always reforming") as a biblical duty.

The "Reformed" are found in a wide range of different schools of thought and denominations, for instance, the United Reformed Church, Dutch, Scottish, and American Presbyterianism, Evangelical Free or Independent fellowships, Baptist and Anglican circles, Princeton and continental Barthian schools, Welsh Calvinistic Methodism, or the Free Church of Scotland.[25] Thus, the Reformed tradition is spread abroad, with diverse manifestations of thought, church structure, and spirituality.

Our particular understanding of the term "Reformed" refers to the theological tradition derived from the "rigorous emphasis" of the Reformers in relation to realigning church and doctrinal belief to scriptural principles.[26] At its heart is the suite of five *solas* (*Sola scriptura*, "by scripture alone"; *Sola fide*, "by faith alone"; *Sola gratia*, "by grace alone"; *Solus Christus*, "Christ alone"; and *Soli Deo gloria*, "glory to God alone"), which serve as a basic summary of Reformed theological belief in their precise contradistinction with Roman Catholicism. Importantly, the Reformed tradition is comprehensive, and although David Cornick uses an ecclesiological denominational approach in his wide representation of the contemporary

---

25. Peter Adam notes the contemporary Reformed scene in Britain has been strongly defined by leaders such as Martyn Lloyd-Jones, Alec Motyer, J. I. Packer, R. C. Lucas, and David Jackman. Adam, *Biblical Spirituality*, 28–29.

26. Cornick, *Letting God*, 11; De Witt, *Reformed Faith*, 3–4.

Introduction

"Reformed," this can be restrictive.[27] Use of the term requires the appreciation of a tradition that extends far beyond denominational labeling, especially since Reformed thought impacts church government, church-state relations, church life, spirituality, ethics, and doctrinal belief. Indeed, the comprehensiveness of Reformed thought is part of its unique vision for the centrality of God in the whole of creation or reality.[28]

In seeking a contemporary understanding of what it means to be Reformed, John R. De Witt asserts there is "no single source to which we can turn for an authoritative expression of the Reformed faith," for no uniform confession has been adopted by all Reformed churches.[29] Yet De Witt looks to the Belgic and the Second Helvetic confessions, the Westminster Standards, the Heidelberg Catechism, and the Canons of Dort as the "closest approximation to a *consensus ecclesiae*."[30] Certainly, these documents all retain the classic representative statements of Reformed theology. However, in the wish to produce a theological outline normative to the Reformed position, it might be overwhelming to assign them all. Therefore, this study proposes the Westminster Confession of Faith (1647), identified by John Murray as "the summation of the Protestant confessions, completing the endeavours initiated by the first Reformers and gathering into itself the fruits of fifteen centuries of theological labour,"[31] and the Westminster Larger and Shorter Catechisms, together with the five *solas*, to demarcate the core of Reformed theological thought. This is in agreement with R. Scott Clark's assertion that "Reformed" "denotes a confession, a theology, piety, and practice that are well known and well defined and summarized in [these] ecclesiastically sanctioned and binding documents."[32]

This work is primarily a *theological exploration* that is seeking to contribute a contemporary feminine articulation relevant to Reformed spirituality. Hence, it is essential to appreciate the role of Reformed theology herein. When considering the doctrine of union with Christ we will carefully examine its place within the whole fabric of Reformed theology. Conducting this study from a distinctively Reformed theological framework is necessary in formulating a distinctively Reformed spirituality.

27. Cornick, *Letting God*, 11.
28. Letham, "Reformed Theology."
29. De Witt, *Reformed Faith*, 3; Niesel, *Symbolics*, 178.
30. De Witt, *Reformed Faith*, 4.
31. Wright, "Westminster."
32. Scott Clark, *Confessions*, 3.

Complementarian Spirituality

Evangelical

We use the term "Evangelical" not in its derivation from original Greek meaning, but in its broader historical-theological rendering as it refers to the community that normatively defines itself in its adherence to a belief structure founded on certain biblical essentials. Importantly, contemporary Evangelicalism is not by any means monolithic but a complex and organic movement with numerous nuances, which John Stott names "the multiple tribes" of Evangelicalism. This is demonstrated in the practice of an Evangelical identity with a preceding adjective, such as "Reformed," "progressive," "open," "post-modern," or "liberal," which qualifies what type of Evangelical is being discussed.[33]

A precise definition of this term is crucial to this study, especially as Evangelicalism and the Reformed tradition can be regarded synonymously, owing to the substantial historicity they share. The wide scope of the contemporary Evangelical landscape, especially in its North American context, demands a distinction between the two terms as well as acknowledgement that there are at the conservative end of the movement figures and organizational bodies with both "Reformed" and "Evangelical" identities. Indeed, the Reformed and Evangelical traditions are integral to one another and history readily confirms this; for even Luther claimed the label *die Evangelischen* and in 1531 Thomas More is said to have given the Reformers the designation *Evaungelicalles*. Additionally, the term was also used to refer to the seventeenth-century English Puritans and the later revivalism of Whitefield and the Wesleys.[34] Evangelical historian Richard Lovelace states that the source of the Evangelical movement *is* the Reformation, although its "spiritual lineage" goes back further to Augustine, Athanasius, and other medieval church fathers.[35]

Therefore, whilst noting this apparent overlap, this work views these terms as distinct. Nonetheless appreciating that the Reformed tradition is, in some way, a theological and denominational subcategory found in the Evangelical movement, we also acknowledge that it is a tradition, sprung from the Protestant affirmation of the biblical gospel tenets, that has carved its own inimitable theological and denominational path throughout the centuries.

---

33. Stott, *Evangelical*, 9.
34. Stott, *Evangelical*, 17–18; Bebbington, *Evangelicalism*, 1.
35. Lovelace, *Dynamics*, 27; McGrath, *Spirituality*, 18; Randall, *What a Friend*, 16–17.

Introduction

Contemporary use of the term "Evangelical" originates from its role as a self-ascribed label by a coalition of opponents again the anti-intellectualism and separatist fundamentalism that marked American Christianity between the two World Wars.[36] This response, which parented the ministry of evangelist Billy Graham, the Moody Bible Institute, Wheaton College, and the National Association of Evangelicals, has been described by the Institute for the Study of American Evangelicals (ISAE) as playing "a pivotal role in giving the wider movement a sense of cohesion."[37] In spite of this, its current breadth has forced molds of Evangelicalism onto a political linear scale, where even the basic Evangelical tenet of the supremacy and infallibility of Scripture is questioned by "leftists" or "modernists," meaning that the Evangelical identity is carried by whoever claims it.[38]

The implication of this in relation to our study means that although "Reformed," "conservative," "broad," and "modernist" labels are not ideal and somewhat reductionist, these classifications prove helpful when considering different personalities and theological positions. It is necessary then that care and justification accompanies any use of these terms. Nonetheless, the fact that this study is specifically examining works from authors who are theologically Reformed but who may not explicitly express a Reformed identity means that the consideration of liberal or broader forms of Evangelicalism is minimal.

In order to supply a suitable working definition we will consider some influential characterizations of Evangelicalism. A definition continually challenged is that given by historian David Bebbington.[39] Bebbington states the "Evangelical religion" to be a popular movement, "not to be equated with any single Christian denomination," yet characterized by four special marks: "*conversionism*, the belief that lives need to be changed; *activism*, the expression of the gospel in effort; *biblicism*, a particular regard for the Bible; and what may be called *crucicentrism*, a stress on the sacrifice of Christ on the cross."[40] John Stott, who pronounces Bebbington's wording to be abstruse, insists that subsuming the essentials under two categories necessarily divides Trinitarian origins from subsequent outworkings. The first category consists of three essentials held together in a Trinitarian soterio-

36. Eskridge, "Defining."
37. Ibid.
38. Luo, "Meaning."
39. Helm, "Bebbington Thesis."
40. Bebbington, *Evangelicalism*, 1–3.

Complementarian Spirituality

logical lock: the authority of God the Father in and through the Bible, the majesty of the person of Christ in and through Calvary, and the Lordship of the Holy Spirit in and through his many ministries. Stott's second category preserves the significance of conversion, evangelism, and fellowship.[41]

A christocentric texture is evident in these evangelical confessions. This is clear in Packer's contention that "all who understand Christianity as faith in, love for, and worship of Jesus Christ as their sin-bearing Saviour are evangelicals; all who affirm his sufficiency to save sinners are proclaiming evangelical theology; and every projection of trustful, grateful Christ-centeredness as the true and only path of life for sinners is evangelical spirituality."[42]

In light of this, our proposed understanding of "Evangelical" or "Evangelicalism" is a biblical Christianity "of the gospel," expressing faith in the unique person and saving work of Jesus Christ for the triune Persons. In order to stress this Trinitarian framework and the need for full acceptance in the uniqueness of Christ for conversion, together with the ecclesiastical values of fellowship and evangelism, we utilize Stott's understanding of Evangelical essentials as defining the Evangelical movement.

Spirituality/Christian Spirituality

The term "spirituality" derives its etymology from the Latin word *spiritualitas*, which in its noun form *spiritus* is translated from the NT Greek noun *pneuma*, "spirit." The term's historical-cultural rendering has a "relatively short pedigree" though in its contemporary understanding it is deemed a "dynamic," "inclusive," and "eclectic" concept.[43] Traced back to its original use within French Catholic circles, at a time when spiritual pursuits were somewhat esoteric, the term "spirituality" is believed to have flourished in its reference to the science of spiritual life with Jesuit Giovanni Scaramelli's division of ascetical and mystical theology in the eighteenth century.[44]

In its contemporary usage, however, it is a fashionable and immensely versatile term that can refer to a range of subjects, for instance: traditional religions, secular faith groups, healthy lifestyle regimes, meditation, yoga, aromatherapy, retreats, pacifism, silence or solitude, superstitions,

---

41. Stott, *Evangelical*, 28.
42. Packer, "Evangelical," 231.
43. Sheldrake, "Spirituality," 21, 37.
44. Albin, "Spirituality"; Carson, *Gagging*, 556; Sheldrake, "Spirituality," 33.

occultism, and political or social activism.⁴⁵ Consequently, the term has become an "ill-defined, amorphous entity"⁴⁶ resisting any universal meaning.

Adding to this, contemporary spirituality as an academic subject has become interdisciplinary, now possessing psychology, sociology, and anthropology as research partners.⁴⁷ This multiplicity of academic assumptions and presuppositions to the subject is exemplified in the recent work by Jungian specialist David J. Tacey, *The Spirituality Revolution*, and strongly affirms the need for substantiated definitions and method in every contribution.

Discourse on the essential structure of spirituality continues to be a subject of much debate and depends largely on whether one approaches spirituality from a secular or institutional/religious standpoint. In relation to the latter is the integral relationship between theology and spirituality. In medieval thought, these two disciplines were not distinct. For "spirituality as living and lived faith was the context and the purpose of all study, both sacred and profane," but as theology moved from the monastery to the academy, in the high Middle Ages, spirituality and theology diverged and the non-rationalistic nature of spirituality stigmatized it from the academy and left it safely behind monastic doors.⁴⁸ This division is weighty to the contemporary understanding of spirituality, particularly within Christendom. Traditionalists understand theology to be the starting point of spirituality and the grounds of its authenticity. On the contrary, other more existential twentieth-century writers, such as R. Newton Flew and Geoffrey Wainwright, argue that spirituality informs theology.⁴⁹ However, one might assert that any spiritual or religious practice, formed by spiritual or religious inclination, must originate in some presuppositional constructs. Louis Bouyer concurs with this premise when speaking of Christian spirituality:

> It [spirituality] does not entertain the pseudo-scientific, and in fact wholly extravagant, prejudice that the understanding of the objects polarizing the religious consciousness is essentially foreign to an understanding of this consciousness itself. On the contrary, spirituality studies this consciousness only in its living relationship with these objects, in its real apprehension . . . of what it believes.

45. Perrin, *Studying*, 16.
46. Carson, *Gagging*, 555.
47. Perrin, *Studying*, 19, 37; Sheldrake, "Spirituality," 21; Schneiders, "Definition."
48. Schneiders, "Definition," 2; Sheldrake, "Spirituality," 32.
49. Albin, "Spirituality," 657; Carson, *Gagging*, 557.

> Dogmatic theology, therefore, must always be presupposed as the basis of spiritual theology.[50]

Having touched on the vital relationship between spirituality and belief, let us consider further the nature of spirituality and the form it takes within the contemporary context.

Sandra Schneiders, a leading researcher in contemporary spirituality, defines spirituality as "conscious involvement in the project of life integration through self-transcendence toward the ultimate value one perceives."[51] Here the ongoing nature of spirituality is emphasized, inferring that it cannot be equated with phases of habit. Further, this "spiritual project" is an inherently positive characteristic reaching outside of the self towards an ultimate value. Schneiders highlights a marked attribute of *contemporary* spirituality, namely, its holism, as it encompasses all of life and rejects the division of the secular and sacred.[52] Another leading scholar in the subject, Philip Sheldrake, equally stresses the holistic characterization of spirituality. Unlike medieval mysticism, "it is not limited to a concern with the interior life but seeks an integration of all aspects of human life and existence."[53] This integration into the whole of life is also apparent in a subjective sense. Rowan Williams comments that the Christian's goal is not enlightenment but a "wholeness" that inspires trust in God's creative outworking in the complexities of life.[54] Again, Kathleen Fischer confirms this to be driving today's spiritual thinking, in the "effort to rid our spiritual lives of dualism—those categories of thinking and living that split the world into disconnected opposites."[55]

These factors are important when considering the influence that contemporary spirituality has upon an explicitly Christian understanding and expression. We shall consider this further in relation to Reformed spirituality towards the end of this chapter, but immediately a provisional working definition of the term "spirituality" must be explored so it can assist a subsequent definition of "Christian spirituality."

---

50. Louis Bouyer et al., *History of Christian Spirituality*, viii, in Carson, *Gagging*, 556–57.

51. Schneiders, "Definition," 1.

52. Ibid., 1–2.

53. Sheldrake, "Spirituality," 37.

54. Williams, *Wound of Knowledge*, 2.

55. Fischer, *Connections*, vi.

Introduction

Walter Principe suggests the following to be a "universally applicable definition of spirituality: the way in which a person understands and lives within his or her historical context that aspect of his or her religion, philosophy or ethic that is viewed as the loftiest, the noblest, the most calculated to lead to the fullness of the ideal or perfection being sought."[56] When dressing this with a specifically Christian identity, this ultimate value becomes the triune God, revealed to humanity through the divine *Logos* outlined in the Bible, driving the individual to a conscious response that is both personal and ecclesial.[57] This is a "quest for a filled and authentic Christian existence, involving the bringing together of the fundamental ideas of Christianity and the whole experience of living on the basis of and within the scope of the Christian faith."[58] It is crucial that one remembers that within Christian spirituality the object of this "quest," to use McGrath's wording, is the enjoyment of a Trinitarian Christian life lived "in Christ." Christian spirituality is the "fostering" and "sustaining" of a relationship with Christ by means of doctrinal, ethical, and practical lifestyle codes.[59]

In light of this, "spirituality" is both conviction and action: it is *the shaping of life by allegiance to a particular religion or faith.* This dynamic, as Schneiders termed it, is "conscious," or "calculated" according to Principe, for it is not passive but is intelligently worked out. In other words, spirituality is the *integration of praxiological elements that confirm and stimulate belief and worship,* and when found in the context of the biblical faith is understood as "Christian spirituality." These praxiological elements may or may not be biblically instructed and might be anything from intercessory prayer, acts of repentance, informal fellowship, scripture memorization, evangelism, the pursuit of self-control, or acts of hospitality and kindness.

Mysticism

Our understanding of a mystical "in Christ" spirituality is not to be associated wrongly with mysticism, a term generally used historically to refer to a particular spiritual philosophy that seeks union with the divine through contemplative spirituality. Dionysius the Areopagite's sixth-century treatise *On Mystical Theology* used the term synonymously with "spirituality," and this understanding continued with Madame de Guyon's salon spiritual

---

56. Principe, "Defining Spirituality," 48.
57. Sheldrake, "Spirituality," 25.
58. McGrath, *Spirituality*, 2.
59. Ibid., 3.

Complementarian Spirituality

societies in seventeenth-century France.[60] A range of religious personalities have been labeled "mystics," from Ann Griffiths, an eighteenth-century Welsh Calvinistic Methodist hymn writer; Florence Nightingale, the nineteenth-century nurse, to the twentieth-century Trappist monk Thomas Merton or activist and philosopher Simone Weil.[61] In both historical and contemporary use, the term and its related terms, "mystic," "mystical," and "mystical theology," are very unstable. Sometimes simply a spiritual writer is designated a mystic, as in the case of Ann Griffiths. With the intention to clarify between mysticism as a spiritual experience and mysticism as a philosophy for spirituality, we will consider historical definitions and then outline a helpful distinction of the term offered by Rudolph Otto in order that the form relevant to this study, namely, mystical or *mystica*, can be employed.

Evelyn Underhill described the term thus: mysticism "in its pure form, is the science of ultimates, the science of union with the Absolute, and nothing else, and the mystic is the person who attains to this union."[62] This personal striving through spiritual disciplines in order to achieve ascent to God represents a broad purview of historical figures and certain ascetic schools, commonly categorized by a particular era and geographical location. The medieval Catholic mystics of Spain, such as St. John of the Cross and Teresa of Avila, are one such school of philosophical mysticism; another example is the German mysticism of the later Middle Ages, including the significant Mister Eckhart.

In its popular current use, the term pertains to an existentialist attitude to the supernatural in both religious and non-religious contexts, seen unfavorably to embody an irrationalism or anti-intellectualism, or—and according to Underhill this is incorrect—mere activities of the supersensual; for mysticism is seen by confessional Christians to "swallow up" meaning in mystery.[63]

On the other hand it is important to note that in Reformed thought the term "mystical" implies incomprehensibility, or even "the relational, spiritual, or experiential aspects of the faith, as opposed to the more cognitive

---

60. Ibid., 5.

61. Jones, "Welsh Spirituality; cf., Dossey, *Florence Nightingale*; Alexandar Nava, *Mystical and Prophetic Thought*.

62. Underhill, *Mysticism*, 72.

63. Ibid., 71–72; Bloesch, *Spirituality*, 50; McGrath, *Spirituality*, 6.

or intellectual aspects."⁶⁴ It is here that the term's relevance to the doctrine of union with Christ, or the *unio mystica*, becomes clear. Hodge describes this somewhat apophatic dimension of the doctrine thus: "The technical designation of this union in theological language is 'mystical', because it so far *transcends all the analogies of earthly relationships*, in the intimacy of its communion, in the transforming power of its influence, and in the excellence of its consequences."⁶⁵

In response to these complexities, Rudolph Otto draws a helpful distinction, proposing the form *Mystik* to encompass "mysticism as a spiritual experience" and *Mysticismus* to refer to mysticism as a "philosophy of life."⁶⁶ "The Christian faith is irrevocably opposed to the latter but not necessarily to the former."⁶⁷ Therefore, these terms will be used in this study at their respective relevance. *Mystik* will denote the mystery of our doctrine in relation to Christian experience, and *Mysticismus* will be the term to describe those who historically hold to philosophical modes of mysticism in relation to spiritual pursuit.

Union with Christ

The doctrine of union with Christ within systematic theology is the pulling together of the NT theme of the believer's spiritual, organic, and permanent oneness with Christ.⁶⁸ It is through this crucial doctrine that Christ's obedience, death, and resurrection can be effectual in the life of the believer, through the act of faith by the work of the Holy Spirit. It is what is meant by the frequent but key and technical NT phrase "in Christ," which describes the securing of salvation through a new status of oneness with Christ, whereby all his merits become readily available to the believer. "The Christian's knowledge, experience and enjoyment of God are through Christ, his baptism is into Christ, his standing and every blessing are in Christ, and his destiny is in Christ."⁶⁹

Essential to its place in biblical teaching is the doctrine's strong corporate implications. Herein the shared status of union with Christ binds believers together in a spiritual accord congruent to church life. Significant

---

64. McGrath, *Spirituality*, 6.
65. Hodge, *Theology*, 483.
66. Bloesch, *Crisis*, n52.
67. Ibid., 123.
68. Berkhof, *Systematic*, 449.
69. Baker, "Union," 697.

here is the belief that this oneness originates in the Trinity. For in the high priestly prayer of John 17, Christ intercedes for believers, pleading that they would become one as he and his Father are one.[70]

The biblical doctrine of union with Christ consists of a number of theological elements, and each Christian tradition has tended to put weight on one theme over and above the others:

Firstly, an aspect accentuated by Eastern Orthodoxy is "incarnational union," whereby the incarnation, in the sharing of our humanity, is the basis of union with Christ.

Secondly, "covenantal union," a theme taken on significantly by the Reformed tradition, sees the development of the OT covenant between Yahweh and Israel to a new covenant. This has strong marital imagery and is based on the federal work of Christ (the Bridegroom) with the elect (the Bride).[71]

Thirdly is the "sacramental union," stressed by Catholicism, which elevates baptism and the Lord's Supper as the means of "initial and continuing union with Christ" appropriated as the partaking believer shares in Christ's suffering and salvific work.

The fourth, "experiential union," pertains more to identification as the Son of God unifies himself to humanity by mutual life experiences and calling, notably in the Evangelical and Catholic traditions.

Finally, underscored by mystic, pietistic, and the Charismatic traditions, Baker describes the contours that make up the "spiritual or mystical union," wherein one seeks intimacy with Christ through a compelling spirituality of disciplines that will lead to true knowledge and delight in God.[72] This is not to be confused with the objective of "mysticism" or the "transformation of the religious consciousness,"[73] whereby God is perceived and known as a Being beyond the personal, therefore bypassing salvific revelation in Christ.[74] Notably, in Reformed belief union with Christ is consistently soteriological in its nature. The union is between Redeemer and the redeemed, not simply the divine and the created.[75]

---

70. John 17:21. All Scripture references are taken from the English Standard Version (ESV) unless indicated otherwise.
71. Baker, "Union," 698.
72. Ibid., 699.
73. McGrath, *Spirituality*, 6.
74. Bloesch, *Spirituality*, 22, 35.
75. Niesel, *Symbolics*, 185.

Introduction

In conclusion, it is briefly added that the kind of union typically accentuated by a particular tradition relates to its specific expression of spirituality.

Importantly, these strands are only aspects of the *one* biblical truth of the believer being "in Christ" and are not to be understood as different unions.[76] We will now summarize the nature of the union from a Reformed perspective.

Wilhelm Niesel employs the thought of Dutch-German theologian Peter von Mastricht on union with Christ, giving us a helpful primary description, which we include at this point without supplementary comment in the aim of offering a basic understanding: the union the believer enjoys with Christ is "real, not imaginary," nor an emotional fancy or a decision of the will. It is "total" or complete, encompassing both the body and soul of Christ and his distinct but indivisible human and divine natures, with the body and soul of the believer. It is "indissoluble," "eternal," and "spiritual", as it is *of* and bestowed *by* the eternal mighty Spirit of God.[77] The Holy Spirit brings this union about in a mysterious and supernatural way that cannot be comprehended by humankind, hence this union is frequently designated the *unio mystica*.[78] It finds its beginning in election and reaches its pinnacle, not end, in the glorification of the saints in Christ.[79]

The specific position of the doctrine of union with Christ in the process of redemption has long been debated among theologians. A Reformed understanding normatively places union with Christ at the starting point of the *ordo salutis* or as the primary undergirding that runs throughout. Reformed theologian Michael Horton, author of *Covenant and Salvation: Union with Christ*, says it is "the wheel which unites the spokes of salvation and keeps them in proper perspective."[80] John Murray remains the chief proponent of the doctrine's centrality in the *ordo salutis*, stating that this doctrine "underlines every step of the application of redemption. . . .

---

76. Wayne Grudem asserts that the phrase "in Christ" "refers to a variety of relationships." Grudem is not pronouncing the existence of more than one union but only several types of relationships stemming from this unique union. Grudem, *Systematic*, 840–41.
77. Niesel, *Symbolics*, 183–84.
78. Berkhof, *Systematic*, 447.
79. Ibid.
80. Horton, "Union," 16.

Indeed the whole process of salvation has its origin in one phase of union with Christ."[81]

We will consider this positioning further by means of a theological explanation in our next chapter.

Feminine

It is crucial to understand correctly the use of a *feminine* approach in this study so that certain assumptions and expectations are not unduly placed upon it. Now we will consider the definition of a "feminine" approach in this project and consider other *related* approaches that are not used.

The integration of a feminine approach in this project is not for the sake of outlining what might be called a "gendered spirituality," whereby a specific spirituality is constructed by gender in its biological, sexual, and cultural makeup. Indeed, a point of emphasis within the study of contemporary spirituality has been its contextual nature since "the lived experience of Christian faith is enormously varied in practice." This is largely because faith has "long been distinguished by state of life or vocation [whereby] individuals and groups have focused their spiritual quest through the lens of these commitments or experiences."[82] In spite of this, our study does not use a gender approach to spirituality because it is initially a response to the dearth in contemporary Reformed theological articulations. Gendered spiritualities are not yet native to a Reformed framework and introducing a gender-specific spirituality into the tradition at this point might prove to be premature and ineffective as it naturally prizes the "data" of gender over and above doctrine. As stated earlier, however, the methodology behind this study is that of a "doctrinal approach" that proposes a recentralization of the Christ-union in Reformed spirituality, thus reacquainting the tradition with its spiritual heritage.

Neither is this approach employing a feminist agenda. For the starting point for the whole feminist project is "feminist consciousness."[83] In feminist ideology this means that patriarchal religious constructs are identified and then destabilized by critical discourse. Although feminist spirituality focuses on the personal state of *being* in relation to the divine and attaining a self-transcendence that results in liberation and well-being, with the

---

81. Murray, *Redemption*, 161.
82. Schneiders, "Definition," 5–6; Perrin, *Studying*, 320–21.
83. Perrin, *Studying*, 322.

Introduction

apparent themes of harmony with God, self, others, and nature, this consciousness still remains the core premise.[84]

The concern of this work is not to engage in the critique and demolition of androcentric articulations of theology and spirituality, or to interact with positive symbols found within feminist spirituality. This study essentially attempts to present female insights and perspectives in a theological and spiritual tradition that has been dominated by male contribution. This demonstrates an initial commitment to the Reformed tradition and its spiritual heritage and not firstly the feminist project. In sum then, the inclusion of "a feminine approach" is the consideration of the *Reformed female voice*, both in the existence of a female researcher and in content that surveys feminine contribution and life experience applicable to pastoral care. Significantly, this project attempts to mark out an initial definition of "Reformed feminine spirituality" in the hope of stimulating a complementarian Reformed church practice in line with complementarian belief, thus profiting Reformed spirituality as a whole, and further academic contribution in this area.

This is not to say that the Reformed tradition has no feminist discourse within it or that feminism cannot be endorsed together with a Reformed confession. The Reformed feminist theologians, led by Amy Plantinga Pauw and Serene Jones, who contributed to the Columbia Series in Reformed Theology work titled *Feminist and Womanist Essays in Reformed Dogmatics*, are all scholars or ordained ministers who pledge allegiance to both the feminist or womanist projects and Reformed theology. From their somewhat broad stance within the Reformed tradition, they name their loyalties as "polyphonic," sharing the conviction that the feminist and womanist discourses can nourish the tradition or traditions.[85] They accordingly name the late Letty Russell of Yale Divinity School to be a leading Reformed feminist theologian, as well as Beverley Wilding and Delores S. Williams. Yet this North American academic and denominational community is not the same arena in which this project operates.[86] Although one may agree with Evangelical John G. Stackhouse's surmise that "among conservative Christians today there is all too little imaginative and scholarly exploration of new ways, *feminist* ways, of reading the Bible and constructing theology,"

---

84. Clifford, "Feminist."

85. Pauw and Jones, *Feminist Essays*, x–xi.

86. Ibid., xi. This broad Reformed position represented by these women, and by Russell, is historico-theologically Reformed though arguably not Evangelical.

instead, this project responds to the wider problem that generally "in biblical and theological scholarship, women seem absent, *both as subjects and as scholars*."[87] One might claim that the feminist voice in Protestant theology and spirituality is increasing in volume, yet there remains little theological consideration that can benefit Reformed women pastorally. Therefore, interacting with feminist interpretations (which are essentially critical), language, and symbols in order to *de*construct is not consistent with this objective. Instead, this project looks to *con*struct a specifically doctrinal spirituality that can fill a vital cavity in the Reformed theological tradition.

To conclude, our feminine approach is exploration into the necessary subject of Reformed spirituality in relation to union with Christ from a female perspective, and the proposed relevance of this to pastoral theology for women, as in line with the aims of this study. Of course, male contributions on spirituality and theology will be consulted at length, yet this feminine approach gives the study freedom to interact with female contributors, listening to their descriptions, experience and expectations. Aspects of this approach might be seen to overlap with methods found in gender-specific and feminist studies in spirituality, this is natural as female perspectivism is important to both of these philosophical approaches to female spirituality. Yet the approach used in this study is theological and therefore not based on the philosophical groundings of feminism and the concept of gender.

CONTEMPORARY SPIRITUALITY

In the West, a spiritual movement has swept through popular culture, redefining the "spiritual" to be syncretistic, personal, and not necessarily religious. This emergent spirituality or "spiritualities" are vogue, consumeristic, and ever changing, seemingly creating or repackaging religion constantly and ensuring that, worldwide, three new religions are born every day.[88]

David Wells describes the flavor of this spiritual quest as "eclectic," drawing insights from the Bible, the Qur'an, the Bhagavad Gita, the medieval mystics, and contemporary writers.[89] Indeed, there is something for all tastes as one can pick and choose from a plethora of spiritual ideology. Although this new spirituality is "personal" and relativistic, it is not entirely individualistic in its penchant towards a sense of "wholeness" in the

---

87. Stackhouse, *Feminist*, 123–24 (emphasis added).
88. Runcorn, *Pilgrims and Seekers*, 1; Wells, *Earthly*, 109.
89. Wells, *Earthly*, 115.

Introduction

"connectedness" of meaningful relationships or community whilst looking to repair the fragmentation of life.[90]

This domestication of spirituality has moved worship, liturgy, and community outside of institutions, religious buildings, and groupings. The accessibility of religious and spiritual paraphernalia in today's bookshops is demonstrative of how popular, novel, and commercial spirituality has become. This hunger is exemplified in the particular popularity of Neale Donald Walsch's bestselling series *Conversations with God*, first published in 1995. Walsch is seen as a modern-day spiritual messenger who dialogues with a God that refines the traditional views and beliefs of organized religion. The popularity of Phillip Yancy's writing serves as an equivalent of a popularized spirituality within a Christian paradigm.

Social scientists and scholars such as David Tacey, Paul Heelas and Linda Woodhead have branded this the "spiritual" or "spirituality revolution," although there is no agreement on what makes up this spirituality.[91] Debate rages on the subjective and objective, or interior and exterior nature of this contemporary spirituality and the consequent bearings of this upon its authenticity.[92] Nonetheless, the rise of this spirituality in Western culture has obviously affected Christianity both as its competitor and its influencer. Some prominent sociologists, such as Thomas Luckmann and Colin Campbell, claim that contemporary spirituality has eclipsed Christianity or at least the spiritual climate indicates that it soon will.[93]

In relation to its source, this spiritual revolution is frequently traced back to the disillusionment of the 1960s, particularly strong in America, where the inner life and consciousness began to hold more significance. "After a long slumber, spirituality was awakened in the West by the arrival of spiritual teachers from the East in the 1960s," Ewart Cousins writes in his foreword for *Contemporary Spiritualities: Social and Religious Contexts*. "Hindu gurus, Buddhist masters and Sufi sheikhs began awakening Westerners from a bland secularism. In this climate, the established traditions of the West—Judaism and Christianity—began searching their roots to find their own meditative practices and spiritual wisdom."[94] Sandra Schneiders pushes the origin of this disillusionment forward a decade or so, declar-

---

90. Raiter, *Stirring*, 36–38, 44, 76; Fischer, *Connections*, vi–vii.
91. Heelas and Woodhead, *Revolution*.
92. Ibid., 5–7; Perrin, *Studying*, 17.
93. Heelas and Woodhead, *Revolution*, 2.
94. Cousins, *Contemporary Spiritualities*, xi.

ing its birth in the social transformation of the 1970s and 1980s, "in the aftermath of the world wars, the depression, the cold war, the theological and ecclesial upheaval of Vatican II," as well as the development of the humanities in the academy.[95] It seems then that this change from traditional religion to spirituality is symptomatic of a huge cultural shift, like that from modernism to postmodernism. Bloesch comments that with modernity's eulogy "God is dead," replacement idols or gods have to "fill the metaphysical and spiritual vacuum of the culture."[96]

Impact upon Christian Spirituality

In his *tour de force* against pluralism, *The Gagging of God*, Don Carson is troubled at the signs of influence of secular spirituality upon the orthodoxy of Christendom. Carson discerns that one fruit of this is the plurality found in Evangelicalism.[97] Outlining the movements concerning Catholicism and Protestantism, Carson claims Vatican II has now universalized spirituality, removing the former notion that it was a part of Christian life reserved only for the mystical elite. This has moved into a post-Vatican understanding that is non-confessional, looking specifically at feminist spirituality and spiritualities with focus on social transformation, the syncretistic, the psychological, the philosophical, and the mystical. Protestantism during the last century has taken on some of this pluralism. "Until the last few decades, when liberal Protestantism's conception of spirituality gradually expanded to roughly the same dimensions as that within post-Vatican II Catholicism, Protestantism's interest in spirituality has largely been that associated with godliness and the devotional life in traditional evangelicalism."[98] This has had a negative effect on confessional orthodox Christianity. Postmoderns look now to "participate in the divine nature," where previous generations strove to become "like" Christ.[99] This potentially has devastating effects upon Evangelical and Reformed theological belief that seeks to align itself with biblical teaching. Eugene Peterson rightly observes this severity: "in the enthusiasm of firsthand experience, spirituality imperceptibly wanders away from its basic spirituality text, the Bible, and embraces the inviting world of self-help," thus what remains is a spirituality "emptied of gospel

---

95. Schneiders, "Definition," 3.
96. Bloesch, *Crisis*, 14.
97. Carson, *Gagging*, 561.
98. Ibid., 559.
99. Stetzer, *Postmodern*, 144–45.

distinctiveness."[100] Equally, Peterson observes that such a "crisis" in Evangelical spirituality has caused frustrated Evangelicals to move into fuller, more lively "Catholic" forms of spirituality, revealed in the influences of the Taizé community, renewed interest in liturgy, spiritual retreatism, and the rediscovery of the Eucharist.[101]

Other influencing characteristics of this emergent spirituality are easily identified in postmodern society and the church's life in it. For example, the prizing of that which is "personal" and "therapeutic" is clearly observed in the delights and drives of consumerism. Such therapeutic approaches to spirituality strongly demean certain spiritual legacies belonging to Reformed faith and practice. For example, this is a long way from the rigorous self-examination of the Puritans, epitomized in Jonathan Edwards' famous resolutions. In addition, force for the personal or relative in current society may account for the individualism and consumer mentality ripe within contemporary Evangelicalism, as spirituality and church are at risk of being merely a means for self-gratification. Wells also stresses that concepts of original sin are lost as the self is viewed as innocent. "Today's spirituality remains a deeply privatised matter whose access to reality is through a pristine, uncorrupted self."[102]

Inevitably, this contemporary spirituality movement has stimulated Christian spirituality in many diverse and unique ways. Apparent in Western Evangelicalism is the innovative worship movements like Hillsong or Vineyard, who have implemented their own unique appreciation of Christian spirituality, and consumer churches exemplified in the Willow Creek phenomenon, or the reinventing of the church in the emergent and emerging church movements. These are all perhaps indicative of the Western Evangelical community trying to keep up with the spiritual pace of the world. Those outside of the church, however, perceive Christianity to be failing in its interaction with the spiritual renaissance. David Tacey writes, "The mainline churches are apparently unable to take up a dialogue with the new spirit of our time, partly because they only acknowledge conventional ideas of the sacred . . . the field of spirituality is open wide and largely unexplored; we have yet to see any committed institutional response to the challenges posed by the new spirituality."[103]

100. Peterson, *Christ Plays*, 13.
101. Green and Stevens, *New Testament*, 4.
102. Wells, *Earthly*, 152, 164–65.
103. Tacey, *Revolution*, 4.

Complementarian Spirituality

It is important to note that there are, on the other hand, areas of positive stimulus in this new spirituality to Christian spirituality, features that may particularly enmesh with Reformed spirituality. Church planter Ed Stetzer explains one example: "Postmoderns want a spirituality that is applicable to all areas of life. Postmoderns do not want spirituality that only lasts for two hours on a Sunday morning, but one that they can rely on all week. A spirituality that does not *work* ([that is, does not] bring peace, make better relationships, and improve our quality of life) does not matter."[104] This desire to defragment life and not separate the sacred from the secular is consistent with the holism expressed in Reformed spirituality.

The impact upon contemporary Christian spirituality by the spirituality movement is alone a potentially mammoth subject. The limitations of this current study, in its concern for Reformed spirituality within a Reformed theological framework, restrict us to one corner of the vast field that represents the subject of contemporary Christian spirituality.

REFORMED SPIRITUALITY/SPIRITUALITIES

As this study is concerned with Reformed spirituality, it is essential that the two terms "Reformed" and "spirituality" are now brought together so that the direction of this book can be understood correctly. Since these two words have independent constructs of meaning in our current cultural understanding, which may imply an uneasy tension, it is crucial that we present a careful definition of "Reformed spirituality." For it is suggested that the term "Reformed spirituality" is an oxymoron, "beyond the mire of ambiguity," as these two words "both find their natural home in the rhetoric of theological or ecclesiastical division."[105] In part, this is due to the Reformed tradition's discrimination of the term "spirituality" as a particularly Catholic expression of the Christian life. Nevertheless, the Reformed tradition is increasingly more comfortable with the term as the use of the tradition's past equivalents (such as "devotion," "piety," "religion," "holiness," and "godliness") are being replaced.[106]

In agreement with Howard Hageman, it is careless to speak of Reformed *spirituality*, inferring the existence of one generic type, but fair to identify many manifestations and expressions of spirituality from this one

---

104. Stetzer, *Postmodern*, 139.
105. McGrath, *Roots*, 13; Cornick, *Letting God*, 11.
106. McGrath, *Roots*, 24.

Introduction

tradition.[107] The differing articulations of spirituality belonging to the two generations of Reformers, of which Luther and Zwingli are representational of the first and Calvin and Bucer of the second, alone implies that limiting Reformed spirituality to one entity even in the Reformation era is historically shortsighted. Indeed, the Puritan piety of the late seventeenth and early eighteenth century remains a unique expression, quite different from that of Calvin, which has proved to be of great consequence to the tradition.[108] Contemporary Reformed writers have instigated a renewed popular interest in Puritan piety, and its marriage of scriptural esteem and heartfelt piety is seen by some as an unsurpassed example of true spirituality; "their legacy excels in basing spirituality, experience, and affections on the Bible."[109]

As we earlier defined Christian spirituality to be the conscious integration of praxiological elements that confirm and stimulate belief in and worship of God (of the biblical faith), so "Reformed spirituality" is this response, in a personal or corporate mode, to the gracious and personal activity of God outlined in Reformed belief and demonstrated in Reformed spiritual traditions.[110] It is a God-centered spirituality because it is fundamentally a response to the gracious act of God in salvation.

The Reformed spiritual tradition has demonstrated expressed loyalty to certain spiritual "praxis," both physical or non-physical, that are not found either to such a degree or at all, in other Christian traditions. Significantly, the Reformed emphasis of *Sola scriptura* ensured the tradition's spiritual life to revolve around the Bible and not tradition per se. However, this in itself brings about aspects and features that are rightly understood as "traditions" or practices, though finding their origin in the Reformed hermeneutic. Thus, it is of course excessive and inaccurate to describe Reformed spirituality to be inherently belief-based and free from tradition.

As stated earlier, the Reformed tradition is widely represented in a rich diversity of schools and denominations and each of these possess its own spiritual expressions. For the sake of this study, however, an umbrella definition of Reformed spirituality is required and therefore it is suggested that these Reformed *spiritualities* are simply *manifestations of the same historical spiritual ancestry with its homogeneous traditional core values taken*

107. Hageman, "Reformed," 138.
108. Ibid.
109. Beeke, *Puritan*, vii–viii; cf. J. Packer, *Quest for Godliness*; Ferguson, *John Owen*.
110. McGrath, *Roots*, 22–23.

from the Reformation's recentralization of Scripture. This consistent essence of Reformed spirituality is identifiable in a number of characteristics, which we will consider briefly. This is for identification purposes and not offered as an exhaustive outline.

Characteristics of Reformed Spirituality

Firstly, in contradistinction to the ecclesiastical elitism of the Roman Catholic Church and founded upon the doctrines of election, salvation, and adoption, the Reformed tradition upholds the priesthood of all believers. A key exemplar of this is the Reformed confidence in the belief of the Bible's perspicuity to laity and clergy alike; the underlying principle behind the Reformed and Evangelical value for the private reading of the word; and the esteem upon all vocation for the glory of God, as opposed to the veneration of the clerical or ecclesiastical. The believer is the servant of God; this is his or her most reasonable service. "This is the motivating heart of Reformed piety: we serve the great King," writes Joseph Pipa, continuing with the instruction, "Recognize that all that you do must be done in His service and for His glory, in whatever calling He has placed you."[111] Following from Pipa's admonishment is the fact that Reformed spirituality is not otherworldly but grounded in everyday reality. That is, "the Reformed faith, with its grasp of the doctrine of the covenant of grace, has insisted upon a multi-faceted, full-orbed Christian life."[112] Christians within the tradition are encouraged to glorify God in the whole of life and not merely by what might be deemed as sacred spheres of life. This means Reformed spirituality is essentially relevant to social realities such as education, politics, and the family unit. McGrath highlights this in its original context of the Reformers: "the key elements of Reformation spirituality—most notably, the doctrine of justification by faith and the work ethic—brought new levels of meaning and significance to even the most routine of domestic duties."[113] Further palpable in the maxim *ecclesia reformata, ecclesia semper reformanda*, we see the Reformed church must be a church that is always reforming, that is, returning to its biblical roots. Reformed spirituality also is a continual questioning of the authenticity of one's spiritual life in relation to the Bible and the interplay between faith and practice.[114]

111. Pipa, "Glory and Beauty," 16.
112. De Witt, *Reformed Faith*, 13.
113. McGrath, *Roots*, 47–48.
114. Ibid., 19.

Introduction

Another integral characteristic of Reformed spirituality is its regard for corporate spiritual life, which extends beyond a strong sense of community and distinguishes it from the individualism of Evangelical spirituality.[115] For the elect are united as the Bride of Christ and this catholicity is liturgically outworked in the Word and in the sacraments, accounting for the Reformed regard for the visible church and church membership.[116]

The Reformed imperative for the unity of Word and Spirit is most significant. This is what is meant by Luther's assertion that the Spirit of God "works in the hearts of whom he will, and how he will, but never without the Word."[117] This draws a line of paramount distinction between Reformed spirituality and other approaches:

> Mysticism makes a place for the experiential dimension in Christian faith, but in its radical form it subverts the paradoxical unity of Word and Spirit, subordinating the former to the latter. Rationalism also fosters a break in dialectic of Word and Spirit, and it ends with a purely logos Christology. Evangelical catholicity strives to unite Word and Spirit by viewing them as inseparable and indissoluble.[118]

Joel Beeke describes Reformed spirituality to be essentially the outworking of 2 Timothy 3:16, deeming any spirituality not founded in Scripture to be "unbiblical mysticism." "Reformed Christianity has followed a path of its own, largely determined by its concern to test all things by Scripture and to develop a spiritual life shaped by Scripture's teaching and directives."[119] This continuation of the Reformational rediscovery of the sufficiency and authority of the Bible conveys that which is quintessential to Reformed spirituality.[120]

Equally, when considering Spirit in its juxtaposition with the Word we note the theocentricity of Reformed spirituality through gospel revelation, practically established in private and corporate worship, Bible

---

115. Peter Adam highlights that Evangelical spirituality focuses on an intense personal relationship with God, with worship that is suspicious of formality, whereas Reformed spirituality is concerned with one's spiritual state before God. Adam, *Biblical Spirituality*, 37.

116. Cornick, "Reformed Spirituality"; McGrath, *Roots*, 63–64.

117. Kepler *Tabletalk of Martin Luther*, 143, cited in Bloesch, *Spirituality*, 86.

118. Bloesch, *Spirituality*, 49.

119. Beeke, *Puritan*, vii.

120. Adam, *Biblical Spirituality*, 23, 34.

Complementarian Spirituality

reading, prayer, the sacraments, and the sacramental nature of preaching. Cornick remarks that the Reformation brought about a renewed response both theologically and spiritually to the "otherness" of God, contrary to the sacramentalism of Roman Catholicism and its promises of divine presence. "Finite things, the Reformed argued, could not contain the infinite. Only God could bridge the gap between God and humanity, and God had done so in Christ, as the Scriptures and dominical sacraments bore witness."[121]

In addition, this imperative of the "Spirit" in Reformed spirituality is the presentation of the triune Godhead immanent in salvation, distinguishing it from mysticism's quest for the transcendent monotheistic divine. This decisive dialectic between Word and Spirit ties Reformed theology and spirituality together.

As Word and Spirit meet, the evidence of the Christian life is obedience to God and conformity to Christ. "Let our souls not rest until the Word and Spirit do their work. Then we shall be changed 'from glory to glory,' and come forth from God's presence with a radiant countenance, with our lives mirroring Christ's holy image."[122] The pursuit of sanctification is a considerable thrust in historical and contemporary Reformed spirituality. This is because Christian holiness is a fundamental thread running throughout the NT, particularly the Pauline epistles, which the Reformers and particularly the Puritans stressed as the fruit of a life spent "in Christ."

The theme of searching for God in order to *know* him is unarguably the foundational *motivation* of Christian spirituality. This crux of spirituality is native to Reformed spirituality, as recent titles such as *Knowing God, Desiring God, A Heart for God*, and *The Pursuit of God* demonstrate the hunger of Reformed believers to commune with the Godhead. The belief that "knowledge of God" is the starting point for Reformed spirituality stems back to Calvin's stress on the Bible's expression of the spiritual life. This "has been represented and made popular in recent years in the classic *Knowing God* by J. I. Packer."[123] Yet *Sola gratia* pervades Reformed thought so entirely that all of salvation and spirituality is viewed from this doctrinal confession. As Packer succinctly states, "knowing God is a matter of grace."[124] In the centrality of grace, these Reformed writings view the attainment of holiness and Christ-likeness as the prime aims of spiritual

---

121. Cornick, "Reformed Spirituality," 533.
122. Beeke, "Seeing God's Glory," 28.
123. Adam, *Biblical Spirituality*, 34.
124. Packer, *Knowing God*, 40.

Introduction

formation, and not the perfected use of spiritual disciplines or ascent union with God as other Christian traditions might emphasis. When the spiritual disciplines are addressed, they are discussed either as "means of grace" for sanctification or for the glorification of God.

Indispensible to understanding the Reformed motivation in spirituality is the central theme of the glorification of God. Frequent reference in contemporary Reformed literature to the first question of the WSC suggests that the motif or anthem of Reformed spirituality is, "The chief end of man is to glorify God and enjoy him forever." Cornick concurs on the centrality of these two Reformed themes: "Reformed spirituality is captivated by the glory and the graciousness of God."[125]

In summary, the priesthood of all believers, the centrality of Scripture, the ultimate human purpose in the glorification of God, high esteem for the catholicity of the visible and invisible church, the indissoluble union between Word and Spirit, and striving for Christ-likeness in the centrality of grace in all of life are all crucial identifying marks of Reformed spirituality.

Now we turn to the doctrinal legacy of the *unio mystica* passed down through hundreds of years of Reformed thought.

---

125. Cornick, *Letting God*, 80.

2

Union with Christ: A Reformed Legacy

UNION WITH CHRIST IS a doctrine of many facets and elements; it is a doctrine "mysterious and profound," "vast in its dimensions."[1] Said to be "the heart" of Pauline religion, theologians throughout Christian history have implemented this NT theme to construct both systematic soteriologies and spiritual perspectives on the Christian life.[2]

In the Reformed tradition, this doctrine has fundamental significance. It is the union of the Redeemer and the redeemed, corporately and individually; it is the covenant marriage between Christ and his Bride, the church. It is the intimate solidarity of the Christian with his Lord and Savior as biblically portrayed in terms of the vine and the branches (John 15), the head and the body (1 Cor 12), the cornerstone and the building (Eph 2), and the husband and the wife (Eph 5).

Although Scripture teaches and depicts the doctrine of union with Christ, it is vital to acknowledge that the bounds of human language cannot fully communicate it. Puritan John Flavel observes that even as the biblical metaphors seemingly work together in revealing the "in Christ" relationship, they fail to present the divine mystery in its entirety.[3] Indeed, it is the *mysterious* divine nuptial referred to by Paul in the fifth chapter of Ephesians. Since the sacred nature of this doctrine masks it from full comprehensibility, our attempt to describe it is subject to restriction.

It is perhaps in response to the profundity of the *unio mystica* that a tendency remains in contemporary theological discussion to approach union with Christ in relation to other soteriological elements (predominantly

1. Donnelly, *Life*, 12.
2. Stewart, *Man in Christ*, 147.
3. Flavel, "John 17:23."

justification and sanctification).[4] Thus, the nature of union with Christ *in and of itself* is not a frequented subject and the contemporary church in the West understands little of the union she enjoys with Christ.

A HISTORICAL METHOD

The aim of this chapter is to explore the meaning and significance of union with Christ in pre-Reformational and intra-Reformational theology. Here the study will profit from sampling key theologians who have wrestled with this doctrine throughout the centuries in order to comprehend the position of union with Christ in applied soteriology and its wider application to church life in the sacraments.

Owing to the direction of this study, we do not have the freedom to delve at any length into the current scholarly debates that impinge upon union with Christ, for there are many. Areas of ongoing or recent theological discourse, such as union with Christ and its relationship with justification and sanctification, particularly in Calvin's *duplex gratia* or the Finnish interpretation of Luther, will be included appropriately in order to aid the precision of our theological sketch. Equally, the purpose of this chapter and the next to serve as theological outlines of our doctrine, necessary for the development of this project, restricts discussion to a largely descriptive method, so limiting any critical evaluation of the contributions expounded.

Our historical summary will consist initially of a brief survey of pre-Reformation influences, particularly the patristic concept of *theōsis*, "adopted by the Greek Fathers to describe the effect of the incarnation upon the nature of those incorporated into the body of Christ."[5] Then we will highlight the Reformation and the intra-Reformational discourse pertaining to union with Christ, its role in soteriology, and of course the "Supper-Strife." Due to the fact that the *unio mystica* is a dominant theme in Calvin's thought and his marked influence upon the forming of a Reformed conception on the subject, more time has intentionally been set apart in perusal of his contribution. Puritan perspectives on the *unio mystica*, the rise of Reformed Orthodoxy, and the *ordo salutis* method are then outlined in the wake of the Reformation, finishing with a look at a sample of influential contemporary approaches.

---

4. Pink, *Union*, 7.
5. Bonner, "Deification."

TERMINOLOGY

Since Calvin, many Reformed theologians have approached applied soteriology under what William Evans calls the "rubric 'union with Christ.'"[6] In observation of the differing theological uses of this umbrella theme, Evans prefers to view union with Christ as a "theme" or "motif" instead of a "doctrine."[7] However, owing to the clear prominence that the "in Christ" relationship has in the NT and its historical place in Reformed systematics, we will continue to manage it as a biblical doctrine belonging to the discipline of systematic theology and not merely as a soteriological theme.

This study will use the terms *unio mystica*, *unio Christi*, *unio cum Christo*, "Christ-union," "in Christ," and "union with Christ" synonymously. Importantly, the doctrine of "union with Christ" in the Protestant Reformed tradition is our subject and therefore concepts of "union with the divine" belonging to other fields of thought, such as the *Mysticismus* theme of *Eros*, are not deemed to be relevant.[8]

PRE-REFORMATION INFLUENCE: INCARNATION AND THEŌSIS

"In the period spanning late medieval mystical theologies and the new Reformation model(s) of salvation, a number of 'unions with Christ' [that is] incarnational/natural, justifying, Eucharistic, ontological, marital [amongst others] . . . belonged to the ordinary discourse of both professional (academic) and popular spiritualities."[9] In recognizing this apparent diversity and yet the familiarity of a basic concept of union with Christ at a time of such profound theological upheaval as the Reformation, it is important to see the prior influences passed down, especially those of the patristics.

Athenagoras (ca.133–190), Irenaeus (c.130–c.200), Gregory of Nyssa (c.335–c.394), and Basil (330–379), all possessed a concept of "union" or "unification" (*henosis*) in the hypostatic union of Christ's divine and human nature. However, as Norman Russell demonstrates in his important work *The Doctrine of Deification in the Greek Patristic Tradition*, these concepts differ.[10] It is in relation to this understanding of the hypostatic union of the divine with humanity that Athanasius (c.293–373) discerns the intimate

---

6. Evans, *Imputation*, 2.
7. Ibid.
8. Cf. Bloesch, *Spirituality*, 86, 91, 147.
9. Garcia, *Life in Christ*, 85.
10. Russell, *Deification*, 1–2.

Union with Christ: A Reformed Legacy

union or *theōsis* between the divine and the believer, following Clement of Alexandria (c.150–215), who was the first to use the term technically.[11] Clement's stance on *theōsis*, like Origen, has more philosophical qualities than that of Athanasius, who expresses a more apophatic union of participation with the divine, through union with the body of the incarnate Christ.[12] Thus, the union of divinity and humanity in the incarnation is of immense significance to a patristic rendering of union with Christ, and the atonement as a whole. "Many Fathers, particularly of the Alexandrian tradition, considered the concepts of the Incarnation of God and the deification of man to be correlative to one another."[13] For Athanasius and Irenaeus, the latter also building on the Pauline concept of Christ as the second Adam, the entirety of redemption centers on the incarnation.[14] Athanasius' celebrated axiom, "He, indeed, assumed humanity that we might become God," encompasses the belief that the clothing of the divine *Logos* in human flesh is the climactic or "decisive moment, the supreme efficacious intervention" for the work of redemption to effectually take place.[15]

This deference for the incarnation has remained a strong soteriological theme, followed by Anselm (1033–1109), John Calvin (1509–1564), and Karl Barth (1886–1968).[16]

The principle of deification, which one might regard in its Cappadocian form as an early equivalent of the later Protestant doctrine of union with Christ, did not receive any formal definition until the sixth century by Dionysius the Areopagite.[17] The early concept operated on a metaphorical level and it was not until early Byzantine thought that *theōsis* became a dogma.[18] In "deification" the believer shares the divine life or "nature" (2 Pet 1:4) and Eden is reversed as the restored believer enjoys union with God. Importantly, the soul is not "deified" ontologically through the mingling of substance, but ascends to God in a participatory transformed life initiated

---

11. Michel Dupuy, "Union à Dieu," cols. 40–61, cited in Garcia, *Life in Christ*, 49–51; Russell, *Deification*, 1.

12. Russell, *Deification*, 12–13, 177.

13. Ibid., 7.

14. Letham, *Christ*, 28.

15. Athanasius, *Incarnation*, 8:5; Marquart, "Luther and Theosis," 184.

16. Letham, *Christ*, 28–29.

17. Dionysius defined deification as "the attaining of likeness to God and union with him so far as is possible." Russell, *Deification*, 1.

18. Ibid., 1.

through baptism and the work of the Holy Spirit. Robert Letham designates this emphasis on the indwelling Holy Spirit as "pneumatocentric soteriology," stating that such an emphasis accounts for the Eastern perspective in the *filioque* controversy.[19]

Theōsis is explicitly Trinitarian as it relates the Trinity directly to union. "To know the mystery of the Trinity in its fullness is to enter into perfect union with God and to attain to the deification of the human creature: in other words, to enter into the divine life" and partake in the divine nature.[20] Importantly then, *theōsis* is not an ontological interpenetration as in Trinitarian *perichoresis*, but a communication of God's energies to the believer bringing about transformation.[21] St. Basil elucidates, "it is by His energies that we say we know our God; we do not assert that we can come near to the essence itself, for His energies descend to us, but His essence remains unapproachable."[22]

A. N. Williams notes that Cyril of Alexandria's notion is substantially similar to that of Athanasius. She writes, "together with the latter and Gregory of Nyssa, he is the outstanding proponent of the physical concept of deification: perfection entails the remission of both fleshy corruption and fleshy passion."[23] Yet Gregory of Nyssa like the other Cappodocians took a much different approach, which Russell categorizes as "ethical" as it focuses upon the imitation of Christ, almost synthesizing Alexandrian ideas with Platonic thinking.[24] "For the Cappadocians, deification never went beyond a figure of speech. Gregory of Nazianzus made extensive use of it in his discussion of the Christian life. Gregory of Nyssa, by contrast, while accepting it in the case of the physical body of Christ and, by extension, of the bread of the Eucharist, was unwilling to apply it to the believer."[25]

It is difficult to know which pre-Reformation writings had most influence on the Reformers. Only Calvin's employment of St Bernard of Clairvaux (1090–1153) on union with Christ is explicit, which many contemporary scholars view as biased in his omission of Bernard's

---

19. Letham, *Western Eyes*, 254.
20. Lossky, *Mystical Theology*, 67.
21. Bray, "Deification," 189–90; Lossky, *Mystical*, 9–10.
22. "Epistle 234 (ad Amphilochium)," *PG*, XXXII, 869 AB, cited in Lossky, *Mystical*, 72.
23. Williams, *Union*, 30.
24. Russell, *Deification*, 9, 13, 206.
25. Ibid., 13; Bonner, "Deification," 265.

contemplative spirituality.[26] In addition, Calvin's stress on the non-soteriological union of God with man in the incarnation seems to reflect Athanasius above, yet there is no firm evidence for this. J. Todd Billings, author of *Calvin, Participation, and the Gift: The Activity of Believers in Union with Christ*, is suspicious of giving Calvin "hidden sources" and only asserts that "through a gradual and eclectic appropriation from various church fathers, Calvin develops theological presuppositions which do not neatly fit into the generalized categories of 'Thomist', 'nominalist', or 'voluntarist.'"[27] Yet, many influential sources are unhidden as Calvin quotes his predecessors. This is well exemplified in Calvin's numerous citations of church fathers in his scriptural approach to sacramental theology in the 1536 edition of the *Institutes*.[28]

Augustine and the Reformation

The influence of Augustine (354–430) upon Reformation thought is unarguable. We know that Calvin read Augustine from his significant quotation of him, and for this reason he probably stood at the "forefront" of Calvin's retrospection of the church fathers.[29] From Augustinian writings, one observes that the union of Christ's human and divine natures in the incarnation is the apex of Augustine's soteriology. William Mallard writes of Augustine: "The rightly conceived mediator, divine and human, was saving mediator for *him* . . . To know the incarnation truly, regardless of speculative models, is to know one's salvation."[30] On this note, Augustine brings verisimilitude to Athanasius: "Christ takes on the human condition in order that humanity may take on a heavenly condition."[31] Considerable to Augustine's perception of union is that he sees Christ and the church to be *totus Christus*, the whole Christ.[32]

Deification is a theme in Augustine's theology of participation, which is influenced by Platonic thought but grounded in the incarnate Mediator. Deification also has ecclesiastical relevance, as it is the gradual process of

---

26. Tamburello, *Union* ; Lane, *John Calvin*, 11–12, 81; Billings, *Calvin*, 21.

27. Billings, *Calvin*, 38, 26.

28. Ibid., 39.

29. Billings claims that in Calvin's early years his use of Augustine is slight, compared to his later decades. Ibid., n39, 40.

30. Mallard, "Christ."

31. Ibid., 469.

32. Augustine, *De Trinitate* 4.14.19; Ferguson, *Holy Spirit*, 109.

grace found through the church and the administration of the sacraments.[33] Gerald Bonner contends that Augustine's notion, fixed on "the priority of divine grace and action" and "the marriage-union between the Redeemer and his redeemed," is nothing less than Pauline adoption.[34]

At any rate, one can readily observe the impact of Augustinian theology into the late medieval period. "By the later Middle Ages, the *unio mystica* was a common theme in theological literature whether of the *Devotio moderna* or of the *Via moderna*."[35]

Current debate continues on whether the West has a definition of deification akin to that of the East or, as Billings warns, "there may be different, yet legitimate, conceptions of deification in the West, arising from the common sources for theologies of deification: scripture and the church fathers."[36] In her work, *The Ground of Union: Deification in Aquinas and Palamas*, Williams responds, "The West has no grounds for rejecting deification, not only because it can be found in Aquinas but also because it figures extensively in the patristic corpus and derives ultimately from scripture."[37] The truth behind this matter has ramifications on the weight of influence that patristic *theōsis* has on Protestant "union with Christ." Yet Billings deems it safe to observe that deification "can be an appropriate term for Calvin's theology of union with God through Christ, if understood as a soteriology that affirms the unity of humanity and divinity, such that redemption involves the transformation of believers to be incorporated into the triune life of God, while remaining creatures."[38]

Thomas Aquinas and the Sacraments

The thought of Thomas Aquinas (1225–1274) is another key antecedent authority upon the Reformers, although it is "far from clear," says A. N. Williams, whether Aquinas holds to a doctrine of deification. Following suit from the Greek fathers, Aquinas looks at length at the union of the divine and human natures in the incarnation, and its corollaries, in his *Summa Theologica*.[39] Union with Christ is also particularly prevalent in his theology

---

33. Clancy, "Redemption," 702–4.
34. Bonner, "Deification," 266; Garcia, *Life in Christ*, 57.
35. Garcia, *Life in Christ*, 57.
36. Billings, *Calvin*, 53–54.
37. Williams, *Union*, 174.
38. Billings, *Calvin*, 54.
39. Williams, *Union*, 34.

Union with Christ: A Reformed Legacy

of the sacraments, which receive their efficacy from the Word made flesh.[40] "Baptism is a sign of Christ's suffering and death bringing men to new birth in Christ; whereas the eucharist is a sign of Christ's suffering bringing men into finished unity with the Christ who suffered. Baptism is *the sacrament of a faith*, which lays the spiritual life's foundation; the eucharist is *the sacrament of a love*, which is *the bond of perfection*."[41] Joseph Martos sums up Aquinas on the Lord's Supper, distinguishing our doctrine of interest, with a perspective resembling Calvin: the Eucharist gives "Christians a means of spiritual nourishment. *The reality of the sacrament was therefore a grace, the grace of union with Christ experienced in the reception of communion*."[42] This will be drawn upon later in our study.

THE REFORMATION

Louis Berkhof observes that the Reformation stimulated new systems of thought for the study of redemption, characterizing "soteriology" as we know it in contemporary theology as well as specific attention to "new life in Christ."[43] As we will see, Reformation thought instigated richer and fuller theological rationales for salvation through union with Christ. The plural "rationales" is used owing to early Protestantism's varying perspectives on the "in Christ" relationship and its posture in soteriology. Indeed, the differences between Calvin and his contemporary Lutherans, noted in Calvin's dialogue with Melanchthon, which since grew into the Calvinistic and Lutheran traditions, demonstrate such diversity.[44]

Martin Luther

The influence of mystical theology upon Martin Luther does account for the notable posture of the *unio mystica* (distinguishable from the mysticism "quasi-ontological" concept) in Luther's doctrine of justification.[45] Luther emphasizes justification by faith through union with Christ in his work *Von der Freiheit e. Christenmannes* ("The Freedom of a Christian Man"), defin-

---

40. Berkouwer, *Sacraments*, 11; Aquinas, *Summa Theologica* 60:1, 546.
41. *Summa Theologica* 73:3, 569.
42. Martos, *Doors to the Sacred*, 237, cited in Bloesch, *Church*, 149–50 (emphasis added).
43. Berkhof, *Systematic*, 417.
44. Garcia, *Life in Christ*, 7.
45. Ibid., 62–63.

Complementarian Spirituality

ing faith as the "wedding ring" that takes hold of Christ, *fides apprehensiva Christi*.[46] Luther writes, the "incomparable benefit of faith is that it unites the soul with Christ as a bride is united with her bridegroom. By this mystery, as the Apostle teaches, Christ and the soul become one flesh."[47] This union of "one body and flesh" is the "most perfect of marriages" where everything is held in common.[48] Through faith then the *unio Christi* secures justification by the imputation of Christ's righteousness onto the believing sinner. The activity of the Spirit of Christ is also crucial to the believer apprehending Christ by union. Similar to Calvin's view, such a tangible union is necessary since salvation is inseparable from Christ. "Without this concrete presence, Luther believed that the redemptive work of Christ in the flesh would lose its graciousness. We would be trapped in a new legalism, with the salvation won by Christ as the elusive prize that we must seek anxiously to appropriate by good works and devotion."[49] The believer's sanctification also stems from this union, as Luther states the eternal Word imparts the believer's soul with qualities like a heated iron glows in its union with fire.[50]

Luther's contribution moved the concept of Christ-union from its mystical elitist form of final elation to a universal doctrine of justification domesticated for every believing household. In the words of Garcia, *unio* shifted from the "monastery to the farm."[51]

The New Finish Interpretation

The New Finnish School, headed up by Professor Tuomo Mannermaa, has presented a new interpretation of Luther as it considers traditional readings to be too heavily influenced by post-Kantian thought. "Faith as volitional obedience rather than as ontological participation is all that a neo-Kantianized Luther could allow. [Whereas] the Finns have found that Luther's texts, when read critically against the background of late medieval philosophy and theology," advocate a *theōsis* concept akin to Orthodoxy.[52] Mannermaa and the "Helsinki Circle" accentuate mystical and ontological features in

---

46. Luther, "Freedom," 352.
47. Ibid., 351.
48. Ibid.
49. Yeago, "Luther," 333.
50. Luther, "Freedom," 349.
51. Garcia, *Life in Christ*, 65.
52. Braaten and Jenson, *Finnish Interpretation*, viii–ix; Mannermaa, "Luther."

Luther and avoid his forensic thought.⁵³ Mannermaa defends, "the indwelling of Christ as grasped in the Lutheran tradition implies a real participation in God and it corresponds in a special way to the Orthodox doctrine of participation in God, namely the doctrine of *theōsis*. This conclusion was not a commonly accepted understanding of how one might find the point of contact that we were seeking."⁵⁴ Though Mannermaa and his colleagues seemingly open themselves up to the criticism of mere ecumenism under the guise of a rereading of Luther on union, this new position has caused an important contemporary debate within the wider Protestant traditions on Luther's soteriology.⁵⁵ Carl Trueman asserts that Mannermaa does present some valid points, particularly in identifying post-Kantian trajectories upon Luther.⁵⁶ Nevertheless, in their task of representing an "authentic Luther" from his considerable writings, covering the length of his life, the Finns tend to focus on early pre-Reformation extracts and "decontextualized readings" of *theōsis* without any methodological justification.⁵⁷

However unclearly Luther might purport identification with the divine *Logos*, he clearly rejects an ontological participation:

> The Logos puts on our form and figure and image and likeness, in order that He might clothe us with His image, form, likeness . . . We who are flesh are made Word *not by being substantially changed into the Word*, but by taking it on [*assumimus*] and uniting it to ourselves by faith, on account of which union we are said not only to have but even *to be* the Word.⁵⁸

In response to this Mannermaa is careful to assert that Luther displays a sort of *theōsis* that may "not simply be equated with the patristic-Orthodox doctrine of deification."⁵⁹ This position sees faith to beckon the believer into the presence of Christ and complete participation with his righteousness and that of the Godhead. Contrary to a forensic Melanchthonian stance on justification as declared righteousness, this communication of the divine righteousness is *actual* as the believer shares in the "divine life."⁶⁰

53. Metzger, "Luther and the Finnish School."
54. Mannermaa, "Luther," 2.
55. Trueman, "Finnish Line."
56. Ibid., 234.
57. Ibid., 235–37, 242–43.
58. WA 1 28:25–32, 39–41, cited in Marquart, "Luther," 186–87 (emphasis added).
59. Marquart, "Luther," n186.
60. Mannermaa, "Luther," 2.

However, Reformed theologian Mark Garcia says, on the contrary, that Luther is only centralizing faith in order to teach *Solus Christi* in his response to the ontological union of his contemporaneous high mysticism.[61]

John Calvin

Calvin engaged in numerous discussions and controversies with other Reformers, Protestant theological dissenters, and Rome pertaining to the "sacred wedlock" of the *unio cum Christo*.[62] In relation to this, it is essential to recognize that Calvin's discourses do not exist in a theological vacuum. In other words, one must be careful not to take Calvin out of his historical-theological context with its disputes and emphases, acknowledging that his presentations of union with Christ are culturally conditioned by the theological interchange of his time.[63] There are, of course, pre-Reformation influences upon Calvin as well as those contemporary to him. For example, Garcia demonstrates that the Augustinian *duplex iustitia* gives precedence to Calvin's *duplex gratia* structuring of union with Christ.[64] Equally, significant is Calvin's somewhat patristic emphasis on the incarnation as the necessary "non-redemptive platform" for union with Christ, which has, in the challenge of being named "incarnational universalism," called for a division in Calvin's redemptive and non-redemptive modes of union.[65] A further example is Calvin's pneumatic Christology, shaped by his adherence to Chalcedonian Christology, evident in the Eucharist and Servetus controversies.[66] In sum, enquiries into Calvinistic thought must consider the determinative theological atmosphere, including that of our present day as well as that contemporary to Calvin.

In Calvin scholarship, new interpretations of Calvin's *unio mystica* never fail to emerge, affecting his dogma and spirituality. There have been recent trends "to focus on Calvin as a relational theologian or as a theologian of union with Christ, even ontological union with Christ," which Thomas L. Wenger has named "the New Perspective on Calvin."[67] Articles such as that from Charles Partee have explored whether the *unio mystica* is

---

61. Garcia, *Life in Christ*, 64.
62. *Institutes*, 3.1.3
63. Garcia, *Life in Christ*, 25.
64. Ibid., 47.
65. Ibid., 26–27.
66. Cf. ibid., 24–25.
67. Clark, "Election," 97–98; Wenger, "New Perspective," 311.

in fact central to his discourse. Partee views the "vigorous" assertion of this doctrine to be "the central mystery of Calvin's theology" "and understanding of the Christian faith" as it serves as a "pivot" to the *Institutes*.[68] Many have similarly considered this doctrine to be the "controlling principle" in Calvin's applied soteriology.[69] Wilhelm Kolfhaus states it to be the cohesion of Calvin's soteriology, and similarly Brunner declares it the "centre of all Calvinistic thinking."[70]

Indeed, readers do not have to delve long into the *Institutes* to see the weight of the *unio mystica* in Calvin's soteriology. Deeming the Christ-union as the necessary means for the efficacy of the work of the cross to be applied to the sinner, he writes, "we must understand that as long as Christ remains outside of us, and we are separated from him, all that he has suffered and done for the salvation of the human race remains useless and of no value for us."[71] For Calvin then one has to *possess* Christ—his person, not merely his benefits—in order to be secure.

> Therefore, that joining together of Head and members, that indwelling of Christ in our hearts—in short, that mystical union—are accorded by us the highest degree of importance, so that Christ, having been made ours, makes us sharers with him in the gifts with which he has been endowed. We do not, therefore, contemplate him outside ourselves from afar in order that his righteousness may be imputed to us but because we put on Christ and are engrafted into his body – in short, because he deigns to make us one with him.[72]

Gaffin summaries this point again: "So central and pivotal is this union for the application of redemption that, again expressing it negatively, he can

---

68. Partee is careful not to give this doctrine an unfair monopoly in Calvin's theology as he states that Calvin did not set out to present his theology around any one doctrine. Partee, "Calvin's Central."

69. Carpenter, "Calvin and Trent," 363–64.

70. Tamburello, *Union*, 85.

71. *Institutes*, 3.1.1.

72. *Institutes*, 3.11.10. In his *Institutes* Calvin uses a range of terms to convey this doctrine: *Insero* or *insitio* rendered "engrafting"; "communion" appears twenty times, and the Latin *communio* or *communico* appears sixteen times. *Societas* or "fellowship" is used nine times and *participes* or "partaking with Christ" ten times. Interestingly, Calvin uses the term *unio mystica* only twice, perhaps most significantly in 3.11.10.

even say that without it the saving work of Christ 'remains useless and of no value.'"[73]

The Crux of Faith and Spirit

Calvin's definition and approach to the *unio cum Christo* centers on the Holy Spirit and faith; so vital is faith wrought by the Spirit that it renders this union essentially *"Spirit-effected" unio cum Christo*.[74] It is important to remember that the work of faith and the Spirit are fully intent upon Christ, however, and that Calvin's articulation is christocentric since union is not with the "divine" but entirely and solely founded on the God-man Jesus Christ.

Faith is so crucial to Calvin's understanding of union that some scholars, such as Kolfhaus, have held that for him faith *is* union with Christ.[75] Yet Calvin sees a clear logical distinction between the two. For faith, the *instrument* that ties the believer to Christ is "the principal work of the Holy Spirit."[76] It is this saving faith that renders union to be soteric. Even with Calvin's emphasis on the incarnation, shared humanity is not sufficient without the binding of the Spirit. This soteric inseparability of Christ and the Spirit *of Christ* or "pneumatic Christology" is somewhat characteristic of Calvin's Trinitarian thought and demonstrates his biblical Christology:

> Calvin's doctrine of union with Christ lies embedded in a theology governed by trinitarian presuppositions. This trinitarianism, moreover, is coupled *with a pneumatic Christology that determines the shape of his soteriology*. In other words, Calvin's insistence that salvation is trinitarian does not compromise but strengthens his exhortation to look to Christ alone: salvation comes to us from the Father through Christ by the Holy Spirit. The fact that it is through Christ alone accounts for the shape of his teaching on union with Christ.[77]

Thus, Jesus came with the Spirit who sanctifies and the Spirit is "the root and seed of heavenly life in us."[78] He marries Christ to the believer not in a "crass mixture of substances" but in a "spiritual" real union.[79]

73. Gaffin, "Justification," 259.
74. Garcia, *Life in Christ*, 14; Gaffin, "Justification," 259, 262.
75. Tamburello, *Union*, 85.
76. *Institutes*, 3.1.4
77. Garcia, *Life in Christ*, 24 (emphasis added).
78. *Institutes*, 3.1.2
79. Tamburello, *Union*, 87.

This unified trinitarian appreciation of union as it originated in the eternal counsel between the persons of the Trinity gives us some understanding of the "integral relationships between the forensic and transformative aspects of redemption as distinctively displayed in the operation of each divine person."[80]

In Dialogue with Osiander

Initially involved in intra-Lutheran disputes with Luther and Melanchthon (1497–1560) on justification, Andreas Osiander's (1498–1552) later dialogue with Calvin offers much insight into the French reformer's view of the nature of *unio mystica*. Indeed, Garcia purports that these interactions demonstrate "with clarity the precise points where Christology, pneumatology, and soteriology intersect in the matrix of Calvin's thought" as well as its sacramental relevance.[81]

Essentially Osiander combines justification and union with Christ in the notion that Christ's indwelling divinity imparts "essential righteousness." In Calvin's refutation of this "strange monster" or "wild dream" of transfusing "the essence of God into men," he labors to demonstrate a Spirit-based union that does not demean Christ's substitutionary death.[82] "He [Osiander] has clearly expressed himself as not content with that righteousness which has been acquired for us by Christ's obedience and sacrificial death, but pretends that we are substantially righteous in God by the infusion both of his essence and of his quality."[83] Further, Osiander declares that all triune Persons dwell in the believer through this union. Yet Calvin maintains a triune indwelling only to the degree that "the Father and Spirit are in Christ, and even as the fullness of deity dwells in him, so *in him* we possess the whole of deity."[84] In other words, whereas Osiander's union with Christ's divinity infers the soul joining in with the Trinity's *perichoresis*, Calvin's Trinitarianism and Chalcedonian Christology founds his position that union with Christ through the incarnation is the only means of divine indwelling. That is, the believer's union *with Christ* is essential but not based on shared essence.

---

80. Horton, *Salvation*, 131.
81. Garcia, *Life in Christ*, 45.
82. *Institutes*, 3.11.5
83. Ibid.
84. *Ibid.* (emphasis added).

> For the fact that it [this union] comes about *through the power of the Holy Spirit* that *we grow together with Christ, and he becomes our Head and we his members*, he [Osiander] reckons of almost no importance unless Christ's essence be mingled with ours. But in his treatment of the Father and the Holy Spirit he more openly, as I have said, brings out what he means: namely that we are *not justified by the grace of the Mediator alone, nor is righteousness simply or completely offered to us in his person*, but that we are made partakers in God's righteousness when God is united to us in essence.[85]

To summarize, we observe features imperative to Calvin's view on union with Christ, determining his soteriology, ecclesiology, spirituality, and pastoral theology. Firstly, justification is dependent on one mediator (which is one person of the Trinity, Jesus Christ), clothing the believer in sufficient righteousness. Secondly, this union is incumbent on the work and power of the Holy Spirit bringing about faith in the believer, so incorporating the believer into a unified body under a particular leadership.

Calvin, Trent, and the Duplex Gratia

The Council of Trent, which significantly formalized "grace-assisted" merits within Romanist justification, first convened in December 1545, taking up the doctrine of justification in its first period and resulting with sixteen chapters and thirty-three canons on the subject.[86] Trent understood justification to involve the sinner actually becoming righteousness "in himself" and not "merely reckoned," therefore leaving no necessary distinction between forensic declaration and actual spiritual state.[87] Conversely, the Protestants held that "the legal, forensic character of salvation (imputation of righteousness) must occur" "prior to the subjective, renovative character of salvation (infusion of righteousness)."[88] Basic to Calvin's contribution here is his belief that justification and sanctification are indispensible to and yet distinct from union with Christ as they are integral elements in the soteric matrix that makes the believer one with Christ.[89] Calvin expounded these elements in his *Antidote to the Council of Trent* (1547), and more fully in his later edition

---

85. *Ibid.* (emphasis added).
86. Carpenter, "Calvin and Trent," 366–67.
87. Ibid, 368–69.
88. Ibid.," 362; McGrath, *Iustitua Dei*, 182.
89. Carpenter, "Calvin and Trent," 371.

of the *Institutes*, centralizing union with Christ as the "antidote" to human depravity within a Trinitarian soteriological framework.[90]

Directly related to this is Calvin's unique positioning of the *unio mystica* in the double grace—the *duplex gratia*—of justification and sanctification, in a way that "union with Christ has precedence in the sense that the twofold grace is rooted in union and flows out of it."[91] Much discussion continues in the present day on the mutual relationship between the definitive (legal) nature of justification, in that Christ's alien righteousness is imputed from outside the believer (*extra nos*), and the *in nobis* (within us) element of Christ's sanctifying and transformative work *in* the believer. The "persistent argument is if justification is truly rooted in union with Christ it cannot be strictly forensic or legal because the union itself is personal and dynamic."[92] Yet in his technical study on the *duplex gratia* Garcia accounts for this, inferring that Calvin's fluid dealings with union with Christ in the *Institutes* clearly fails to see any such tension. "Indeed, the closest idea in the sixteenth century that would approximate this non-imputative and anti-forensic understanding is found in the theology of Andreas Osiander, whose doctrine of union with Christ Calvin adamantly rejected."[93]

For Calvin understands Christ living in believers in two ways: the first by his governing, enlivening Spirit and the other by participation in his righteousness. These two distinct outworkings of union, constituting the synthetic whole, form a triangulation with union with Christ, so union is not subsidiary to justification or sanctification. Horton underlines the harmony of the forensic and transformative, observing its substantiation in later Reformed federal theology:

> In classic covenant theology, the solidarity of the body with its head is simultaneously legal and relational, judicial and familial. In such a union, there can be no facile oppositions between law and love, the courtroom and the family room, a verdict of righteousness *extra nos* and an organic, living, and growing relationship in which the justified grow up into Christ.[94]

However, we shall see later in our study that not all scholars regard this tension to have been fully accepted by later federal thought.

90. Ibid., 374, 379.
91. Gaffin, "Justification," 252.
92. Garcia, *Life in Christ*, 13.
93. Ibid., 85–86; Gaffin, "Justification," 268–69.
94. Horton, *Salvation*, 130.

Complementarian Spirituality

In Dialogue with Vermigli

Unlike his interaction with Osiander, Calvin agreed in his correspondence with Italian reformer Peter Martyr Vermigli on the nature of our doctrine.[95] Vermigli wrote to Calvin expressing his own opinion of a threefold union, of which Calvin responded in complete accord.[96]

The first union is that of incarnational flesh and blood as Christ unites himself to humanity by taking on human nature. Both Vermigli and Calvin deny that this union has any redemptive value as it merely serves as the natural physical "platform"[97] upon which a saving union can occur. The saving union, however, takes place through faith by the work of the Holy Spirit and is spiritual and not ontological or essential. Between these unions, one non-redemptive, the other redemptive, Vermigli then articulated a third intermediate union. Calvin understands the third union to be the "fruit" of the former, yet both Calvin and Vermigli do not give any clear qualification for the distinction of the latter two unions, only that this "immediate union," is Christ again "exert[ing] a second influence of His Spirit, enriching us by His gifts" for the growth of the Christian in hope, patience, sobriety, temperance, love for holiness and righteousness and devotion, prayer and hope of heaven.[98] Seemingly, Vermigli and Calvin agree that this second union is one of belonging or possession, whereby Christ puts the mark of his Spirit on the believer in order to sanctify them and bring them under his divine headship.

Before moving to Calvin's stance on the Lord's Supper and its relevance to the *unio mystica*, let us first summarize the contours of Calvin's thought on this fundamental doctrine. Calvin sees union with Christ to be the fountain from which justification and sanctification spring, obtained in the presence of faith by the work of the Holy Spirit.

> The 'triangulation' of union, justification, and sanctification could hardly be expressed more clearly; the controlling priority of Spirit-worked union is plain ('you must first possess Christ'), involving the integral inseparability, without confusion, of justification and sanctification. There is no partial union with Christ, no sharing in only some of his benefits. If believers do not have the whole Christ,

---

95. Anderson, "Peter Martyr."

96. Some scholars are in disagreement that Calvin holds to a threefold union concept; see Tamburello, *Union*, 86–87; and Willis-Watkins, "*Unio Mystica*," 78.

97. Garcia, *Life in Christ*, 275.

98. CO 15.723, cited in Garcia, *Life in Christ*, 277–78.

they have no Christ; unless they share in all his benefits they share in none of them.[99]

In addition, although the doctrine is crucially Trinitarian in all its soteriological bearing, the Calvinistic perspective portrays a "pneumatic Christology," whereby one possesses Christ in his humanity yet benefiting from his divinity by the Spirit.

"Supper-Strife": The Eucharist Debate

The Marburg Colloquy in 1529 witnesses to disagreement regarding the Eucharist between Luther and Zwingli. Luther maintained a view of "consubstantiation" where Christ's body and blood have a presence "'with, in and under' the bread and wine, instead of replacing them," whereas Zwingli (1484–1531), Calvin, and Bucer (1491–1551), on the other hand, saw some distinction between the spiritual reality and the symbols.[100] From his symbolic memorialist position, Zwingli went as far to deny the communication of grace through the elements, although his view seemingly changes later. Conversely, Calvin held in accordance with Augustine and Peter Lombard (c.1100–c.1164) that all sacraments are "the visible Word" or the "visible form of an invisible grace."[101] For Calvin, the Eucharist is the "special remedy" of a "real" "spiritual presence" of Christ that assures the believer of the profound reality of union with Christ.[102]

Significant also to the Reformation emphasis on the sacraments is their role in the incorporation of believers into membership of the visible church, revealing the Reformation value for corporate life, for "the Eucharist is an *agape* feast in which communicants cherish each other and testify of the bond that they enjoy with fellow believers in the unity of the Body of Christ."[103] Owing to the three differing views of Lutheran "consubstantiation," Zwinglian "memorialism," and Calvin's "spiritual presence," no universal Reformed view exists on the Eucharist. However, the standard confessional view as expressed in the Heidelberg Catechism (1563) and

---

99. Gaffin, "Justification," 269.

100. Beckwith, "Eucharist." In his examination on the Eucharist in the Reformation, Thomas J. Davies asserts that Luther's central issue or "real concern" in the eucharistic celebration is "not the ubiquity of Christ's Body but the power of the Word." Davies, *My Body*, 15–16.

101. *Institutes*, 4.14.1, 4.14.6; Reymond, *Systematic*, 918; Beeke, *Sacraments*, C–D.

102. Davies, *Body*, 72; Hesselink, "Reformed View."

103. Beeke, *Sacraments*, A–F; *Institutes*, 4.17.44

WCF is ostensibly Calvinistic, and so Calvin's "spiritual partaking of the flesh and blood of the risen Christ," also held by Bucer, Theodore Beza, and Peter Martyr, is generally seen as the Reformed view.[104]

Of course, the Eucharist together with baptism has significant bearing on the *unio mystica*, to which the role of the Holy Spirit, from the Godhead, and faith, from the believer, are vital. The question of how one can partake or "feed on" the resurrected Christ in the Eucharist is particularly weighty. In the consideration of a "local presence," one divides Christ from his Holy Spirit, leaving faith as a nonessential instrument. Thus, Heshusius's disagreement with Calvin circled on the assertion that "if the body of Christ is in heaven, it is not in the Supper, and that instead of him we have only a symbol."[105] Calvin retorted that it never occurred to the Apostle Paul that Christ needed to bodily leave heaven "because he knew that he is united to us in a different manner"; "the bond of our union with Christ is faith . . . so that instead of subjecting Christ to the figments of our reason, we seek him above in his glory."[106] Here we observe the governing position of union with Christ in soteriology shaping Calvin's Eucharist theology. The believer is already one with Christ through the *unio mystica* and therefore true ontological participation, such as the stance of Joachim Westphal, one of Luther's students, with whom Calvin exchanged a series of pamphlet dialogues, is superfluous. Garcia affirms this, "because the grace of salvation and the grace of the sacraments are the same grace, one anticipates the mutually interpretative language of union with Christ that pervades Calvin's thought."[107]

In addition to this, it is important to note that Calvin is concerned to stress that Christ's person is fully received, not just his benefits, exemplified in his call for "a greater communication of Christ in the Sacraments" in Bullinger's *Tractatio*.[108] Yet unfortunately Calvin's articulation of Christ's spiritual yet real presence in the Eucharist has been considered too complex, as Beeke points out his failure to "precisely explain" how the believer partakes of Christ.[109] This, together with the consideration that Calvin is

---

104. Hesselink, "Reformed View," 59–60.
105. Schaff, "Calvin and Heshusius."
106. Ibid.
107. Garcia, *Life in Christ*, 150.
108. Anderson, "Peter Martyr," 48.
109. Beeke, *Treatises*, E.

Union with Christ: A Reformed Legacy

too mystical by many nineteenth and twentieth-century theologians, has left Calvin's Eucharist teaching forsaken in recent centuries.[110]

Union with Christ and the Eucharist

An important element of Calvinistic thought to our discourse is the pneumatological consistency found in the role of the Holy Spirit of Christ as the "Bond" both in the Eucharistic partaking of Christ and the salvific *unio cum Christo*, suggesting that Calvin deems these two as intrinsically linked. For the Christian partakes in Christ's *substance* physically through the Spirit, as Romans 8:9 "teaches that the Spirit alone causes us to possess Christ completely and have him dwelling in us."[111] Therefore, we see that what Garcia termed as Calvin's "pneumatic Christology," which determined his soteriology, also extends into his Eucharist theology.[112]

In order to offer a historical Reformed understanding on the Eucharist we will briefly consider the subject from the thought of Scottish reformer Robert Bruce (c.1555–1631), who in delivering sermons on the subject was disengaged in the *intra*-Reformed debate on the Continent. Bruce's contemporary editor, Thomas F. Torrance, notes that in Bruce's teaching union with Christ or the believer's participation in Christ has much import. He writes, "this is just as strong in Bruce as it is in Calvin or in any of the Church Fathers which both loved to cite . . . Holy and eternal life from God resides in the Humanity of Christ, and we are given to share in it as we are united to Christ."[113] Hence, says Torrance, both Bruce and Calvin apprehend the role of the Spirit in enabling the believer to feed on Christ in the Lord's Supper.

The sixteenth-century reformers maintained that the Eucharist should always accompany the preached Word, for the "Word alone cannot be a Sacrament nor the element alone, but Word and element must together make a Sacrament."[114] In this, the giving of Christ's words of institution is necessary, whilst the sacrament, observed as a "holy sign and seal," should be "annexed to the preached Word of God" as a whole.[115]

---

110. Hesselink, "Reformed View," 59.
111. 4.17.12
112. Garcia, *Life in Christ*, 24.
113. Torrance and Bruce, *Lord's Supper*, 23–24.
114. Ibid., 33.
115. Ibid., 30, 46, 58–62.

Complementarian Spirituality

Like Augustine, the Reformers believed the sacraments to be visible forms leading the believer to Christ "by the eye," by means of a sacramental union between the element and the thing "signified."[116] The purpose of the Eucharist is spiritual nourishment as the Christian exercises the instrument of faith and the Holy Spirit offers the body and blood of Christ to him or her.[117] Equally, testifying to one's union with Christ, both sacraments are also a means of inserting the believer into the total Christ, that is, Christ and his church.[118] According to Calvin, the exhibition of Calvary in the elements of the Holy Supper "ratifies" the sacred union between Christ and his redeemed, which was bought by the cross.[119]

Akin to Calvin, Bruce understood it to be Christ *himself* that is given and not just the merits flowing from the bread and the wine as signifying and pointing to Calvary. In sum, Christ's benefits are not given apart from his person. Although, as Torrance notes, Calvin and Bruce emphasize union with Christ's *humanity* in the *unio mystica* and the Eucharist, Bruce avows that it is the whole Christ, his deity and humanity with the inseparability of his two natures, that is received.[120]

Overall, one might attribute Bruce's articulation of the Lord's Supper to be less complex than that of Calvin as he is seemingly quicker to declare that mystery of the Eucharist:

> There is no Sacrament but contains a high and divine mystery. Because a Sacrament is a mystery, then, it follows that a mystical, secret and spiritual conjunction corresponds well to the nature of the Sacrament. Since the conjunction between us and Christ is full of mystery, as the Apostle shows us (Eph 5:32), it is a mystical and spiritual conjunction that is involved. . . . It is not possible to show you by any ocular demonstration how Christ and we are conjoined. Whoever would understand that conjunction must have his mind enlightened with a heavenly sight . . . unless you have this heavenly illumination you can understand neither your

---

116. Ibid., 30, 45, 53–58; Reymond, *Systematic*, 917. Bruce highlights that Irenaeus described the thing signified as "the heavenly and spiritual thing, namely, *the whole Christ with His whole gifts, benefits and graces*, applied and given to my soul." Torrance and Bruce, *Supper*, 37; Calvin, *Treatises*, 172–73.

117. Torrance and Bruce, *Supper*, 40, 71, 91–92.

118. Ibid., 71.

119. Calvin, *Treatises*, 574.

120. Torrance and Bruce, *Supper*, 38.

own conjunction with Christ, nor the conjunction between the sign and the things signified in the Sacrament.[121]

However, Bruce fails to enlighten his readers on the origin of union with Christ in these sermons, inferring at least methodologically that his starting point is the Lord's Supper itself.

In concluding our outline of Calvin, it is reasonable to say that Calvin's contribution to the doctrine of union with Christ was influential, especially in its holding together of justification and sanctification, continuing in the theology of his pupils and evident in the theology of his contemporaries, of which John Knox is representative. "After Knox, the theme was carried forward by a series of gifted Scots clergy, whose literary remains were to influence Scottish religious life for generations."[122] The doctrine was held in high esteem by Puritans Samuel Rutherford (1600–1661) and William Guthrie (1620–1665), and the later Thomas Boston (1677–1732), moving us aptly on to the generations of Reformed Orthodoxy (RO) and Puritanism.

THE BEGINNINGS OF REFORMED ORTHODOXY

The generations that followed the Reformation saw the "rise of scholastic method, the advent of *ordo salutis* schemas, the development of federal theology, and the influence of pietist concerns"; thus, having an impact on Reformed thought as the sixteenth-century categories and methods were replaced.[123] One example of the effect of these technical scholastic categories upon Reformed soteriology, says William Evans, was the "eclipse" of "the concerns of Calvin—particularly his focus on union with the incarnate humanity or *substantia* of Christ."[124] However, in his stress of this Evans fails to acknowledge Richard A. Muller's challenge against such a dichotomizing between Calvin and the posterity of his thought, stating that post-Reformation history has been negatively misread.[125] This approach of setting Calvin against the thinkers of RO consequently dominated Calvin studies and the resultant understanding of the RO from the middle of the nineteenth century to the late twentieth, as R. Scott Clark and Letham

---

121. Ibid., 45–46.
122. Evans, *Imputation*, 65.
123. Ibid., 44.
124. Ibid., 51–52.
125. Muller, *After Calvin*.

observed, but this has now been outdated by Muller's critique.[126] Muller expresses the "variegated" but uniform nature of the Reformed tradition and declares that distinguishing the history of confessional thought from controversial theological thought is a methodological safeguard from misinterpretation like that which has taken place.[127] Nevertheless, the rise of a deemed "technical" approach to soteriology is significant when examining a new generation's approach to union with Christ. Thus, scholars have viewed a tendency in RO to focus on sequence and relationship befitting the *ordo salutis*, with a syllogistic dogmatic handling that replaces Calvin's more organic pastoral manner.[128] Evans notes that this change of treatment shaped both Reformed and Lutheran theology considerably, as a preoccupation with the wider *ordo salutis* replaced the prior centrality of *unio cum Christo*. Modification of the *unio cum Christo* within both traditions subsequently took place.[129]

Scottish theologians Thomas F. Torrance and James B. Torrance account for the simplification of union with Christ to a legal meaning to be down to the emergence of federal theology.[130] Torrance discerns this shift to be apparent in the tradition's confessional theology; wherein earlier Reformation catechisms state Christ *himself* to be the direct means of his benefits, the Westminster Standards state that it is through Christ's *benefits* that the believer partakes of Christ.[131] As Robert Letham points out, Torrance's method has "surprising holes" as he fails to incorporate the Larger Catechism (WLC 65–90) into his critique of Westminster, focusing only on the WCF.[132] Letham interjects that "the strictly logical and sequential pattern of the Confession is balanced by a focus on union with Christ in the Larger Catechism," and he later adds, "these two perspectives exist side by side, the Assembly did not view them as incompatible."[133] Even then, WCF 29.7 points to the heart of the Lord's Supper as "receiving and feeding on Christ" and WCF 26.2 underlines corporate responsibilities in shared union with Christ. The theological rupture here, from Torrance's viewpoint, is the loss

---

126. Clark, *Confessions*, 29; Muller, *After Calvin*, 3; Letham, *Westminster*, 107.
127. Muller, *After Calvin*, 8.
128. Evans, *Imputation*, 52.
129. Ibid., 54–55.
130. Ibid., 62.
131. Torrance, *School of Faith*, xlii, cited in ibid., 63.
132. Letham, *Westminster*, 106–9, 269.
133. Ibid., 110, 111.

of a Calvinistic emphasis upon the incarnation as the means of union, or the believer's union with Christ's humanity dispensing over into the sacraments, to an inadequate merely legal rendering.[134]

One might assume that the downgrade of Calvin's holistic and more organic or synthetic understanding of union with Christ (holding the double grace of forensic justification and spiritual transformation together) to the later emphasis on the federal or contractual has led recent theologians to fragment the doctrine into distinct unions.[135] Although initially this splitting of union with Christ into two or more distributaries was at the start, following from Calvin, only implicit, Evans claims that by the mid-seventeenth century Samuel Rutherford (1600–1661) and others began explicitly to distinguish various different unions with Christ.[136] Some, however, only attributed a plurality of forms or aspects of one unified union. A contemporary of Rutherford, English Puritan Thomas Watson (1620–1686) described the "mystic" or "conjugal" union as twofold: "natural" (the incarnational union described in Heb 2:16) and "sacred," with the latter containing both "federal" and "effectual" forms.[137] Jonathan Edwards (1703–1758) referred to three unions, distinguishing between "vital" and "spiritual," and then the "natural" union of incarnation, as seen in Calvin. The much later A. W. Pink (1886–1952) is representative of those who conceive the doctrine somewhat divisively, distinguishing between "mediatorial union," "mystical union," "federal union," "vital union," "saving union," "practical union," "experimental union," and "glory union," though considering them all aspects of one compound union.[138] This approach of presenting the *unio mystica* in such a multifaceted way is alien to Calvin's unified perspective.

PURITANS

In perceiving with Calvin the Christian's union with Christ as both the means of Christian salvation and beginning of all Christian life, the Puritans rarely treat union with Christ apart from communion with Christ.[139] However, although the two sit closer in Puritan thought than any other, union

---

134. Evans, *Imputation*, 62–63.
135. Ibid., 81.
136. Ibid., 82.
137. Watson, "Mystical Union."
138. Pink, *Union*, 7–17. Berkhof presents a multicity of unions but in a unified organicism. Berkhof, *Systematic*, 449.
139. Kay, *Trinitarian*, 119.

has "logical precedence" over communion.[140] Tudur Jones demonstrates this in his study "Union with Christ: The Existential Nerve to Puritan Piety," whilst offering evidence that union with Christ was "woven into the fabric of Protestant thinking in Britain in the sixteenth century."[141] For example, Jones draws from the important monograph of William Perkins (1558–1602), *A Grain of Mustard Seed*, wherein Perkins speaks of being "incorporated" into the body of Christ.[142] From similar case studies Jones interestingly deduces two dominant concepts in the Puritan understanding of the Christ-union, firstly that of covenant or federal headship, and secondly the notion of marriage, noting that they seemingly addressed the objective and subjective aspects of the doctrine, respectively.[143]

Perhaps the most popular Puritan contribution on union with the divine comes from John Owen (1616–1683), who published his work *Of Communion with God the Father, Son, and Holy Ghost, Each Person Distinctly, in Love, Grace, and Consolation* in 1657. Here Owen considers the nature of intra-Trinitarian unity and communion and the union and communion of the believer with the members of the Trinity. His emphasis on the Trinitarian nature of soteriology means he does not avoid or neglect the reality of the believer's union with God founded in union with Christ. However, not all his Puritan contemporaries made this distinction. Henry Scougal's (1650–1678) treatise *The Life of God in the Soul of Man* interestingly has a God-union at the heart of it. Scougal declares that true religion, or the Divine life, is the union of the soul with God, that is, "the very image of God drawn upon the soul," in order to reflect the divine perfections.[144] He does not develop on union with Christ but unpacks a concept of union in spirituality resembling a *Mysticismus* view of union with God.

Returning to Owen's strong Trinitarian stance on the *unio mystica* and his focus on the soteriological self-disclosure of the Trinity, Brian Kay claims Owen's emphasis on "the Trinity as the foundation substructure upon which is constructed almost the entirety of Christian soteriology" renders his contribution groundbreaking.[145] In this Trinitarian substructure, Owen understands each person of the Trinity relating to the believer

---

140. Ibid., 118; cf. Flavel, "John 17:23," 33, 35–36.
141. Jones, "Existential Nerve," 187.
142. Ibid., 187.
143. Ibid., 202.
144. Scougal, *Life of God*, 47.
145. Kay, *Trinitarian*, 113

in a distinct way, although Kay comments on his weak biblical argument for this. "Our communion, then, with God consisteth in his *communication of himself unto us, with our returnal unto him* of that which he requireth and accepteth, flowing from that *union* which in Jesus Christ we have with him."[146] Kay attributes Owen at this juncture with a "Spirit-centered Christology," whilst extending Christ's communication to the believer as encompassing the whole of the Trinity. For Owen then, "union with Christ turns out to be therefore an explicitly trinitarian affair itself."[147]

Characteristic of a Puritan perception of the "in Christ" relationship is the close connection of sanctification and union worked out in piety. "Our sanctification is not only from him meritoriously, but efficiently, yea, and in a kinde materially too, for . . . through our union with him there is a kinde of flowing of sanctification from him into us, as the principle of life."[148] Similarly, Walter Marshal writes in his *Gospel Mystery of Sanctification* (1692), "it is by our being in Christ, and having Christ himself in us; and that not merely by his universal Presence as he is God, but by such a close Union as that we are one Spirit, and one flesh with him, which is a Privilege peculiar to those that are truly sanctified."[149]

Influenced by medieval spirituality, Evans purports that the Puritans valued contemplation upon Christ and communion with him to the theological belittlement of union with Christ.[150] At this point, however, Evans seems unfair and his lack of primary sources to exemplify his point does his argument no justice. For Thomas Goodwin (1600–1680), Owen, and John Flavel (1627–1691) wrote lengthy theological contributions, providing new articulations in covenantal frameworks.

Goodwin and Owen believed the nature of union between the Father and the Son to give insight into the nature of the *unio mystica* between Christ and his church.[151] Goodwin particularly held to a threefold economic indwelling, lead by the Spirit, whereby all three members of the Godhead indwell the believer.[152] Flavel, who describes *unio mystica* as "supernatu-

---

146. Owen, *Works*, 8–9.

147. Kay, *Trinitarian*, 7.

148. Jeremiah Burroughs, *The Saints Treasury*, 46 (1654), cited in Kevan, *Grace*, 236.

149. Marshal, *Gospel Mystery of Sanctification*, London, 1692 (1714), cited in Kevan, *Grace*, 237.

150. Evans, *Imputation*, 76–78, 81.

151. Kay, *Trinitarian*, 180.

152. Ibid., 178.

ral," "immediate," "fundamental", "efficacious," "indissoluble," "honorable," "comfortable," "fruitful," and "enriching,"[153] stresses its mystery; "it is the singular honour of that blessed and holy flesh of Christ, to be so united as to make our person with him; that union is hypostatical, this only mystical."[154]

The Puritans strictly rejected the deification of the believer and any ontological union, though Anthony Tuckney, a member of the Westminster Assembly, delivered a sermon on 2 Peter 1:4 that reflected on ideas akin to Eastern deification, surmising that Peter wrote of something "inward and inherent."[155] One Welsh radical Morgan Llwyd is said to have a view of the actual mixture of natures.[156] Richard Baxter, however, named the concept of deification as an abuse of Christ's oneness and "aspiring arrogancy of Adam" and "beyond that of devils."[157]

The incarnation was important to the Puritans. Tudur Jones highlights this fact that those such as Edward Reynolds (1599–1676), Thomas Cole (1627–1697), and John Bunyan (1628–1688) deemed the incarnation as a necessary forerunner to union with Christ. Another perspective from John Everard (c.1575–1640) describes the indwelling Christ transformative to the believer as one suddenly acknowledging himself to be in the intimate presence of a King and accordingly humbling himself.[158]

A generation or two after Jonathan Edwards (1703–1758) the doctrine of union with Christ began to fall into decline, which Evans asserts was due to the degradation of the doctrine of imputation and the issues of legalism, Arminianism, and the overtures of Evangelical conversionism bidding for attention.[159] For example, Evans rather darkly concludes that Samuel Hopkins' (1721–1803) New Divinity ended up with a doctrine of union with Christ devoid of any *mystik*. "What remains is an extrinsic, moralistic, voluntary union that fit well the increasingly individualistic and moralistic tenor of the times."[160]

---

153. Flavel, "John 17:23," 39–41.

154. Ibid., 34–38.

155. Letham, *Westminster*, 291.

156. Jones, "Existential Nerve," 203.

157. Mursell, *English Spirituality*, 368.

158. John Everard, *The Gospel Treasury Opened*, Collection of Sermons (1656), 357–59, cited in Mursell, *English Spirituality*, 370.

159. Evans, *Imputation*, 126, 134–37.

160. Ibid., 129.

The Westminster Standards

In its articulation of the intimacy of union with Christ, the WCF reasons any ontological equality to be "impious and blasphemous" (26.3).[161] Such Reformed confessions of the Puritan era also illuminate the corporate as well as saving nature of our doctrine. This is readily apparent in Questions 65–90 of the WLC. Q.65 declares that the members of the invisible church enjoy both union and communion with Christ, whilst Q.66 and 69 state the gracious communication of Christ for those united to him by a real yet mystical irrevocable union.[162] Q.69 also echoes the golden chain in Romans 8, inarguably the root of the *ordo salutis*, stating, "the communion in grace which the members of the invisible church have with Christ, is their partaking of the virtue of his mediation, in their justification, adoption, sanctification, and whatever else, in this life, manifests their union with him."[163] Indeed, WLC 65–90 demonstrates, contrary to Torrance, that "the prime benefit of salvation is Christ himself. Salvation consists in union and communion with Christ in grace and glory."[164]

The corporate nature of the Body of Christ is also realized in Puritan thought in the sacrament of the Lord's Supper, wherein the body of believers in "examining themselves of their being in Christ" "feed" on the body and blood of Christ in a "spiritual manner."[165] Describing this holy ordinance and that of baptism instituted by Christ to "signify, seal, and exhibit" Christ's New Covenant work, the Westminster Assembly documents express the sacramental relevance for the believer: ". . . Judging themselves, and sorrowing for sin; in earnest hungering and thirsting after Christ, feeding on him by faith, receiving of his fullness, trusting in his merits, rejoicing in his love, giving thanks for his grace; in renewing of their covenant with God, and love to all the saints."[166]

To conclude then, in line with Calvin's pneumatic Christology, it is by the operation of the Holy Spirit that the sacraments "strengthen and

---

161. Clark, *Confessions*, 222.

162. WLC Q.66, "The union which the elect have with Christ is the work of God's grace, whereby they are spiritually and mystically, yet really and inseparably, joined to Christ as their head and husband; which is done in their effectual calling."

163. WLC Q.69.

164. Letham, *Westminster*, 324–25.

165. WLC Q.170, 171.

166. WLC Q.174.

increase" faith and "all other graces; to oblige [believers] to obedience; to testify and cherish their love and communion one with another."[167]

A DOWNGRADE

In his *Imputation and Impartation: Union with Christ in American Reformed Theology*, Evans distinguishes a downgrade in the sacramental aspect of union with Christ in the decades following the early Puritans:[168]

> Puritan piety tended to push Reformed theology in particular directions. Calvin's view of union with the humanity of Christ as an instrument in the application of redemption largely disappears; instead, the humanity of Christ is viewed as the *conditio sine qua non* of redemption and as an object of devotion. Calvin's robust view of sacramental presence of Christ's humanity through the power of the Holy Spirit tend[ed] to be replaced by a "virtue presence" and by conceptions of psychological efficacy.[169]

Indeed, a downgrade of the sacrament of the Lord's Supper and partaking of Christ is clear in the divergence of Charles Hodge's (1797–1878) understanding from that of Calvin's communicated grace. The "union with the visible church, and participation of the sacraments, are not the indispensible conditions of our union with Christ, neither are they the means of communicating, in the first instance, his benefits and grace, but rather the appointed means by which our union with Christ is acknowledged, and from time to time strengthened."[170]

His son, A. A. Hodge (1823–1886), while ostensibly holding a higher view than his father, says that Calvin's use of "spiritual" is ambiguous and his speculation on the nature of Christ's presence is unnecessary in the mystery.[171] Hodge does name the presence nonetheless to be "relational," and not spatial, though failing to esteem the Eucharistic presence as a *unique* communication of divine grace. "This is not confined to the sacrament. He [Christ] makes manifest to our faith the reality of his presence with us, and communicates the same grace to us, on many other occasions and at

---

167. WLC Q.161, 162.
168. Evans, *Imputation*, 76.
169. Ibid., 80–81.
170. Charles Hodge, "Idea of the Church," cited in Evans, *Imputation*, 220.
171. Hodge, "Presence of Christ."

other times, here and now and in this breaking of bread we have a personal appointment to meet our Lord."[172]

Robert Lewis Dabney (1820–1898) depicts a lower view of the Eucharist, denying any spiritual "feeding on Christ" or spiritual enlivening. Critical of any "literal and substantive intromission" of Christ, Dabney purports that "real presence" and the misapplication of John 6:51 is the palpable legacy of the patristics, naming Calvin's stance an "impossible theory."[173] The biblical understanding, says Dabney, is the position of the bread and wine as "commemorative signs" or "divinely appointed seals of covenant blessings" "summed up in our legal and spiritual union to Jesus Christ" and "constituted solely" by the Holy Spirit's indwelling.[174]

John McLeod Campbell's (1800–1872) universalist and somewhat creative perspective of saving union with Christ solely by means of the incarnation is perhaps a significant example of a downgrade in theological orthodoxy in the nineteenth century.[175] Much less unorthodox is *The Mystical Presence: A Vindication of the Reformed or Calvinistic Doctrine of the Holy Eucharist* from Mercersburg theologian John Williamson Nevin (1803–1886). This work made a unique contribution upon the Eucharist's relationship to union with Christ. Influenced by Schleiermacher and tensions in his own move from Presbyterianism to the German Reformed tradition, Nevin advocated an organic corporate union with Christ whilst reproaching modern Puritanism's "unchurchly, rationalistic tendency" to depart from the Reformational stance on the Eucharist.[176] Understanding the importance of the Reformation's "Supper-Strife," Nevin regarded the Eucharist as "intertwined particularly with all the arteries of the Christian life."[177] So he sought to challenge the downgrading of the Eucharist in his emphasis on the *unio mystica*. Nevin held views consistent with a Reformed understanding; believing union with Christ to be more intimate than any other union, but not ontological in the continuation of person individuality. He maintained union with Christ as wrought by the power of the Holy Spirit through the "instrumentality" of faith.

---

172. Ibid.
173. Dabney, "Union."
174. Ibid.
175. Letham, *Christ*, 31–32.
176. Nevin, *Mystical*, 48; Evans, *Imputation*, 141, 146–54.
177. Nevin, *Mystical*, 47.

Nevin's attempt to revert to a Calvinistic appreciation of union with Christ meant denial of federal aspects of the doctrine that undermined the importance of Christ's humanity to be merely a *condition sine qua non* for redemption.[178] He maintained union with Christ to be more than the moralism found in New England ideas, as well as rejecting the "compound" federal view that split union into legalism and spiritualism.[179] Instead, he promoted a corporate perspective that upheld union with the "substance" of Christ in the prominence upon Christ's humanity, as Calvin did.[180]

Although subject to criticism by Reformed theologians, Nevin helpfully reasserted elements of a synthetic Calvinistic perception of union with Christ with biblical emphases on the incarnation and the corporate life.

Later in the nineteenth century and outside of the Reformed tradition, Albert Schweitzer in his *The Mysticism of Paul the Apostle* brought union with Christ to the forefront in its Pauline "in Christ" formula.[181] This has since had ramifications on contemporary reading of Reformed theology and Reformed theology itself. Schweitzer reread the Apostle Paul as having *unio mystica* as the center of his soteriology and spirituality borrowed from Hellenistic thought, relegating justification to be only a "subsidiary crater."[182] "Forcing a choice between forensic and participationist soteriologies, the basic outlines of Schweitzer's thesis reappear in myriad calls to give priority to union with Christ over justification," Michael Horton insightfully remarks. Horton's observation is realized in the New Finnish interpretation on Luther and perhaps Thomas Torrance's equivalent approach to Calvin. These notions, in driving forensic and participatory ideas poles apart, perceive "mystical union as an ontic participation in the Trinity's being" over and above forensic justification.[183]

TWENTIETH-CENTURY TO THE PRESENT

In his *Church Dogmatics*, influential Reformed theologian Karl Barth (1886–1968) expounds the doctrine of election with great comprehensiveness, viewing this "election of grace" as "the sum" of the gospel.[184] With

---

178. Ibid., 159–66; Evans, *Imputation*, 147, 152.

179. Evans, *Imputation*, 158.

180. Ibid., 159, 163.

181. Reid, *Life in Christ*, 11–12.

182. Kruse, *Paul*, 30–31; Horton, *Salvation*, 129; Ridderbos, *Paul*, 59.

183. Horton, *Salvation*, 130.

184. Barth, *CD* II.2.VII, 10–14. Barth's contribution together with Barthian

his characteristically strong Christology, Barth affirms Christ as both the "electing" God and the "elected" man, rendering the incarnation a significant theme as Christ reconciles humanity to an otherwise "alien God."[185] Consequently, Christ is "very God and very man, and as such He is the Representative of the people which in Him and through Him is united as He is with God."[186] Consequently, the "goal of vocation" for the Christians is their fellowship with Christ through the *unio cum Christo*.[187]

In relation to the sacraments, Barth's early conception of the sacraments are said to be "neo-Calvinist" as he maintained that the sacraments could not be separated from the preaching of the Word, which he saw as the "chief sacramental reality." However, in his later theology, Barth designated Christ as the only sacrament and viewed baptism and the Lord's Supper as commemorations of the incarnation. Like Zwingli, this later Barth disregards the communication of grace in the sacraments.[188]

John Murray (1898–1975) was a key Reformed theologian who was extremely influential in centralizing union with Christ in the *ordo salutis*. Murray established the Christ-union to be particularly distinct from the other applications of salvation in the *ordo* due to its unusual architectonic posture. In light of this, recent studies on union with Christ have tended to consider its particular relationship with other aspects of redemption and rarely by itself (although new studies focusing on union are beginning to emerge). Due to the noteworthy acceptance and influence of Murray's contemporary contribution on the *ordo salutis* and union with Christ, we shall draw from his writings significantly in our theological outline.

Louis Berkhof (1873–1957), William Evans critiques, follows the "federal textbook" tradition of Abraham Kuyper and Herman Bavinck handed down by Charles Hodge.[189] In his emphasis on the *ordo salutis*, Berkhof recognizes a distinction between spiritual aspects and the legal. Using the term "mystical union" he states, critical of that reminiscent of Calvin:

> It is sometimes said that the merits of Christ cannot be imputed to us as long as we are not in Christ, since it is only on the basis of

---

scholarship continues to be subject to interpretative examination, therefore bringing about new perspectives. Cf. Morgan, *Karl Barth*.

185. *CD* II.2.VII, 3, 10, 94.
186. *CD* II.2.VII, 7.
187. *CD* IV.3.2, 540.
188. Bloesch, *Church*, 152–53.
189. Evans, *Imputation*, 233–34.

our oneness with Him that such an imputation could be reasonable. But this view fails to distinguish between our legal unity with Christ and our spiritual oneness with Him, and is a falsification of the fundamental element in the doctrine of redemption, namely the doctrine of justification.[190]

As a result, Berkhof's stance is considered to be too narrow, wherein "union with Christ has, for all intents and purposes, ceased to function as an umbrella category unifying all of salvation. For Berkhof, the term 'mystical union' applies only to sanctification, and not at all to justification."[191] This fragmentation is exemplified in Letham's critique of Berkhof, and Hodge for that matter, in separating union with Christ from election, a "departure from Scripture." Unlike Calvin, Berkhof and Hodge do not consider union to be a spiritual reality in election; that is, they deny that God elects only *in* Christ but that union comes after election. They therefore restrict "union with Christ to the existential union effected through faith in our own life histories," contrary to Ephesians 1:4–5.[192]

Some New Interpretations and Challenges

As we have seen, discussion in Calvin and Luther scholarship has exposed the doctrine of union with Christ to contemporary interpretation. Robert Letham is one example of a Reformed theologian who is bridging the gap between Western union with Christ and Eastern *theōsis*.[193] The contribution from Dutch Reformed theologian Lewis B. Smedes (1921–2002) is also worth mentioning as a recently contemporary interpretation. Smedes has constructed a "situational" christological approach to the doctrine in his *Union with Christ: A Biblical View of the New Life in Christ* or *All Things Made New: A Theology of Man's Union with* Christ, defining the "in Christ" relationship as a new world order in Christ. "Being 'in Christ' is not primarily a subjective moral experience, nor a mystical experience, but existence within a radically new situation in the continuing turmoil of human history."[194]

---

190. Berkhof, *Systematic*, 452.

191. Evans, *Imputation*, 236–37.

192. Letham, *Christ*, 86.

193. Letham, *Westminster*, 110, 290–92, 323; Letham, *Holy Trinity*, 472–73; Letham, *Western Eyes*, 253–63, Letham, *Union with Christ*.

194. Smedes, *Union*, 91.

Union with Christ: A Reformed Legacy

In its dialogue with the Reformed tradition the New Perspective on Paul (NPP), a debate revolving around a reinterpretation of Pauline justification, implicates his use of the *unio mystica* in relation to imputed righteousness. The Reformed "categorically distinctive conception" of union with Christ comprehends the doctrine and the imputation of Christ's righteousness to be "distinct-yet-inseparable facets" of a saving "faith union with Jesus Christ."[195] On the contrary, the NPP proponents, such as N. T Wright (b. 1948), view both doctrines as "functional equivalents," drawing a distinction between a Pauline and Reformed understanding.[196] The NPP is one example of a present-day discussion on the nature of the imputation of Christ's righteousness and the relationship between this justification and sanctification additional to the *duplex gratia*.[197]

CONCLUSION

In this historical outline we have witnessed a shift in the dominant approach to union with Christ over the generations. At its peak in a Calvinistic unified and organic form, later generations moved into a federal emphasis with a legal prejudice, calling into question the complementary organic and soteric aspects of justification and sanctification. This demise of a holistic understanding of salvation and the Christian life in union with Christ has left the doctrine neglected in recent centuries.

In response to this, this project, in its concern for an applied approach to soteriology favors the prior Calvinistic understanding of union with Christ as opposed to the latter technical method contextualized in the *ordo salutis*. Sinclair Ferguson usefully notes the danger of an excessive technical approach to our doctrine: "it may be possible to trace various levels of orders of nature in which, logically, one element in our union with Christ appears to be the prerequisite for another. But to seek to reduce the elements to a string of causes and effects has the immediate impact of flattening out the dimensions of grace involved."[198]

This historical-theological background paves the way for a systematic description of union with Christ in its contemporaneous Reformed form. Focusing on the features of this union in and of itself, we will also briefly

---

195. Tipton, "Union," 24.

196. Ibid., 39, 46.

197. This debate is demonstrated in Piper, *Counted Righteous*; and Garlington, "Imputation or Union."

198. Ferguson, *Holy Spirit*, 106.

Complementarian Spirituality

consider key theological structures to the Christ-union, the role of union with Christ in conversion, communion with God, and the significance of the doctrine in the sacraments.

3

Possessing Christ: Union with Christ in Contemporary Reformed Thought

It is becoming clear that the doctrine of union with Christ, as it appears in Reformed theology, displays Christ as the "embodiment" of salvation in the "wide span of salvation from its ultimate source in the eternal election of God to its final fruition in the glorification of the elect."[1]

The christocentricity of the Reformed tradition is established in the fact that union with Christ lies at the core of its soteriology. The NT palpably indicates, for instance in the "golden chain" of Romans 8:30, that all aspects of salvation, secured in the work of Christ at Calvary, are efficaciously applied to the believer by Christ-union. Thus, "every spiritual blessing" is *in Christ Jesus* (Eph 1:3): Believers are elected and predestined in Christ (Eph 1:4, 5), called to God in Christ (1 Cor 1:9; 7:22; 2 Tim 1:9), and regenerated (Eph 2:5; Col 2:13) and justified in Christ (Rom 8:1; Gal 2:17; 1 Cor 1:30). They are created for good works in Christ (Eph 2:10), sanctified in Christ (1 Cor 1:2, 6:11; Rom 6:5), persevere in Christ (Rom 6:4; 1 Cor 4–6; Phil 1:6), and die in Christ (Rev 14:13; 1 Thess 4:17). In the future they are to be raised and glorified in Christ upon his return (1 Cor 15:22; Rom 6:5, 8:30).[2] As James Montgomery Boice asserts, "in one sense 'union with Christ' *is* salvation."[3]

This centralizing of union with Christ in applied soteriology might instigate criticism for an overemphasis on Pauline theology. However, further to the defense that union with Christ is a NT theme not exclusive to Paul, Richard B. Gaffin avers, "Reformed theology has always thought

---

1. Murray, *Systematic*, 165; Barth, *CD* IV.3.2, 543.
2. Cf. Tipton, "Union," 25; Boice, *Foundations*, 390.
3. Boice, *Foundations*, 392 (emphasis mine).

itself to be distinctively Pauline, more sensitive than other traditions to the deeper motives and trends of the apostle's teaching and more consistent in its expression of them."[4]

INTRODUCING UNION WITH CHRIST IN SCRIPTURE

The Bible presents our doctrine in an array of rich pictorial language and metaphors that enjoy continual theological reflection.

Firstly, there is the figure of the physical body of which Christ is the head and the church the members of the body (1 Cor 12:12; 14–27; Eph 4:15–16). Secondly, the church is likened to a building (1 Cor 3:9), with Christ its cornerstone (Eph 2:19–22; 1 Pet 2:4–5). Thirdly, there is Christ's self-designation as a vine and his disciples as the branches (John 15:1–8). Fourthly, we note the analogy of a husband-wife relationship modeled by Christ and the church (Eph 5:22–23). Fifthly, there is the federal or covenantal headship of the first Adam with humankind (Rom 5:12–19; 1 Cor 15:22, 48–49). Additionally, Robert Reymond includes the Trinitarian discourse of the Gospel of John (14:23; 17:21–23) as a figure of the believer's union with Christ, and James M. Boice highlights Christ's self-reference as the spiritual bread to be eaten (John 6:35) and water to be drunk (John 4:10–11) in his institution of the Lord's Supper.[5] Similarly, Donald Guthrie sees the Pauline exposition of spiritual baptism as a metaphor for union with Christ.[6] Drawing from this collection of biblical imagery, Herman Bavinck concludes that the church does not exist apart from Christ and Christ does not exist without the church, which "together with him can be called the one Christ."[7]

METHOD

In contemporary systematic theology the *ordo salutis* is the typical structural context for the study of our doctrine. In this there is a tendency to represent union with Christ in its relationship to other aspects of applied soteriology and rarely by its own measure. For this reason, this study has purposefully avoided an *ordo salutis* model in the hope to represent the

---

4. Gaffin, *Resurrection*, 11.

5. Reymond, *Systematic*, 738; Boice, *Foundations*, 390.

6. Guthrie, *New Testament*, 644.

7. Bavinck, *Dogmatics*, 474. Although Dutch Reformed theologian Herman Bavinck is not contemporary to our designated era, his thought is included owing to his profound influence upon Reformed theology.

doctrine in its synthetic and organic Calvinistic form, whilst reducing a mechanistic approach. This is not to say that this study stigmatizes the *ordo salutis*. On the contrary, the *ordo* is a helpful instrument in considering the features of redemption "distinctly, inseparably, simultaneously, and eschatologically" in their logical sequence whilst demonstrating the "central redemptive significance" of the Christ-union.[8] Nevertheless, the *ordo* is not by itself adequate for presenting a complete picture of salvation in Christ according to the Reformed tradition. This is further accounted for in the observations of Reformed theologians Geerhardus Vos and Herman Ridderbos, who reason from their studies in Pauline theology that the Apostle's main thrust is not justification by faith or a single aspect of the *ordo*, but his chief concern is the *historia salutis* realized in the person of Christ.[9] Ridderbos is particularly helpful in his conclusion that Paul's *heilshistorisch* propounds a governing redemptive-historical framework that demonstrates the organic coherence of the gospel.[10] This said, however, one should of course acknowledge that Paul does at times utilize a *heilsordelijk* method. As Tipton stipulates, both the *historia salutis* and the *ordo salutis* are preserved in the Reformed tradition, so the tradition "offers an expansively rich conception of salvation in Christ."[11]

CRUCIAL THEOLOGICAL SUPPOSITIONS

Before launching into the nature of the *unio mystica* in present-day thought, we will initially highlight three crucial theological suppositions found in Reformed applied soteriology that shape our understanding of union with Christ powerfully. Firstly, the trinitarian nature of the *unio mystica* will be considered and its origin in the divine initiation of the Godhead, and secondly, stemming from this trinitarianism, the pneumatological-christological quality of the "in Christ" relationship. Thirdly, the important theological structure of the incarnation as the basis of union with Christ's humanity will be underlined. These brief expositions are included to summarize their significant posture in the historical survey above and in order to establish their position in contemporary Reformed theology.

---

8. Tipton, "Union," 23–24; Letham, *Westminster*, 245.
9. Letham, *Westminster*, 245.
10. Gaffin, *Resurrection*, 13–14; Ridderbos, *Paul*, 39, 44.
11. Tipton, "Union," 23.

Complementarian Spirituality

Trinity-Initiated

Fundamental to the Reformed approach to soteriology is the belief that God the Father is the author of salvation and union with Christ is at the center of his salvation plan, visible in the incomprehensible grace of the incarnation.[12] It is through union with Christ's death and resurrection and the reversing of Adam's federal condemnation that sinners are reconciled to God (Col 1:18–22). Barth reminds his readers that redemption is God-initiated in Christ's self-giving: "We do well to begin, not below with the Christian, but above with Jesus Christ as the Subject who initiates and acts decisively in this union. We do well to begin with the union of Christ with the Christian and His self-giving to the Christian, and not *vice versa*. It is here that the union and self-giving of the Christian have their roots."[13] Lane Tipton concurs:

> It is "of his doing" that you are "in Christ Jesus." The point is that no flesh can boast before God, because, for one thing, it is of him or of his doing that believers are in Christ Jesus. It is sovereign power or activity of God, and nothing resident within the flesh, that effects union with Christ. Therefore, a decisive, divine activity lies at the basis of the believer's union with Christ.[14]

Importantly, this Christ-union is established upon the triune unity of the Father, Son, and Holy Spirit and, as emphasized above, the "essential and immovable foundation" of Christ's indivisible divine and human natures.[15] Consequently, union with Christ is of the whole Trinity in the soteric outworking of all three members in redemption and the fruit of union in joining the believer to the Godhead, as Christ prayed in John 17:21.[16] John Murray elucidates on the importance of this trinitarian perspective:

> The atonement as a completed work of Christ must always be viewed in the light of the inter-trinitarian economy of salvation. We cannot over-emphasize the importance of this orientation. For only thus can the atonement be placed in its proper context, its relationships properly constructed, the distinctive functions of the three persons of the Godhead understood and appreciated.[17]

12. Murray, *Systematic*, 162–63, 166.
13. Barth, *CD* IV.3.2, 541.
14. Tipton, "Union," 32–33.
15. Douty, *Union*, 2.
16. Pink, *Union*, 9.
17. Murray, *Systematic*, 143.

Possessing Christ: Union with Christ in Contemporary Reformed Thought

In sum, the overemphasis of one or two members of the Trinity renders a view of salvation that is grossly warped and uncharacteristic of a Reformed view.

Pneumatic Christology

In order to build appropriately on the trinitarian nature of union with Christ, it is essential to integrate the "pneumatic Christology" or "Spirit-centered Christology" pattern of thought demonstrated in Calvin and Owen above. Boice in his *Foundations of the Christian Faith* declares union with Christ to be "indispensible" to the vocation of the Holy Spirit in applying Christ's work to the believer.[18] Indeed, in a Reformed trinitarian framework, union with Christ is a Spirit-wrought union. "The Spirit is the living contact between the victorious Jesus and all who are united with Him. There is a Spirit *of* Jesus Christ. Between Him and us there is no gulf in time or space. This Spirit brings us into so intimate an association with Jesus Christ that Paul can speak of Christ being in us."[19] Smedes is so emphatic on this that he claims living in Christ is the same as living in the Spirit.[20] Furthermore, the Spirit is not merely the Bond working in believers, but in his intra-trinitarian operation he "animates and regulates" the person of Christ, which governs his work in the rest of humanity.[21]

Sinclair Ferguson says that because the "central role" of the Holy Spirit is the revelation of Christ to the believer in union, "the model we employ for structuring the Spirit's ministry should be that of union with Christ."[22] From this, Ferguson declares strongly, is our fundamental approach to all the aspects of applied soteriology: "The *dominant motif and architectonic principle* of the order of salvation should therefore be *union with Christ in the Spirit*."[23] At this juncture, Ferguson draws from Calvin to underline the necessity of viewing redemption not merely in its christocentricity but through the lens of "direct participation in Christ, in union with him through the Spirit."[24] This again affirms that the Reformed expression of union with Christ powerfully draws on a "pneumatic Christology."

18. Boice, *Foundations*, 389.
19. Smedes, *Union*, 26; cf. 43, 54.
20. Ibid., 43, 54.
21. Douty, *Union*, 59.
22. Ferguson, *Holy Spirit*, 100.
23. Ibid. (emphasis added).
24. Ibid., 101–2.

Complementarian Spirituality

Incarnation as Prerequisite

Another key theological presupposition, in line with the Reformers, is the incarnation serving as a vital platform for salvation in Christ, for without the incarnation there is no regeneration, justification, or sanctification, since union is with the incarnate Christ.[25] Douty expresses this punitively, maintaining that humankind the offender must endure the penalty.[26] The incarnation then paves the way for the "great transfer" from Adam to Christ.[27] As Christ marries human ontology with his divinity, he is truly human—the second Adam, which consequently is "an unspeakable advancement" for human nature.[28] This demonstrates the consistency of the divine initiative in the covenant of grace. Letham explains, "our union with Christ is grounded on his union with us. We can be one with him because he made himself one with us. As always, the divine initiative comes first. Christ's union with us took place in his incarnation."[29]

UNION WITH CHRIST AND CONVERSION

Union and Election

"Long before man fell, even before the foundation of the world, the God of all grace had made provision for his salvation. In the quietude of eternity He ordained the covenant of grace. In this covenant He provided another Adam, another representative or federal head, to accomplish all that was necessary for the redemption of His elect."[30] Consistent with Calvin, contemporary Reformed soteriology begins with the doctrine of election, as the invisible church are the elect "in Christ," the inaugurator of a new humanity, before the foundation of the world (Eph 1: 4–5). Murray states, "hence all phases of union with Christ, and all blessing accruing from union with him, proceed from the union constituted before the foundation of the world in election."[31] Reymond, in dealing with the believer's effectual call and union with Christ in an order that differs to Murray, accounts for

---

25. Piper, *Alive*, 70–72.
26. Douty, *Union*, 85.
27. Donnelly, *Life*, 20.
28. Douty, *Union*, 44–45.
29. Letham, *Christ*, 77.
30. Kuiper, *Body*, 91–92.
31. Murray, *Systematic*, 128; Ridderbos, *Paul*, 58.

this starting place in election: "The elect sinner is not brought by God's effectual summons into the *en Christō*, relationship for the first time. Rather, it is *because* the elect sinner was 'chosen *in Christ* before the creation of the world' and because he was *in Christ* when Christ died for him that God effectually calls him."[32] There is however a distinction between union with Christ in election and a fully realized participation with him upon faith. Reymond clarifies that believers do not actually partake of Christ until faith is present in regeneration. So he sees being "in Christ" and partaking of Christ as "two different things."[33]

Murray asserts, in accordance with Romans 8: 28–30 and the Barthian view, that "the fountain of the whole process of salvation is God's *electing love*."[34] Important here is that God the Father is doing the electing since he is the subject of both Ephesians 1:4–5 and Romans 8, "those whom he foreknew he also predestined to be conformed to the image of his Son" (Rom 8:29). From this, Barth considers the election of Jesus Christ, the first man, as the basis of a corporate election that includes the church.[35] This is Barth's christocentric theme of Christ as both "electing and elected" and the "sole object" of God's "good pleasure" or "the will of God in action."[36] Thus, the incarnation of the Son of God is indispensible to the election of the church. In agreement with Barth, Smedes writes, "Christ and Christians, the Lord and His subjects, the King and His kingdom, the Reconciler and the reconciled, the Leader and His followers, the Head and His body are elect together."[37]

Union and Call

The "effective summons" or "effectual call" is the *gracious* call of the sinner into saving fellowship with Christ, distinct from any human response.[38] In the same way one is elected "in Christ" one is also called "in Christ," and so able to "repent and believe."[39] Importantly, Murray sees a distinction

---

32. Reymond, *Systematic*, 716.
33. Ibid.,
34. Murray, *Systematic*, 129 (emphasis added); Barth, *CD*. II.2.VII, 10–14.
35. Barth, *CD* II.2.VII, 94.
36. Ibid., II.2.VII, 103–4; cf. 115–16.
37. Smedes, *Union*, 90.
38. Reymond, *Systematic*, 715; Douty, *Union*, 126.
39. Reymond, *Systematic*, 715.

between union with Christ and its call.[40] Reymond rejects, however, Murray's insistence that the call actually unites the believer to Christ and that regeneration and the other aspects of the *ordo* follow from this point. Reymond, in accordance with the WCF, states that regeneration is the "effecting force" of the call and that Pauline texts clearly affirm that there is "no question" that regeneration flows from the "in Christ" relationship (2 Cor 5:17; Eph 2:5, 10).[41] This well exemplifies that Reformed theologians fail to be unanimously agreed on the procession of the *ordo salutis*. Yet, whatever the differing views of order, the nature of regeneration as "the Holy Spirit working directly, efficaciously and irresistibly upon man's heart and mind, making the man over again, and creating him anew after the image of Christ in holiness and righteousness" is uniformly appreciated.[42]

Union and Faith

We must acknowledge the Reformed imperative of faith in uniting Christ and the believer. In his historical death at Calvary, the elect were united to Christ through their future saving faith.[43] The contemporary Reformed understanding is therefore akin to Calvin as faith is the "spiritual means" or "bond" engrafting the believer to Christ and Christ to the believer.[44] "Faith is indispensable to union. . . . Faith is the *how*. Union with Christ is the *what*."[45] The act of faith, "which is never bare intellectual assent, or 'unformed,'" is the necessary response to God's call in Christ to bring about and sustain the union.[46] It is not the work of believers but the work of God by the Holy Spirit, which, according to Hoeksema, Christ merited for believers in his perfect obedience.[47]

THE NATURE OF UNION WITH CHRIST

Now we will broach the pressing need to present a description of union with Christ in current Reformed theology. This description consists of

40. Murray, *Systematic*, 164.
41. Reymond, *Systematic*, 715–16; Murray, *Redemption*, 93.
42. Murray, *Systematic*, 171.
43. Boice, *Foundations*, 392.
44. Hoeksema, *Dogmatics*, 479.
45. Smedes, *Union*, 144–45.
46. Carpenter, "Calvin and Trent," 379.
47. Hoeksema, *Dogmatics*, 1:479.

twelve characteristics discussed in relevant systematic soteriological discourse, and will serve as a theological anchor for our following chapters on spirituality. The order given below possesses no particular theological quality, only the author's discretion.

A Covenantal Union

Union with Christ in its Reformed context has strong covenantal import. This starts with the *pactum salutis* (covenant of redemption), which is the pact between the persons of the Trinity for the salvation of the elect.[48] Through this divine initiation God's promise of salvation made to his covenant people in Scripture is accomplished by a unity of covenants: the covenant of law (Adamic and Sinaitic) and the covenant of grace (Abrahamic-Davidic-New), in which God's gracious and eternal purpose of election is executed.[49] As Horton reminds, the promise of salvation in the eternal intra-Trinitarian covenant is by means of law *and* gospel, which "meet" in the Father's Son.[50] Salvation is then unilateral as it is entirely of grace, but bilateral in the covenantal obligation of joining faith. The Holy Spirit "so engages our whole being that in belonging to Christ there is a 'mutuality,' or 'covenantal bond,' so that the Spirit's work and the believer's faith are absolutely correlative in the union."[51]

Hence, established in Christ their federal head, the elect of God are saved through their oneness with his body and blood. Here, in soteric union with Christ, is the covenantal reversal of Adam's headship (or the Adamic covenant of law) of sin, death, and condemnation. Murray stresses this continuity of headship: "analogy is drawn between Adam and Christ. They stand in unique relations to mankind. There is none before Adam—he is the first man. There is none between—Christ is the second man. There is none after Christ—he is the last Adam."[52] Christ's obedience now obscures Adam's disobedience.[53]

Hence, redemption is based on Christ's representative identification so that his obedience successfully secures righteousness, justification, and life

---

48. Horton, *Salvation*, 131.
49. Ibid.,
50. Ibid., 134.
51. Ferguson, *Holy Spirit*, 111.
52. Murray, *Systematic*, 49.
53. Ibid., 58.

for those he represents through union (1 Cor 15:22).[54] Therefore, before the creation of humankind, it was the will of the Father to establish redemption through the covenant union of his Son. Barth underlines the incarnation at this point as the means of this covenant of redemption. For only by the new "racial solidarity" owing to the incarnation does Christ become the Head and his obedience becomes our obedience, his life our life.[55]

A Soteric Union

This union is essentially soteric because Christ's person and work is "saving" and union is with *Christ*. Thus, this union brings about a "fundamental change in relation to the sinner and the Godhead through the remission of sins."[56] The status "in Christ" assures the believer that God's perception of him or her is that of his Son. The Christian therefore "stands absolved in heaven's court in the absolution of Christ Himself."[57] The saving nature of this union renders it one of equality, for there is no such thing as salvation *in* Christ to a greater or lesser degree. "This union pertains to *all* the redeemed: the least as well as the greatest Christian, the humblest as well as the highest, is *equally* united to Christ and participates in what belongs to Him."[58]

A Forensic Union

This union is legal in nature as "imputation is the judicial ground for justification and is given distinctly, inseparably, simultaneously, and eschatologically *in* union with Christ."[59] It is through union with Christ that the justified sinner stands acquitted by his work. That is, "incorporation into Christ includes within it the possession of Christ's own righteousness, which is imputed to the believer by virtue of his solidarity with the crucified, resurrected, and righteous Son of God."[60] As Calvin viewed the legal and transformative character of redemption as compatible in the common core of union with Christ, so contemporary Reformed theology predomi-

---

54. Ibid., 49–50.
55. Barth, *CD* II.2.VII, 101.
56. Douty *Union*, 154.
57. Ibid., 161.
58. Pink, *Union*, 16.
59. Tipton, "Union," 24; Boice, *Foundations*, 395 (emphasis added).
60. Tipton, "Union," 38.

nately maintains that "union with Christ allows Paul to speak in relational and judicial categories simultaneously, without conflating each other," whilst acknowledging the distinctiveness of the two.[61]

An Intimate, Mutual and Personal Union

The union between Christ and the church is an intimate and personal union, like that between a husband and a wife (Eph 5:31). Edward Donnelly describes this union as "so all-embracing that it includes our physical flesh," a point he concludes from Paul's exhortation in 1 Corinthians 6: 15–16 to not join Christ to a prostitute by one's own body—a "member of Christ" (6:15).[62] "You are his, *body and soul*, for time and for eternity"; the believer is "inextricably linked with him. You are now inside him."[63]

Barth expressly avoids the terms "attachment" and "co-ordination" as too weak to portray the intimacy of the *unio mystica*.[64] He characterizes it as where Christ and the believer "become and are a *single totality, a fluid and differentiated but genuine and solid unity*."[65] He continues, confirming that the union pertains to space-time but also is beyond it; for though the *in* "must indeed indicate on both sides that the spatial distance between Christ and the Christian disappears . . . [and that they are] not merely alongside but in exactly the same spot," the biblical evidence suggests it also transcends the local.[66]

Through the *mutual* nature of this union its intimacy is distinguished, for it is a mutual indwelling. Christ is in the believer and the believer in Christ, rendering a dynamic, "deep personal intercommunion."[67] It is also important to note that individuality is not lost since Christ and the believer do not merge into one person.[68] Both Christ and the Christian maintain their "own independence, uniqueness and activity."[69] If personal distinction was lost, then, when applied to the church, the communion of believers

---

61. Ibid.; Berkhof, *Systematic*, 452; Horton, *Salvation*, 147–48.
62. Donnelly, *Life*, 27.
63. Ibid., 22–23; cf. Horton, *Salvation*, 148.
64. Barth, *CD* IV.3.2, 540.
65. Ibid. (emphasis added).
66. Ibid., IV.3.2, 547.
67. Letham, *Christ*, 83.
68. Barth, *CD* IV.3.2, 539; Kuiper, *Body*, 93; Kelly, *Systematic*, 309.
69. Barth, *CD* IV.3.2, 540.

would also be dissolved and only Christ Himself would remain, rendering much NT teaching obsolete.[70]

Robert Letham amplifies this point, stating that union with Christ is not union with the divine *essence*, which would result in the breakdown of "creator-creature distinction," but union with the divine *energy*.[71] "This union no more deprives us of our humanity than does the assumption of human nature by the Son negate the reality of the humanity he assumed. It erodes our personal distinctiveness no more than the indivisibility of the holy Trinity erases the distinctiveness of the three persons."[72]

A Vital Union

In Reformed thought, union with Christ is vital in its regenerational properties through the vocation of the Spirit, observed in its pneumatic-christological condition. The believer's union with the Son of God is "inaugurated" by the vocation of the Spirit.[73]

The life-giving nature of this union is a marked theme in the Bible. Boice confirms that union is necessary for the Christian's regeneration or new birth. This is what is meant by Christ in his conversation with Nicodemus on rebirth (John 3:5) and what Paul infers in his teachings on the Christians as a "new creation" (2 Cor 5:17).[74] Similarly, Horton deduces the vitality of the *unio mystica* from Romans 8:10; 2 Corinthians 13:5; Galatians 4:19.[75] The life efficaciously bestowed onto the believer at the moment of faith is historically founded upon the Christian's union with Christ at his death on the cross.[76]

A Mysterious Union

In Ephesians 5:32 Paul writes that the union between Christ and the church is a profound mystery. Indeed, this union is of God and so beyond human comprehension.[77] "The oneness of the Church with Christ is a blessed real-

---

70. Kuiper, *Body*, 93.
71. Letham, *Western Eyes*, 260.
72. Ibid., 256.
73. Ferguson, *Holy Spirit*, 116.
74. Boice, *Foundations*, 391.
75. Horton, *Salvation*, 148.
76. Boice, *Foundations*, 391.
77. Pink, *Union*, 7.

ity, which none but the Spirit of God can open to the renewed mind and give right views of it."[78] Similarly, Barth asserts that, like the unity of Christ's human and divine natures, union with Christ is "concealed" for human comprehension and physical sight.[79] Although identified commonly with the covenantal fellowship of human marriage, the *unio mystica* transcends all earthly associations and unions. "The organic union of Christ and His church is a profound mystery. Therefore, he who seeks to describe it must exercise the greatest care to speak soberly. On the one hand he must indeed aim to do justice to the intimacy of this union, but on the other hand he must beware lest he completely identify Christ and the church."[80]

A Spiritual Union

The union that the church enjoys with Christ is not visible by sight, as "is not a gross, fleshly, corporeal union, but a mystical spiritual, and inward one."[81] Since "he who is joined to the Lord becomes one Spirit with him" (1 Cor 6:17). It must be spiritual as it is of God and a source of his power for the church.[82] Equally, it is spiritual also because it is of the Holy Spirit: "As Jesus Christ speaks with man in the power of the Holy Spirit, His vocation is effective to set man in fellowship with himself."[83]

A Real Union

This state of union with the person of Christ is real and not merely theoretical; it is "true" and not "merely psychical or intellectual."[84] Nor does it depend on individual experience and knowledge. Moreover, the Christian's *unio cum Christo* is not a sought-after peak of Christian experience, for it has been real since eternity. Barth reminds us, "we are presenting the last and most exact formulation of what makes us Christians whatever our development or experience."[85]

---

78. Ibid., 12.
79. Barth, *CD* IV.3.2, 540.
80. Kuiper, *Body*, 93.
81. Pink, *Union*, 16; Barth, *CD* IV.3.2, 540; Kelly, *Systematic*, 309.
82. Boice, *Foundations*, 395.
83. Barth, *CD* IV.3.2, 538.
84. Kelly, *Systematic*, 309; Barth, *CD* IV.3.2, 540.
85. Barth, *CD* IV.3.2, 548.

Complementarian Spirituality

A Permanent and Irrevocable Union

Union with Christ is a permanent union that cannot be rendered asunder by any power, as the "Holy Spirit brings it to pass in time and maintains it to eternity."[86] Unlike human marriage or the union of body and soul, which are both terminated by death (Rom 8:35; 2 Cor 5:8; Rev 14:13), the *unio mystica* is "an abiding reality determinative for the whole of the Christian life."[87]

A Sanctifying Union

By the work of the indwelling Spirit, union with Christ brings about transformation in the believer (Matt 16:24; Rom 6:5; Gal 2:20; Col 1:24; 2:12; 3:1; 1 Pet 4:13).[88] This sanctification is not divorced from the cross but secured, with justification, through Christ's obedience. Reformed Baptist Norman Douty amplifies this: Christ "did all this (Calvary) in our name, as our representative, so that we, being joined to Him, might, first, have the credit of His performances, and then, secondly, *be conformed, increasingly, to His likeness*."[89]

One theological key in the sanctifying aspect of union is the change of headship from Adam to Christ, resulting in the fact that sin no longer has mastery over the believer. The "in Christ" relationship removes the power of sin and sets the Christian free due to the victory of Christ with whom they enjoy union.[90] Tipton clarifies this further from Romans 6:

> Union with Christ effects a principial breach with the enslaving *dominion* of sin (Rom 6:4, 9–11). By virtue of union with Christ, the believer has died to sin with reference to its controlling power. Just as Christ has died to sin once for all and is alive to God, so also the believer should consider himself dead to sin and alive to God in Christ Jesus. Hence, the believer is no longer a slave to sin but to righteousness, so that he must now present his bodily members 'as slaves of righteousness unto holiness.'[91]

---

86. Boice, *Foundations*, 395; Kelly, *Systematic*, 309.
87. Ridderbos, *Paul*, 59.
88. Horton, *Salvation*, 148; Berkhof, *Systematic*, 450–51.
89. Douty, *Union*, 80 (emphasis added).
90. Boice, *Foundations*, 392.
91. Tipton, "Union," 47.

The death of the Christian to sin and its dominion is a strong theme in Evangelical and Reformed spirituality. As the faithful bridegroom, Christ incurs the penalty that belongs to his bride and so consequently the marriage between Christ and the church brings about a change in relationship to sin.[92] There must be complete fidelity to Christ as spouse and therefore no freedom for adulterous consorting with sin.

Christian holiness is the vocation of the Holy Spirit, which Christ gave to his church for her sanctification. The third person of the Trinity regenerates the elect, unites the elect to her Spouse, and makes her worthy of him. As we shall observe further later, this "giving" of his Spirit by Christ (Acts 1:4–5, 8) is essential to Christ's position as Head and Bridegroom of the church. The "Spirit is proof of [Christ's] continued, though invisible, presence with her, pledges His perfect fidelity to her, and constantly reminds her of His many precious promises . . . prone as she is to infidelity, the selfsame Spirit, abiding with her and in her, keeps and prepares her for that day."[93]

So union with Christ is the "foundation" or "cause" from which all the benefits or "effects" of salvation flow, including justification, sanctification, adoption, and glorification.[94] The progression into Christ-likeness starts with union to Christ himself, for "whoever abides in him sins not" (1 John 3:6). This sanctification through union with Christ is a corporate reality, however. "This progression has respect, not only to the individual, but also to the church in its unity and solidarity as the body of Christ. In reality the growth of the individual does not take place except in the fellowship of the church as the fellowship of the Spirit."[95]

An Eschatological Union

"This union brings us into the orbit of the eschatological change effected by Christ in his resurrection-transformation and glory. . . . As God's workmanship (Eph 2:10) we are brought into the sphere of the divine regeneration of all things which has already been inaugurated in Christ's resurrection."[96] This is the promise of future glory in Christ and eternal life. Accordingly, personal union with Christ is necessary for the resurrection of the saints on

---

92. Boice, *Foundations*, 393–94.
93. Kuiper, *Body*, 362.
94. Letham, *Christ*, 80; Pink, *Union*, 9.
95. Murray, *Systematic*, 299.
96. Ferguson, *Holy Spirit*, 111.

the last day. Union with Christ links the church to Christ's own resurrection and then is the qualification for her glorification and physical renewal at the marriage of the Lamb.[97]

An Experiential Union

Union with Christ is a practical union experienced by the Christian. Here there is a distinction between the experiential fruit of *unio cum Christo*, that is, communion, and its own experiential *qualities*. Gaffin stresses this element of union with Christ in reasoning from the believer's solidarity with Christ in his death and resurrection in Pauline teaching. "These references describe the actual life experience of the individual believer. Therefore the union basic to this experience, of which this experience is an expression, is likewise experiential."[98]

COMMUNION: THE FRUIT OF UNION

A key biblical teaching pertaining to the fruit of the believer's union with Christ is good works.[99] Christ's teaches in John 15:5 that union with Christ is essential for the church to bear fruit and "be useful to God in this world," for "apart from [him we] can do nothing."[100]

Yet prior to the fruit of good works is that of communion. It is essential to observe the theological distinguishing between union and communion. Pink declares union to be greater and foundational as he corrects the Puritan merging of the two, for if you "take away union, and there can be neither communion nor communication."[101] Therefore, the fruit of saving union with Christ is the enjoyment of Christ in fellowship with him. This fellowship with God in Christ also has its own fruit as it causes spiritual transformation in the life of the believer.[102]

Union with God

Union with Christ must be seen in relation to its purpose, namely, fellowship with God. Reformed soteriology acknowledges the goal of the eternal

---

97. Gaffin, *Resurrection*, 33.
98. Ibid.,, 50.
99. John 15: 2–5, 8, 16; Rom 7:4; Eph 2:10; 1 Tim 6:18; Titus 3:14; 2 Pet 1:8.
100. Boice, *Foundations*, 394.
101. Pink, *Union*, 9–10.
102. Douty, *Union*, 191.

pactum salutis and vocation of the three persons of the Godhead in salvation is the elect's uninhibited union and communion with the triune God. However, the distinction of persons of the Trinity is crucial here in the scriptural admission that the *unio mystica* is union with *Christ*. Smedes purports, "Paul is Christocentric in his whole theology of our relationship with God. He does not have a doctrine of our union with God. God was in Christ, but it is Christ who is in us."[103] Similarly, Letham, in advocating a position of *theōsis* or deification akin to Athanasius, declares it to be a "way of affirming that *in Christ a real, personal intercommunion takes place. We are introduced in Christ to the fellowship of God himself.*"[104] Kelly agrees, yet perhaps with a little less sympathy for the Eastern view, in his brief comparison of Protestant union with Christ and Eastern deification. The Holy Spirit's "mighty invisible presence 'evacuates' the bonds of space and time, and mysteriously—but truly—works a personal, spiritual union with the Almighty God—'from the Father, through the Son, and in the Holy Spirit.' We are thus united to the Lord Himself."[105]

ECCLESIASTICAL SIGNIFICANCES

The Sacraments

Union with Christ has a huge bearing on the sacraments, as we saw above. In Reformed tradition, the sacraments are the holy "signs and seals" of God's promises in Christ instituted *by* Christ for the strengthening of faith *in* him.[106] These signs and seals represent Christ and his benefits, "confirm[ing] our interest in Him" as well as, in the words of Reymond and in line with the WLC, "to put a visible difference between those that belong unto the church and the rest of the world."[107]

Christ's words of institution, found in the Synoptic Gospels and Paul's letter to Corinth, witness to Christ's institution of these two sacraments and these only.[108] In short, baptism is the initiation into the Christ-community,

---

103. Smedes, *Union*, 114.

104. Letham, *Christ*, 83, 84 (emphasis added).

105. Kelly, *Systematic*, 309.

106. As found in the Reformed confessions (e.g., Heidelberg Catechism, Q.66); Berkouwer, *Sacraments*, 13; Hoeksema, *Dogmatics*, 656–57, 705.

107. Reymond, *Systematic*, 917; Roberts, *Union*, 104.

108. Matt 26:20–30; Mark 14:17:26; Luke 22:14–23; 1 Cor 11:23.

representing the believer's sharing in Christ's burial and resurrection, and the Lord's Supper is the remembrance and giving of thanks *eucharisteō* (Matt 26:27; 1 Cor 11:24) for the Christ-event. Both are "by virtue of divine institution involved with the New Covenant, with the coming of the Kingdom of God in the Messiah. . . . Baptism and the Lord's Supper are signs that proclaim the all-sufficiency of the work of Christ."[109] The Reformed unity of Word and Spirit is realized as the sacraments are indispensably related to the Word. "Preceded by the preached word . . . the Lord's Supper draws us into ever closer union with him who is 'the eternal theme of praise.'"[110] As the believer participates in the visible signs and seals of the invisible and inward truth, the Holy Spirit conjoins the reality of the elements with the spiritual reality of Christ and imparts grace to him or her as Christ "*really spiritually present* offers himself" whilst strengthening faith.[111] Notably, the sacraments are essentially "Christ's sacraments," as they were established by him and he is their "truth" or significance.[112]

Due to the constraints of space upon us, the interdenominational differences regarding baptism and the Lord's Supper will not be discussed. In the Paedobaptist and Baptist standpoints, the theological significance of union with Christ and baptism is the same, as Christ remains the covenant head. Nevertheless, in adhering to the Westminster Standards and Swiss Reformation thought as representing a Reformed theological position (see chapter 1), we must acknowledge that the baptism of infants in a covenantal framework is germane to Reformed belief, in its role as the new covenant rite.[113]

This great ecclesiastical significance of baptism in union with Christ demands that it be considered at this point of our discussion. Nevertheless, Calvin's specific proclivity for the Lord's Supper as the direct and special reception of Christ and affirmation of union with him determines its particular relevance to our discourse. This will become apparent in the following chapter as we focus on this sacrament as a manifestation of the corporate Christ-union. This favoring is due to the direction in our work, and not because of any theological discrimination, for both sacraments are established in this doctrine and have weighty corporate ramifications.

109. Berkouwer, *Sacraments*, 91.
110. Letham, *Supper*, 63.
111. Reymond, *Systematic*, 922; Hoeksema, *Dogmatics*, 657.
112. Berkouwer, *Sacraments*, 10.
113. Roberts, *Union*, 107; Murray, *Systematic*, 374; Reymond, *Systematic*, 935–50.

Nonetheless, the examination of both sacraments in relation to a corporate spirituality would alter the concentration of this study considerably, given that this study is not essentially a spirituality founded on the sacraments. Instead, the Lord's Supper is only *one focus* incorporated into our corporate Reformed articulation of union with Christ.

Baptism and Union

Baptism is the "pivotal sacrament for incorporation into the mystical body of Christ."[114] As a sign of the remission of sin by the work of Christ and "regeneration and renewal by the Spirit of Christ," baptism is also the engrafting of the believer into Christ himself.[115] The physical act pertains to union with Christ as it demonstrates and seals the "spiritual baptism" that incorporates the believer into Christ.[116] Indeed, as Reymond states from Pauline passages on the subject (Rom 6:3–6; 1 Cor 12:13; Gal 3:27–28; Col 2:11–12), it is evident that baptism pertains to a strong affiliation with the one in whose name the baptism takes place. Reymond avers that the nature of this intimate affiliation or relationship is "one of *union with* Christ, more particularly, union with Christ in his crucifixion, death, burial and resurrection. Of this basic union baptism is the sacramental sign and seal."[117] Bloesch concurs, "this symbol is not an empty one, for it is used by the Spirit to prepare for and confirm the union with Christ realized in faith."[118] Further is its trinitarian qualities; Reymond verifies with Murray that union penetrates into the *entire* Godhead, so bringing the believer into union with the Father and the Son and the Holy Spirit as the believer is baptized into the triune Name.[119]

Therefore, the washing of baptism is more than merely a symbolic testimonial relevance or a re-enactment of Christ's burial and resurrection. "Baptism is an initiation, not an imitation."[120] Still Murray contends the importance of baptism as the "putting on of Christ" (Gal 3:27), which includes the totality of Christ's mediatorial work, for the completeness of union with

---

114. Bloesch, *Church*, 154.

115. Hoeksema, *Dogmatics*, 677.

116. Ibid., 676–77; cf. Bloesch, *Church*, 154–55.

117. Reymond, *Systematic*, 925.

118. Bloesch, *Church*, 154.

119. Reymond, *Systematic*, 925; Murray, *Baptism*, 7; Murray, *Systematic*, 371; Hoeksema, *Dogmatics*, 675.

120. Smedes, *Union*, n101.

Christ.[121] It is a confirmation of the union that was fully realized at the moment of faith and is not in itself salvific.[122]

In sum, the rite of water baptism represents the spiritual reality of spiritual baptism, wherein the believer is joined to Christ and shares in his crucifixion, death, burial, and resurrection. The symbol is empty without the work of the Holy Spirit in joining the believer to Christ and his redemptive crucifixion, death, burial, and resurrection. This efficacy for the Holy Spirit in bringing about and confirming union with Christ demonstrates the *pneumatic christological* nature of union with Christ as it is in the sacraments.

Sharing in Christ's Death and Resurrection

The Apostle Paul teaches that union with Christ entails participation with him in his historical death and resurrection.[123] In Romans 6:3 Paul stresses the corporate nature of Christ's death so that faith in Christ instantaneously identifies the believer with Christ's historical death.[124] Significantly, Donald Guthrie reminds his readers that Paul is not writing of a group of individuals united with this in common but a community itself identified to Christ corporately.[125]

From Paul's writing in Ephesians 1:19–20 and 2:5–6, Lane G. Tipton explicates the believer's experiences as mirroring those of Christ:

> Believers are united to the person of Christ. Yet more specifically believers are united to his person as crucified and resurrected. Therefore, extending the preceding observation, *union with Christ is a soteric replication in the structure of the believer's life-experience of what happened antecedently in the life-experience of Christ, namely, death and resurrection.*[126]

By means of union with Christ, then, Christ is a soteric model for the church so that salvation is not merely moral imitation but a redemptive "replication" of his life experiences. For "what obtains in the life-experience

---

121. Murray, *Systematic*, 372–73.
122. Guthrie, *New Testament*, 646.
123. Rom 6:4, 6, 11; Gal 2:20; Eph 2:4–6; Col 2:12, 20; 3:1, 3–4; 1 Cor 15:15–18, 20–23.
124. Guthrie, *New Testament*, 644–45; Ridderbos, *Paul*, 59–60.
125. Guthrie, *New Testament*, 645.
126. Tipton, "Union," 25.

of Christ as resurrected and seated in the heavenlies pertains to the church's life-experience in union with Christ."[127]

As Calvin does not separate Christ's death from his resurrection, contemporary Reformed theologians also accentuate the paramount and pivotal truth of the resurrection. Smedes centralizes the resurrection as the power to apply the two-thousand-year-old cross to the contemporary Christian believer. "The past events can save us only because *they do not remain mere past events*. Without a risen and therefore living Christ, there is no point of contact between past event and present faith."[128] Christ's resurrection is crucial, christologically speaking as well as soteriologically, because he "did not rise again as a single and private person, but as the Head of His Church."[129]

The Lord's Supper and Union

The Lord's Supper is a memorial ordinance for the "perpetual remembrance" of Christ's atoning death at Calvary.[130] Finding its roots in the regular OT Passover meal, as opposed to the one-time initiation of circumcision and baptism, the Lord's Supper is the equivalent NT meal of the eternal Lamb.[131] "Just as baptism incorporates us into the community of faith, so the Lord's Supper sustains us in this community."[132]

In his words "the new covenant in my blood" Christ is pointing to himself as the covenant fulfillment of the redemption of humankind. His instituted supper is a meal of remembrance or "recollection," thanksgiving, and "proclamation" (1 Cor 11:26), celebrating the perfect fellowship between Christ and the church.[133] Consistent with Calvin, the supper is the giving of Christ himself to his people for "spiritual nourishment and growth in Him" as "a bond and pledge of their communion with Him, and with each other, as members of His mystical body."[134] It is a corporate meal, and a sacramental encounter with Jesus.

---

127. Ibid., 27.
128. Smedes, *Union*, 144.
129. Pink, *Union*, 11.
130. Reymond, *Systematic*, 955.
131. Roberts, *Union*, 107.
132. Bloesch, *Church*, 160.
133. Barth, *CD* IV.3.2, 542; Murray, *Systematic*, 377–78; Smedes, *Union*, 13.
134. Reymond, *Systematic*, 955; cf. Bloesch, *Church*, 160.

Complementarian Spirituality

Reading John 6 sacramentally in his work *The Lord's Supper: Eternal Word in Broken Bread*, Letham declares that in partaking of Christ's body and blood in the Lord's Supper through faith, "*We are granted union and communion with Christ by the Holy Spirit.*" He continues, "as we eat, food becomes one with us. It enters our system, we digest it, and so we produce energy that enables us to live an active life. So when we eat and drink Christ, he enters our system. He indwells us and, in turn, we remain in him. We grow into union. There is mutual indwelling—he in us his church, we in him. This is a great mystery."[135]

Reymond states, "the celebrant 'communes' by faith with his Lord's slain body and blood" or a "renewed appropriation" of Christ and his benefits.[136] Both faith and the Holy Spirit are vital for feeding on Christ. Hence, the Supper is a vital channel for the Holy Spirit to increase, nourish, sustain and confirm the believer's faith. Second to our union and communion with Christ, Letham underlines, "we are introduced into the living fellowship of the Triune God."[137] This Trinitarian meal also has eschatological meaning, as "the Lord's Supper and the Lamb's Supper are two sides of the same reality."[138]

The Lord's Supper has a crucial part to play in Christian spirituality, as demonstrated in our next discussion chapter. As Murray highlights, bad practice of the Lord's Supper can demise the partaking of Christ in the meal. "So frequently, believers become so introspective, that preoccupation with themselves excludes preoccupation with Christ."[139]

A Corporate Meal

"The spiritual unity of Christ's church is an undeniable reality. It is one body, even the mystical body of Christ. Nothing can destroy this spiritual unity."[140] Corporate worship unites the church and the sacraments are God-given means for this. Letham accounts for the neglect of the Lord's Supper in corporate church life as due to Evangelical conversionism, resultant from eighteenth-century revivalism, which relegated corporate life and the

---

135. Letham, *Supper*, 13–14.
136. Reymond, *Systematic*, 966.
137. Letham, *Supper*, 14.
138. Ibid., 63.
139. Murray, *Systematic*, 378.
140. Kuiper, *Body*, 46

sacraments to "secondary importance."[141] David Peterson highlights the corporate nature of this sacred meal in its display of shared union with Christ:

> The Lord's Supper, which has so often throughout church history been understood as a means of deepening the personal communion of believers with their Lord, is clearly meant to focus the eyes of the participants *on one another as well as on God*. We do not simply meet to have fellowship with God but to minister to one another as we express our common participation in Christ.[142]

It is in the Lord's Supper, by the Holy Spirit, that all believers are "elevated into the presence of Christ as we repent of our sins and join our fellow believers in an act of praise and thanksgiving."[143] Thus, the Lord's Supper is elementary to NT corporate spirituality.

Because of this, in the following chapter we explore the *unio mystica* in the Lord's Supper and the correlative issues of confession, repentance, and corporate church life.

CONCLUSION

In the historical handling of the doctrine in Reformed theological circles, we see that the *unio mystica* is a doctrine basic to salvation, with requisite Trinitarian dimensions, ensuring the partaking or possessing of Christ by the believer through the work of the Holy Spirit in faith. The doctrine has corporate relevance exercised in the sacraments and affirmed in the nature of the church as a corporate entity under Christ.

Significantly, our outline has demonstrated that "the theme of union with Christ brings together the temporal tenses of our salvation—past, present, and future, as well as the objective and subjective, historical and existential, corporate and individual, forensic and transformative."[144] This offers appropriate substantiation for an exploration into a Reformed expression of the Christian life anchored on this doctrine, to which we now look.

---

141. Letham, *Supper*, 1–2.
142. Peterson, *Engaging*, 218.
143. Bloesch, *Church*, 161.
144. Horton, *Salvation*, 131.

4

Jesus Christ the Bridegroom

RECENT WORKS ON PROTESTANT spirituality observe a famine in vibrant spiritual experience, such as Michael Raiter's *Stirrings of the Soul*, which questions whether traditional churches have presented "an emasculated gospel, doctrinally pure, but stripped of all *its relational and experiential dynamism*?"[1] As he looks at Evangelicalism and the new spirituality movement, Raiter declares that many Christians find the spirituality of their own churches or traditions "stultifying, and long for a more *experientially* satisfying relationship with God through Christ."[2] Similarly, Alister McGrath laments that he has witnessed many spiritually dissatisfied colleagues leave Evangelicalism and explore other Christian spiritual traditions. "There is a popular assumption that Evangelicals, who in theory depend so much on the Bible, do not have any spirituality, and so they must take as much as they can from Eastern Orthodox or Roman Catholic spirituality, or even from the religions of the East."[3]

The wide influence of Evangelicalism on the Reformed tradition has ensured that Reformed spirituality has also suffered in this way. Criticism from within the tradition, as well as outside of it, clearly reveals the need for renewal and reawakening in Reformed spirituality as it struggles to excite any significant contemporary expression anchored in Word and Spirit. In its effort to maintain a biblical orthodoxy untainted by modern liberal and postmodern theology, Catholic or Charismatic expressions of worship, or the increasing secularization of society, the contemporary Reformed tradition has neglected investing in the rich heritage of spiritual theology given by preceding generations. Thus, a caricature of the Reformed tradition has

1. Raiter, *Stirrings*, 31.
2. Ibid., 29.
3. McGrath, *Roots*, 21; Metzger, "Luther and the Finnish School."

taken form, portraying an overly dogmatic and cerebral community that avoids any meaningful interest in spirituality. This leaves the Reformed community with a challenge to be self-reflective, critically observing any tendency towards mere credence. For biblical Christians "should be rightly suspicious of forms of theology that place all the emphasis on coherent systems of thought that demand faith, allegiance, and obedience, but do not engage the affections, let alone foster an active sense of the presence of God."[4]

It has been suggested that an enhanced understanding of the Christian's union with Christ will deepen and nurture spiritual life. Whilst expounding a Western perspective on the Eastern concept of *theōsis*, Douglas Kelly writes that "churches of the West . . . need humbly and earnestly to seek *to experience the full reality of holy life* in an unholy and needy world, *by means of a fresh and constant awareness of our union with Christ in and through the Holy Spirit*."[5] Evangelical commentator Richard Lovelace likewise purports that modern Evangelical spirituality needs to recover the core of its Reformation heritage in the theme of "new life in Christ."[6]

This belief that a recovery of the *unio mystica* will actually benefit and shape spiritual life stems from the Reformed principle that theological truth governs the Christian life. Subsequently, the thirteenth-century divorce of theology and spirituality in academia has not impeded upon Reformed thought. Operating within this premise, this study looks to rearticulate theology in order to inform Reformed Christian life. As underlined earlier, "a restatement of spirituality will involve a restatement of the meaning of the gospel, the nature of God, the person and work of Jesus Christ, the work of the Holy Spirit in the appropriation of the fruits of Christ's sacrifice and the role of the church in our salvation."[7] This pivotal chapter looks to respond precisely to this conjecture from Bloesch, by presenting a theological restatement of union with Christ, in a Trinitarian and especially pneumatic-christological capacity, whilst presenting a uniquely feminine perspective of a "churchly" or corporate spirituality in the next. This will reassert the Reformed ideal for corporate life in Christ, true to the Reformers, which has indeed been lost in today's individualism, and may counteract the common perception of the local church in relation to a series of programs and

---

4. Carson, *Gagging*, 567.
5. Kelly, *Systematic*, 310 (emphasis added).
6. Lovelace, "Evangelical Spirituality."
7. Bloesch, *Spirituality*, 13.

events instead of a significant visible expression of the invisible spiritual Body of Christ, living and breathing in shared union.

The discussion below, together with chapter 5, attempts to interpose a doctrinal basis for both a *relational* and *experiential* spiritual life into the Reformed tradition, responding to Howard Hageman's concern that the Reformed return to a corporate sense of worship and spirituality in line with a Calvinistic understanding.[8] Importantly, this corporate articulation does not undermine personal or private forms of spiritual life, but only looks to complement and strengthen the spirituality of the individual by readdressing the corporate sphere. This will perhaps contribute to rescuing the Reformed tradition from Beeke's diagnosis of a "dry Reformed orthodoxy," and encourage a Reformed spirituality that reflects a "vibrant" "vital, spiritual union with the God of doctrine."[9]

METHODOLOGY

The aim of this chapter and the next is to explore a distinctively female approach to the Reformed theological understanding and expression of union with Christ, particularly in relation to spirituality. In other words, we will now delve into a feminine Reformed articulation, or more correctly a *re*articulation, of the doctrine and its significance for the enjoyment of a more experiential knowledge of Christ, drawing from the systematic theology outlined in our previous chapters. This chapter looks particularly at the role of the divine initator in union with Christ, that is, the triune Godhead, and specifically Jesus Christ as the soteric Bridegroom. The next chapter then complements this by looking at his complementarian redeemed partner, the Bride the church.

Before delving into the discourse of this chapter, however, we briefly clarify further what is meant by a "feminine approach" in this study. We will also consider some recent feminine Evangelical writings on spirituality and discuss their relevance to our exploration in employing the parallelism of union between Christ and the church and husband and wife in Ephesians 5.

---

8. Hageman, "Reformed."
9. Beeke, *Puritan*, viii.

The "Feminine" Approach

As this chapter and the next *particularly* seek to explore a feminine articulation of the Reformed doctrine of union with Christ, the "feminine approach" employed possesses a twofold practice.

Firstly, by means of a female author this project looks to counterbalance the strong male presence in Reformed theology by uniquely responding to the dearth of female academic contribution. As noted earlier in chapter 1, other Christian traditions (in particular Roman Catholicism) have established female voices in their theological arenas but Evangelical Reformed theology still has little to contribute in this way. This book looks to serve as a prolegomena that will encourage further scholarly writing from Reformed women.

Secondly, suggestions are given for the application of this work in response to the indigence of specific consideration of women in Reformed pastoral ministry and for the presentation of an initial definition of a feminine Reformed spirituality. This will demonstrate that offering a pastoral ministry deliberately to women that centers on pastoral issues applicable *to* women (e.g., marriage breakdown, infertility, abortion, self-esteem, depression) and the role *of* women in undertaking this pastoral care is judicious to contemporary church life and growth and advantageous for female Reformed spirituality. This is particularly pertinent in the ongoing controversy regarding the ordination of women. The subject of female ordination has not be broached in this work, particularly as a theological complementarian stance is crucial to this project and its use of marital union. The inclusion of this controversy would cause our discourse to stray from the aims unique to this project. This work is concerned with feminine spirituality, which, it is suggested, has been neglected owing to the dominance of this political issue in contemporary Protestant discourse.

As outlined in the first chapter, the use of a feminine approach in this study does not mean the presentation of a "gendered spirituality" or a spirituality constructed upon a cultural understanding of gender. Whereas a spirituality established upon gender considers the biological and sexual makeup of the believer in his or her cultural setting, this is not the method of the current study. For if the question were asked under which cultural setting does this study operate, the initial answer would be the contemporary Reformed community in the United Kingdom and North America. This work does not examine current cultural constructs of the female sex but instead looks to consider the application of a theological exploration to Reformed female spiritual experience.

Neither does this discourse in its "feminine approach" belong to feminist spirituality. Feminist spirituality, like feminist theology, draws upon "the broader project of feminist theory," and the prevailing method in feminist theory is the identification of cultural systems oppressive to women, the critique of androcentric constructs and subsequent reconstruction.[10] However, no hermeneutic of suspicion exists in this study's methodology.

Some may assert that feminist theological discourse does actively seek to include female perspectives on experience and praxis as "primary sources" and therefore the method used in this study is akin to the feminist agenda. Of course this is true to some extent. However, feminist methodology commonly starts with the questioning of *basic assumptions concerning religious thought* and practice and responds with a feminist reinterpretation.[11] Our objective is not challenging theological dogma in and of itself but exploring a modern feminine articulation of it and subsequent spiritual expression. Furthermore, the aim of this work is not the presentation of an exclusive project but an *inclusive* contribution to the contemporary Reformed tradition, relevant to both male and female Christian experience, yet chiefly imparting to Reformed women. This is an investigation into a uniquely feminine expression of the soteriological doctrine of union with Christ, initially committed to the Reformed tradition, its spiritual heritage, and its theological and spiritual practice at a time where "spirituality" is offered in fashionable assortment.

Themes in Recent Evangelical Writings by Women

In many current feminine writings in the conservative Evangelical/Reformed arena, we see a noticeable proclivity for the issue of "biblical womanhood," an epithet frequently applied to texts that discuss female roles. This approach, exemplified in *Biblical Womanhood* by Sharon James, *The Legacy of Biblical Womanhood* by Susan Hunt and Barbara Thompson, and *Disciplines of a Godly Woman* by Barbara Hughes, explicitly and sometimes implicitly interacts with egalitarian or feminist ideas of gender roles as it defends a Reformed complementarian stance. In this contention, biblical teaching on submission to Christ mirrored in feminine submission to one's husband, as instructed in Paul's letter to the Ephesians, together with key

---

10. Dickey Young, *Method*, 11–12, 16ff., 21.
11. Hogan, *Women's Experience*, 10.

texts on womanhood, are of paramount importance.[12] Consequently, the spiritual application of these biblical texts in the Christian pursuit of holiness is, in this feminine context, largely executed in relation to being a godly wife.

This deliberation of the Christian life in relation to "biblical womanhood" clearly places the subject of spirituality in an expressly *feminine* framework. Furthermore, this approach makes quick use of the biblical language and imagery of Christ as the spiritual husband or lover, which we designated as a type of "Christ-husband" spirituality. This is clearly perceived in popular works, such as Leslie Ludy's *Authentic Beauty: The Shaping of a Set-Apart Woman*, the Dee Brestin and Kathy Troccoli trilogy,[13] and the broad Evangelical work *Captivating* written by John and Stasi Eldredge. It is in relation to this "marital" union with Christ, essentially devotional in nature and somewhat lacking in theological subscription, that these popular feminine works employed the doctrine of union with Christ. Drawing again from Ephesians 5:31–32, Linda Dillow expresses this profoundly as she asserts that the oneness of Christ and the believer in spiritual life should reflect that of the physical union of man and wife. She writes, "I yearned for a joy unspeakable, *for a deeper union and oneness, for spiritual, bridal union*."[14]

To many this approach to union might seem stereotypically "feminine" as it possesses a strong air for the devotional and intimate. It is however significant that in starting from the biblical texts these works utilize the bride/wife role in developing a spiritually authentic response to the bridegroom/husband Christ. A literature review undertaken by the author failed to discover any theological or academic Reformed discourse on the *unio mystica* by female writers and yet these popular feminine works posture union with Christ in this Pauline "marital" sense. Therefore we identify this to be characteristic of a contemporary feminine Reformed approach and incorporate this into our theological exploration, contributing to our contemporary feminine angle. This Pauline parallelism is especially advantageous to a discussion on spiritual theology, for interacting with the spiritual saving union with Christ and the earthly human marriage union creates

---

12. Such as Prov 31; 1 Cor 7; 14; 34–35; 1 Tim 2:9–15; 5:2–16; Titus 2:3–5; 1 Pet 3:1–7.

13. Brestin and Troccoli, *Falling in Love with Jesus* (2000), *Living in Love with Jesus* (2002), and *Forever in Love with Jesus* (2004).

14. Dillow, *Satisfy*, 19, 20 (emphasis added).

Complementarian Spirituality

opportunity to apply the *unio mystica* directly to feminine life experience, in a strong biblical theological framework.

Ephesians 5:22–33

Since Ephesians 5:22–33 features strongly in feminine complementarian works and is crucial to understanding the biblical doctrine of union with Christ, we will consider the text further.

The doctrine of union with Christ is the "heart" or "center" of the Apostle Paul's "personal religion," thus exploration will possess a marked Pauline quality.[15] One fundamental aspect of this profound doctrine in Paul's letter to the church in Ephesus is his analogy of the union and relationship between Christ and the church with earthly marriage in his section regarding household codes (*Haustafel*). As always, part of Paul's intention here is pastoral exhortation to his brothers and sisters in Christ for godly conduct and practice in their marriages, issuing distinct relational duties to husband and wife. Paul offers the *unio mystica* between Christ and the church as the prototype for the marriage union and exacts the responsibility or dutiful roles between Christ and the church to that of the husband and wife.[16]

In development from his command in Ephesians 5:21 to "submit to one another out of reverence for Christ," Paul delivers the exhortation that wives should specially submit to their husbands as their head as the *ecclesia* submits to Christ as her Head and Savior. He confirms this parallel of submission in verse 24, stating that as the church submits to Christ in "everything" so too the wife's submission is complete and comprehensive.

The husband's correlative duty is to love his wife (v. 25) and so reflect Christ's love for his Spouse. F. F. Bruce notes, "the Church's obedience to Christ, which is the wife's model for her duty to her husband, may fall short of what it should be; [however] there are no shortcomings about the love of Christ for His Church."[17]

Here Paul does not fail to stress the gospel imperative of the love of God in salvation. Christ's love for the church is indeed the motivating factor in his role as Savior, a title rare in Pauline use.[18] Muddiman confirms that this nuptial "saving" is to be understood in the present and future

---

15. Stewart, *Man in Christ*, 147.
16. Patzia, *Ephesians*, 267.
17. Bruce, *Ephesians*, 115.
18. Muddiman, *Ephesians*, 262.

senses, "Christ saved the Church when he sacrificially offered himself for her and he will save her finally when the fruit of his work appears, holy and blameless, at the last judgment."[19] In this love, he has the purpose "that he might sanctify her, having cleansed her by the washing of water with the word" (v. 26). This means that the preaching of the Word is vital to church life as the primary means of removal of sin, assuming the unity of Word and Spirit. This sanctification, wrought by the Spirit of Christ, is in order to "present the church to himself [Christ] in splendor, without spot or wrinkle or any such thing, that she might be holy" (v. 27). Thus, the Spirit of Christ prepares the church for her marriage to the Bridegroom so she becomes the virgin bride worthily dressed in the white of Christ's own righteousness.

Rebecca Jones elucidates this "specific parallel" stating that God sought to teach his people about the relationship between Christ and the church by instituting the marriage union as well as teaching about marriages.[20] Arthur Patzia and many others concur: "The analogy works in the opposite direction as well. Throughout the epistle he has been expounding on the nature of the church and how Christ, the Head, is related to his body, the church. Marriage gives him an illustration—albeit imperfect—of how his readers can understand his ecclesiology . . . the analogy has both a domestic and an ecclesiological function."[21] The union between Christ and the church is therefore the original model of this physical and spiritual union between husband and wife. William Hendriksen builds on this parallel in his commentary on Ephesians, agreeing that this mysterious archetype informs the earthly expression:

> The fact that this marvelous love, this blissful Christ-church relationship, is actually reflected here on earth in the union of a husband and his wife, so that by the strength of the former bond (Christ-church), the latter (husband-wife) is now able to function most gloriously, bringing supreme happiness to the marriage-partners, blessing to mankind, and glory to God *that*, indeed, is the Mystery Supreme![22]

Paul centralizes the duty of love in the marriage union in his charge to the husband to fulfill the same role and calling as Christ, who in his sacrificial love nourishes and cherishes the church because it is his own flesh

---

19. Ibid., 263.
20. Jones, *Christianity*, 165.
21. Patzia, *Ephesians*, 267; cf. Clowney, *Church*, 225; Hoehner, *Ephesians*, 746.
22. Hendriksen, *Ephesians*, 257.

Complementarian Spirituality

(v. 28–29). Importantly, this "nourishing," says Muddiman, is an "oblique allusion" to the eucharistic meal. Muddiman reasons that it would be "surprising if there were no allusion anywhere in Ephesians to the Eucharist as a means of union with Christ and unity in the Church, given Paul's understanding of it."[23] The husband's sacrificial love calls the wife to respond appropriately in submission and respect, as the church does to her Lord and Spouse.

Then Paul confirms that all believers belong to Christ and are part of him, "because we are members of his body" (v. 30), indicating that Christ and the church is the "whole Christ" or *totus Christus*.[24] Perhaps the climax appears, however, when Paul expresses that the *unio mystica* is a "holding fast" or "one flesh." "'Therefore a man shall leave his father and mother and hold fast to his wife, and the two shall become one flesh.' This mystery is profound, and I am saying that it refers to Christ and the church" (Eph 5:31–32 ESV). John Muddiman surmises that the reference to Genesis 2:24 here "understands marital love as arising from the physical derivation of Eve from Adam's body," just as the church finds physical and spiritual life in Christ both in creation and ecclesiology.[25] Nonetheless typical of Paul's constant pastoral concern, he again returns to practical guidelines for husbands and wives, encouraging the correct godly response to each other (v. 33). As Patzia states, Paul "fluctuates" between the two analogies, "at times the husband-wife relationship served an ecclesiological function by illustrating Christ's relationship to the church; at other times, the Christ-church analogy illustrated a domestic ideal."[26]

It is noteworthy that this text is inherently corporate, for Paul constantly refers to "the church" as united to Christ and never the individual believer: Christ gave up himself for *the church* and *the church* submits to Christ in everything. Equally, it is *the church* that Christ purifies through the Word and he will present *the church* to himself. Therefore, it is the duty and responsibility of Christ as the Head and Savior of *the church* to nourish and cherish her.

Owing to the overly individualistic mindset of Christians when considering new life in Christ, a renewed corporate sense of union with Christ is required in contemporary thinking. The binding of the believer to the

---

23. Muddiman, *Ephesians*, 268.
24. Mallard, "Jesus Christ," 468.
25. Muddiman, *Ephesians*, 260–61.
26. Patiza, *Ephesians*, 275.

"in Christ" community is equal to the believer's union with Christ, for the two are not separate; one cannot occur without the other. As we have seen from Ephesians 5, the individual's incorporation into the Body of Christ by means of union with Christ is a critical completion of Christ's work of justification in sanctification. For Christ instituted the church for the sanctification, edification, and service of his people. Thus, union with Christ is a soteriological, transformative, pastoral, and ecclesiastical doctrine.

The Need for a Feminine Spirituality of the Church

"It has been suggested that Christian spirituality is simply the human response to the salvation offered by God in Jesus Christ, *a response that occurs through the working of the Spirit in the church.*"[27] As we have seen, contemporary Reformed feminine discussion makes full use of the Pauline teaching on the union between Christ and the church as it portrays a biblically authentic model for feminine spirituality in exhibiting the response of the "feminine" church to Christ as spiritual Head and Spouse. In other words, the parallelism of the Ephesians 5 model means that the individual Christian woman in seeking a spirituality of biblical womanhood can take on the persona of the church as she enjoys her union with Christ as well as that with her husband. One might say that she is a "miniature" of the church in her individual spirituality in marriage to Christ *and* in her marriage to her husband as her quest for biblical womanhood is informed by both unions. However, this parallelism is perhaps most at home, as the *unio mystica* is, in the corporate consideration of the church and not merely that of the female believer. In a corporate model, a spirituality based upon union the church takes up the persona of the wife. This means that a feminine spirituality based on the Christ-church marriage is also deeply applicable to those who are single, for the divine marriage is the prototype informing the earthly pale reflection and not the other way around. We will consider this further in chapter 6. In sum, our distinctly feminine approach to the Reformed doctrine of union with Christ pertains theologically to the church as the Bride of Christ.

---

27. Carr, *Transforming Grace*, 201 (emphasis added).

Complementarian Spirituality

A FEMININE REFORMED THEOLOGICAL UNDERSTANDING AND EXPRESSION OF UNION WITH CHRIST

Jesus Christ is Head over his covenant people, the community purchased with his own blood. In becoming its Savior, it was the eternal plan of the Holy Trinity, the Three in perfect union, to unite the pre-eminent Son of God to humanity by means of the incarnation. The incarnation of Christ meant he could be made one with the elect, by the power of the Holy Spirit, in a spiritual saving union. Hence, the pre-existent Son took on human flesh. In marrying his divinity to humanity, an irreversible union of these natures took place. There was no loss of trinitarian union in this clothing of Christ with humankind, "in him the whole fullness of deity dwells bodily" (Col 2:9). In making himself one with humanity, the Son of God graciously and humbly became the "Son of Man" and obediently died on a cross to save those given to him by the Father. So by his *body of flesh* he reconciled to God those who once were "alienated and hostile in mind" (Col 1:21). Although he suffered a human death, Christ by the power of the Holy Spirit rose from the dead and the elect, soterically bound to Christ by his Spirit, shared in his death and his resurrection.

How secure is this saving union between Christ and the church? Those predestined in Christ are as secure *in Christ* as the eternality and permanency of his incarnate self, for union with Christ is as irreversible as the union of divinity and humanity in Christ's person. Truly, the elect are "hidden with Christ in God" (Col 3:3).

This union sustains the church through the Christian life, waiting for Christ's return. Whilst his Bride awaits him, Jesus Christ the eternal Bridegroom bestows his Spirit on his church (John 14:16–17). The Spirit of God convicts of sin (John 16:8; 1 Thess 1:5), pours Christ's love on his people, and sanctifies them. The church responds to this salvation in union with Christ by living a life worthy of him in love, devotion, and obedience to her Head and Spouse, awaiting his return and her glorification in him.

The focus of our exploration will be this spousal response of the invisible church, represented in a visible local form, to its *unio cum Christo*. Before we delve into this, we must further unpack the role of Christ, the divine initiator, uniting the church to himself. Then we will consider extensively the spiritual and spousal response of the church to salvation.

As we have discerned, the parallels between the Christ-church relationship and the husband-wife relationship teach us about not only a woman's identity but also the identity or character of the church.[28] Although this parallel is incomprehensive, for Adam did not sacrifice himself for Eve as the husband does not save the wife, hence the need for a second Adam, it is a biblical analogy offering mutual theological insight into the profundity of the *unio mystica* and the creation ordinance of marriage.[29] "Marriage was *designed by God* from the beginning to be a picture or parable of the relationship between Christ and the church." Thus, God created marriage "for this great purpose: it would give a beautiful earthly picture of the relationship that would someday come about between Christ and His church."[30]

Christ the Heavenly Bridegroom

It is a soteriological necessity that we begin with the divine initiation in Christ's self-giving and view the Christ-church union in light of this. As Barth reasons, "we do well to begin, not below with the Christian, but above with Jesus Christ as the Subject who initiates and acts decisively in this union. We do well to begin with the union of Christ with the Christian and His self-giving to the Christian, and not *vice versa*. It is here that the union and self-giving of the Christian have their roots."[31] Subsequently, any theology of the church as the Bride of Christ or, similarly, any exploration into a spirituality of the church must start with this. "To be sure, if the church rather than Christ becomes the centre of our devotion, spiritual decay has begun. A doctrine of the church that does not centre on Christ is self-defeating and false."[32]

As stated above, Jesus Christ the heavenly Bridegroom takes the initiative, by order of the Trinitarian *pactum salutis*, in salvation by "taking the form of a servant, being born in the likeness of men" (Phil 2:7). The Son of God therefore, becomes the great pursuer of his people manifesting the covenantal love of the Godhead for his wayward people by bearing ever closer in human form. In the incarnation we see "God's true dwelling is not a tent of goatskins, or a temple of cedar and gold, but the flesh of Immanuel."[33]

28. Jones, *Christianity*, 152.
29. Hoehner, *Ephesians*, 743.
30. Knight, "Husbands and Wives," 175.
31. Barth, *CD* IV.3.2, 541.
32. Clowney, *Church*, 15.
33. Ibid., 45.

Complementarian Spirituality

The profound spiritual union of the incarnate Christ with his church means that when Christ looks upon his Bride he sees *his own flesh*, as well as his own redeeming righteousness (1 John 2:1). As Adam praised the first sight of his spouse Eve, Christ might also delight in the church with the words, "'This at last is bone of my bones and flesh of my flesh' (Gen 2:23), as Paul conveyed, '. . . the two shall become one flesh.' This mystery is profound, and I am saying that it refers to Christ and the church" (Eph 5:31–32). This oneness of flesh is unarguably necessary for salvation and founded in the tri-unity of the Godhead. Pink elucidates, "Divine union—between the Eternal Three—was the foundation of the Mediatorial union. Had there been only one person in the Divine Essence or Godhead, our salvation had been utterly impossible: we could not be joined to the very nature or essence of God, without either ungodding Him or deifying us."[34]

The Permanency of Union—Incarnation

The permanency of union with the incarnate Christ is a reality for every believer that experientally informs the Christian life, issuing confidence in Christ. The experiential aspect of the Christ-union is first found in the fact that the believer was experientially united to Christ in his historical death and resurrection. Otherwise, Christ's historic work would be of no benefit. Gaffin asserts this as he points out that the Pauline text on union describes actual life experience, inferring that the union basic to this experience "is likewise experiential."[35] The Christ-union is not theoretical or limited to the supernatural realm, but actively imparts salvation and spiritual life within space-time. It can be seen experientially by its transformative power, as the sinner's desires change from love for sin to love for Christ. "Thus you shall recognize them by their fruits" for "apart from me you can do nothing" (Matt 7:17–20; John 15:5). A turning away from sinful inclinations is only the work of the regenerative Spirit, witnessing to the presence of Christ by faith.

The Physicality of Union with Christ

As union with Christ is experiential in its spiritual nature, it is also physical, not in an ontological but a possessive sense. Owing to the intimacy and totality of the *unio mystica*, those in union with Christ belong to Christ *physically* as well as spiritually. The Apostle Paul makes this clear in his

34. Pink, *Union*, 31.
35. Gaffin, *Resurrection*, 50–52.

exhortation to the Corinthians to abstain from sexual immorality.[36] "Do you not know that *your bodies are members of Christ*? Shall I then take the members of Christ and make them members of a prostitute? Never!" (1 Cor 6:15). The parallel of *unio mystica* to the marriage union in Ephesians, as Christ and the church are described to be one flesh like husband and wife, affirms the nature of the physicality of the church's union with Christ. For example, upon marriage, the husband and wife do not join ontologically in a mixture of biological properties eradicating any individual physicality. Instead, the joining, physically manifested in the sex act, is the coming together of two individuals in covenantal possession of each other. "For the wife does not have authority over her own body, but the husband does. Likewise the husband does not have authority over his own body, but the wife does" (1 Cor 7:4). The covenantal promises, which they have undertaken as a creation ordinance, are source of the spiritual, physical, emotional, or decisive union rendering them "one flesh." The union is not by any means initially physical.

Just like marriage, union with Christ operates on the unity of that which is distinct and different.[37] The individuality of Christ and that of each believer is not lost. Yet the nature of the Christ-church union as a spiritual covenantal bond significantly bears on the physical realm. Therefore, though union with Christ is a spiritual union, it does not preclude the believer's flesh but incorporates the whole person. It is because the body belongs to Christ that the Spirit indwells it, "or do you not know that your body is a temple of the Holy Spirit within you, whom you have from God? You are not your own, for you were bought with a price. So glorify God in your body" (1 Cor 6:19–20).

This becomes further apparent when deliberating the eschatological resurrection of those in Christ and their final glorification in heavenly bodies. "As our whole nature, body, soul, and spirit, died in Adam, so must our whole nature, body, soul, and spirit, be made alive in Christ before our blessedness can be complete. And if we are in the Lord, our physical restitution is assured to us with equal certainty with our spiritual."[38]

We should therefore not perceive the believer's union with Christ to be physical, as Osiander's notion, but equally we should not subject it to a platonic divorcing of the spiritual from the natural. As we saw in the

36. Donnelly, *Life*, 27
37. Jones, *Christianity*, 31, 152.
38. Gordon, *Christ*, 84.

previous chapter, the church fathers did not let it suffer this way but considered Christ to be uniting himself with human flesh in the non-salvific incarnational union providing a platform for redemptive union with Christ. In Augustinian thought the imperative of the incarnation for the perfect mediator, both "divine and human," meant truly knowing one's salvation.[39]

There remains a need in Protestant theology to address the incarnation as the necessary grounds for union with Christ. The Holy Spirit's work in marrying Christ's divinity with humanity is prior and natural to his uniting of Christ with his church. As we have seen, the indissolubleness of the first cements the indissolubleness of the second. Thus, the doctrine of union with Christ is established on christological ontology. What assurance this imparts. A. J. Gordon asks, "will Christ permit this body to be dismembered? He can suffer in his members; but Faith would feel herself robbed of all her heritage of assurance, were it anywhere written, He can cut off or perish in his members."[40] None can rend the church from Christ, as his deity and humanity are indivisible by the power of the Holy Spirit. It is to the Holy Spirit as eternal Bond that we now look.

The Bond of Union—the Holy Spirit

Christ's discourse with his disciples accounted in the Gospel of John chapters 14–16 frequent his sending of the Holy Spirit in the face of his imminent departure. "And *I will ask the Father, and he will give you another Helper*, to be with you for ever, even the Spirit of truth, whom the world cannot receive, because it neither sees him or knows him. You know him, for he dwells with you and will be in you" (John 14:16–17, 26; 15:26). Importantly, Jesus stresses the necessity for him to leave them in order for the Promise to come (16:7). "But if I go, *I will send him to you*. And when he comes, he will convict the world concerning sin and righteousness and judgment" (16:7–8). In these three chapters John is overtly presenting a pneumatic Christology in which the Spirit is the gift of Christ, establishing that he will continue with his disciples through the ministry of his Spirit. John makes it clear that it is the vocation of the Spirit of Christ to witness of Christ, to glorify Christ, and declare what belongs to Christ to his people (15:26; 16:14–15).

Paul and the NT writers consistently affirm this role of the Holy Spirit as testifying to Christ. Furthermore, it is only by the power of the Spirit

---

39. Mallard, "Jesus Christ," 464.
40. Gordon, *Christ*, 20.

that Christ's person and works are joined to the believer. Hence, the Christ-union is a pneumatic-christological reality for the church as the Holy Spirit soterically binds the Savior to his people. Rebecca Jones concurs in this Spirit-effected marriage, "Christ and the church are the new Adam and Eve, the founding couple for a new humanity. *Their union produces offspring for God by the power of the Holy Spirit.*"[41]

Essentially then, Christ's sending of the Spirit is the wedding of himself to his Bride. Moreover, it is a trinitarian joining as the Father bestows the covenantal Promise, or in other words, the marriage vow of the Spirit, to the elect. This union however must be a *mutual* joining and it is precisely the divine Promise who imparts the gracious gift of mutuality to the undeserving Bride. This is the Spirit's "wedding ring of faith" in the words of Luther, the regenerative existence of faith.[42] "Before the Holy Spirit fixes the heart of a sinner upon Christ He first quickens him into newness of life."[43] The "incomparable benefit of faith is that it unites the soul with Christ as a bride is united with her bridegroom. By this mystery, as the Apostle teaches, Christ and the soul become one flesh."[44] Consequently, the Savior takes hold of the Bride and "in faith" the Bride takes hold of him. Thus, "we do not so much enter into Christ as Christ enters into us; and the gateway is the decision of faith."[45] This consent of faith furnishes the spiritual life with acceptance and assurance. "As a woman accepts the marriage proposal of her wooer by yielding herself and all her future interests into his care, so the [church] is able to say, 'I know whom I have believed, and am persuaded that He is able to keep that which I *have committed unto him* against the day (2 Tim 1:12).'"[46]

It is incumbent upon the trinitarian authorship of union with Christ that the Holy Spirit as the promised Bond of Christ and the faith response of the church are distinct yet inseparable entities making up the core of union with Christ. Such demonstrates the initiative and economy of the Trinity in salvation and the necessary existence of faith. In this Spirit-wrought union with Christ authored by the Father, we find the mystery of the church's covenantal union and fellowship with the whole Godhead.

41. Jones, *Christianity*, 134 (emphasis added).
42. Luther, "Freedom," 352.
43. Pink, *Practical Christianity*, 30.
44. Luther, "Freedom," 351.
45. Bloesch, *Spirituality*, 143.
46. Pink, *Union*, 85.

Complementarian Spirituality

The Spirit's Sanctification of the Body

In his work on Evangelical spirituality, Raiter asserts that Christian spirituality "is the study of the work of the Holy Spirit in the life of the believer."[47] Without the Spirit, indeed the Christian life cannot exist, for he is as Calvin says "the root and seed of heavenly life in us."[48] Crucial to this pneumatic Christology flowing from the *unio mystica* is the fact that Christ supplies his Spirit to his church in order to sanctify her.[49] As Paul demonstrates, the christological duty of the Head is to sustain, nourish, and sanctify the church "by the washing of water with the word, so that he might present the church to himself in splendor, without spot or wrinkle" (Eph 5:26–27). Hence, we arrive at the efficacious unity of Word and Spirit in the purification of Christ's Bride, an imperative to Reformed theology and spirituality. For it is the particular vocation of the Spirit, who inspired the biblical writers, to also illuminate the Word of God in the hearts of believers in order to make them holy. This shows that the Spirit does not merely join Christ and the elect in a once-and-for-all act but continues renewing the church in Christ. "But when the goodness and loving kindness of God our Savior appeared, he saved us, not because of works done by us in righteousness, but according to his own mercy, *by the washing of regeneration and renewal of the Holy Spirit, whom he poured out on us richly through Jesus Christ our Savior*" (Titus 3:4–6).[50]

Jesus Christ the heavenly Bridegroom is only deserving of a spotless virgin Bride and it is the ministry of the Holy Spirit to prepare and present the church in this worthy state. Importantly though, the Bride is *already* justified and worthy as she is righteous by Christ's robe "dipped in blood," and so "it was granted her to clothe herself in fine linen, bright and pure" (Rev 19:8, 13). The Spirit keeps her faithful and steadfast to her Bridegroom. Whilst she abounds in good works she waits for him, and he like the Hebrew bridegroom prepares a room for his spouse in his father's house (John 14:2–3).

---

47. Raiter, *Stirrings*, 195.
48. *Institutes*, 3.1.2.
49. 2 Cor 3:18; 6: 6; Gal 3:3–5; 5:22.
50. Acts 20:23; Rom 5:5; 15:13; Phil 1:6, 19.

A Pneumatic-Christological Spirituality

Through the apostolic instruction of the NT letters we see that the Spirit's work of sanctification is innate to the context of the Body of Christ, as the Christ-union entails membership into the corporate Body of Christ *in the Spirit* in order to grow into a "holy temple" (Eph 2:18, 21–22). "For in one Spirit we were all baptized into one body—Jews or Greeks, slaves or free—and all were made to drink of one Spirit" (1 Cor 12:13).

Indeed, a biblical spirituality that finds its source in the NT documents of the early church will be inherently corporate, shaping both the spirituality of the individual as well as the Body as a whole. For example, contemporary Christians need to approach the Epistles deliberately as the corporate letters they are and not simply view the text in an individualistic devotional manner. For the apostles wrote to each church to rebuke, exhort, and encourage them *pastorally as a Body*, so any application of the Epistles into Christian life should directly impact the Christ-community. As Christian unity is in Christ by the "one Spirit," in any comprehension of the role of the church, both theologically and in relation to Reformed spirituality, the Holy Spirit must be central. This does not confuse the church as the Bride or Body of Christ but only confirms it, as "Christ indwells his church *in the fellowship of the Spirit.*"[51]

As indicated, NT teaching demonstrates that the unity of the Body of Christ in the Spirit is the God-given setting for the preservation and sanctification of his people until he returns. Therefore, it is in the sacred context of the Bride of Christ that the believer's Christian life can manifest its union with Christ to the uttermost. This is apparent in the Spirit's use of the preached Word and the sacraments and his moving of the Body to works of mutual love, service, and edification, and acts of self-examination, confession, and repentance. John Murray acknowledges this, highlighting its eschatological significance:

> In reality *the growth of the individual does not take place except in the fellowship of the church as the fellowship of the Spirit*. Believers have never existed as independent units. . . . Sanctification itself is a process that moves to a consummation which will not be realized for the individual until the whole body of Christ is complete and presented in its totality faultless and without blemish. This points up the *necessity of cultivating and promoting the sanctification of*

---

51. Clowney, *Church*, 29 (emphasis added).

Complementarian Spirituality

> *the whole body, and the practical implications for responsibility, privilege, and opportunity become apparent.*[52]

A Challenge from the East

Our focus on the doctrine of union with Christ as a pneumatic-christological doctrine has led us to contextualize sanctification in the corporate and pneumatic-christological sphere. This might prove to be a challenge for the Reformed community, who in counteraction to the Charismatic overemphasis of the Holy Spirit has perhaps debased the person and work of the Holy Spirit in the spiritual life.[53] A pneumatic-christological understanding of corporate life in Christ such as we are articulating can encourage a correction in Reformed spirituality that reflects a biblical take on "life in Christ by the Spirit." Ralph Del Colle, in his study *Christ and the Spirit: Spirit-Christology in Trinitarian Perspective*, affirms that a Spirit-christology will be of great benefit to Protestant theology and spirituality:

> Spirit-christology focuses theological reflection on the role of the Holy Spirit in christology proper. It seeks to understand both 'who Christ is' and 'what Christ has done' from the perspective of the third article of the creed: 'I believe in the Holy Spirit, the Lord and Giver of Life.' Spirit-christology addresses directly the charge that something is lacking in the church's understanding and faith if in theory and praxis the basic christological confession is not informed by pneumatology. In the realm of religious experience this points directly to the experience of the Holy Spirit as well as of God and of Christ.[54]

The Orthodox tradition has criticized the West's use of pneumatology in salvation, additional to though not divorced from the *filioque* controversy. In relation to spirituality, Vladimir Lossky reproaches Western expressions for belittling the pneumatological and owning an "excessive christocentricity" that falls short of biblical *trinitarianism*. Here the role of the Spirit as the "medium" to Christ in the western perspective of the *unio mystica* is said to reflect a narrow binitarian focus.[55] Although this criticism is to some degree expected in light of the Orthodox widening of the *unio mystica* to a fuller union with the Godhead in deification, Lossky and Del

---

52. Murray, *Systematic*, 299 (emphasis added).
53. Cf. Carson, *Gagging*, 567.
54. Del Colle, *Spirit-Christology*, 3.
55. Ibid., 9.

Colle do helpfully challenge the posture of the Third Person in Protestant theology. An increased awareness of the pneumatic-christological components of union with Christ and subsequent "life in the Spirit" will stimulate Reformed spirituality to a thoroughly Trinitarian spirituality that biblically centers on Christ as the means of union and communion with the Three-in-One.

Mainstream Evangelical and Reformed appreciation of the "in Christ" relationship in popular works was largely limited to an "exchanged life" formula or freedom in Christ concept devoid of any worthwhile soteriological or Trinitarian framework. The pneumatic-christological outworking of the *unio mystica*, however, sets out the Christian life with a biblical-theological holism. Equally, it upholds the Evangelical primacy of the Christ-revelation and his person as the only means to the Father (John 14:6–7). Packer ensures that a Trinity-encompassing spirituality still has Christ at the center (John 5:23; 16:14) and "exalting Christ, then, by worship, witness, and service, as the main focus of our *uplifting of the triune God*, should be our constant aim."[56]

Furthermore, a Trinitarian appreciation of the Christian life roots the church deeper into community, whilst not undermining the place of personal spirituality. Graham Beynon insists the triune God does not believe in individualism but has ordained for believers to live in community as he does.[57]

CONCLUSION

As we have observed, in salvation Jesus Christ steps in as Bridegroom for the whole Trinity, serving as "the gate" and leading his Bride the church into a secure and eternal union with the triune Persons. The essential Trinitarian and subsequently corporate nature of the Christ-union belongs to the Bride, that is, the church body, and so is thoroughly corporate. This union is experiential as it is worked out analogously in the marriage covenant, as well as serves as the blueprint and bulwark for spiritual life and sanctification on earth.

Let us now consider how the Bride biblically responds to this mighty union of grace.

---

56. Packer, *Holiness*, 81 (emphasis added).
57. Beynon, *New Community*, 53.

5

The Church the Bride of Christ

As we have observed, the *unio mystica* is clearly distinguishable in the Body of Christ as the community grows in shared life in Christ and joint possession of his Spirit. Now we shall look to outline specific contours of this union for the Bride of Christ in response to the heavenly Bridegroom, reflected in the feminine "wife" character and her role in the marriage union. This will define a spirituality of the church anchored in the biblical doctrine of union with Christ that can contribute to the need for renewal in Reformed spirituality. This is in line with Bloesch's prescription: "what is needed today is a renewal of devotion to the living Savior, Jesus Christ. Such renewal will take the form of a spiritual reformation that involves the very structure and life of the church. . . . It will also manifest itself in an awakened interest in the sacraments, particularly the Blessed Sacrament of Holy Communion."[1] Bloesch's movement of thought here is significant. For in this theological examination of the church as the corporate Spouse of Christ it is incumbent upon us to consider the unity of Christians in the meal of Holy Communion. For *corporate* participation of Christ in the Lord's Supper finds its roots in the doctrine of union with Christ, as we saw particularly in patristic, Thomistic, and Calvinistic thought in chapter 2.

In addition, a significant feature of union with Christ appropriated in the Christ-feast is the work of the Holy Spirit as the uniting party. Indeed, we have acknowledged repeatedly the vocation of the third member of the Trinity, the Spirit of Christ, as the bond of our union with Christ and his corollary power and presence in the church. The pneumatic-christological fruit of *unio cum Christo* involves the Holy Spirit leading the Body in repentance and conviction of sin, apparent in the requirement for

1. Bloesch, *Crisis*, 15.

self-examination and repentance in the Lord's Supper (1 Cor 11:27–28). Hence, the themes of self-examination, repentance, and confession of sin, as necessary components to biblical spirituality, are integrated into this discussion in their corporate forms.

THE COVENANT BRIDE IN SCRIPTURE

The covenant people perceived and celebrated as the bride or wife of God is an undeniable biblical theme, evident in the OT and NT.[2] In the former, Yahweh covenantally joins himself to Israel his bride, expressing his "conjugal jealousy" through the giving of the Decalogue.[3] He purses her even in her unfaithfulness, evident in the admonishments of the prophets, as she goes after other gods in her idolatry, rebellion, and intermarrying. This intimate relationship starts at the Abrahamic covenant, as God chooses a nation for himself—"Jehovah chose Israel, they are his people; he married her"—and runs throughout the OT, as Israel is described positively and negatively as the "virgin" or "bride" or even "harlot" or "whore," to the coming of Christ.[4]

In the new covenant established upon the body and blood of the Christ, his Bride is Christ's redeemed people, the church. The church is the blessed and beloved community of the Godhead. It is the sacred people of God, saved by the priceless blood of Jesus Christ. There is no dearer treasure outside of the Trinity itself than the Body named in and under Christ. The church is indeed the glory of Christ and his person is incomplete without it.[5]

Practically this means that as Christians love, respect, submit to, and serve the Bride of Christ, they are also expressing love, respect, submission, and service to Christ.

THE CORPORATE IMPERATIVE

The church's existence as the family of God (Rom 8:14–17), the family of families, bestows great responsibility and corporate duty to the individual

---

2. 2 Sam 17:3; Isa 62:5; Jer 2:2; Ezek 16; Hos 1–14; Matt 9:15; John 3:29; Rev 19:7; 21:2, 9; 22:17.

3. Vos, *Biblical*, 258; cf. Ps 45; Isa 1:21; 61:10; Jer 2–3; 18: 13; Ezek 16; Amos 5:2; and the Song of Solomon.

4. Vos, *Biblical*, 256.

5. Acts 9:5; Rom 12:15; 1 Cor 12:12; 2 Cor 8:23; Col 1:18; Eph 1:22–23; 4:12; cf. Bavinck, *Dogmatics*, 474.

Christian life. Any conception or practice in the church that fails to cultivate and celebrate the oneness of the Body of Christ is contrary to the Bible and God's purpose of the church, visible and invisible, local and global. This is particularly pertinent in light of the rampant individuality found in contemporary church culture. Due to the wide influence of Evangelical personalism, the Reformed tradition has much to counteract.[6] American writer Donald Whitney concurs, "the New Testament knows nothing of the individualized spirituality of today and nothing of a Christianity that exists apart from the local church."[7] The Christian life that downplays the role of the church grossly denies God's intention for salvation and sanctification. Clowney reminds us of this imperative in relation to the Spirit's work in union: "Since salvation is only in Christ, there is a sense in which there is no salvation outside the church of Christ, for those whom the Spirit unites to Christ, he unites to all others who are in Christ."[8] Its theological significance is seen as it is the fulfillment of Christ's high-priestly prayer, "Holy Father, keep them in your name, which you have given me, that they may be one, even as we are one" (John 17:11b).

As one dedicates himself or herself covenantally to the life and growth of Christ's Body, a full, spiritually satisfying appropriation of the believer's union with Christ can be realized. However, a covenantal commitment to the Christ-community is not common to the contemporary church. Twenty-first century involvement and conception of the local church differs little from that of society's clubs and fraternities. Undoubtedly, this denigration of communal church life is connected to the same of family life. Contemporary return to a Reformed value for the immediate family unit will inevitably permeate into church life and vice versa. Richard Baxter's call remains apt for today; "A holy family is a place of comfort, a church of God. . . . Oh that God would stir up the hearts of people thus to make their families as little churches."[9] This is an essential feature of Reformed spirituality. The Christian family is to be a miniature church practicing daily corporate worship under the leadership of its head, for the production of holiness. William Hendriksen writes in his commentary on Ephesians 5: "no institution on earth is more sacred than that of the family. None is more basic. As is the moral and religious atmosphere in the family, so will it be

6. Hageman, "Reformed," 155.
7. Whitney, *Simplify*, 35.
8. Clowney, *Church*, 57.
9. Baxter, "Poor Man's Family Book."

in the church, the nation, and society in general."[10] The family is the initial context that tests and displays genuine spirituality, and it together with the church are the divinely established corporate milieu for the well-being of God's people in society, waiting for Christ's return.

There is a dire need for modern day Christians to renew a vision of the church consistent with its soteriological and eschatological purposes. Reformed Christians must dedicate themselves wholeheartedly to their local representations of the Body of Christ, who lives and breathes for her archetypical and final form as the Bride of Christ, the priesthood of God, united in Christ by the Spirit "from every tribe and language and people and nation" (Rev 5:9; 7:9).

The fact that current works on spirituality predominately position the "in Christ" relationship in an individualistic context and not that of the Body renders our theological approach radically corporate, suggesting that increased corporate appreciation and practice would richly benefit Reformed spirituality. A church spirituality that is geared towards the purification of Christ's Bride as one Body will centralize and fully recognize the profound grace of God in the Lord's Supper and its unique context for examination, proclamation, thanksgiving, praise, and mutual growth, re-establishing the Reformed value for the sacraments. Any individualism found in Reformed churches runs against the tradition's resonant sense of community and the gospel it is based on, as Packer clarifies in the reformers' opposition to the medieval concept that "holiness" lay in the eremitic life:

> The Reformers reconceived holiness as the fulfilling of one's relationships, the stewarding of one's talents and time, and the maintaining of love, humility, purity, and zeal for God in one's heart. The ideal of isolationism was then jettisoned completely and replaced by an insistence that holiness – viewed now as the consecrated life of the grateful, forgiven sinner – must be worked out in the way in which, as worshiper, worker, and witness, one relates to one's family, church, and wider community.[11]

We see constantly in the NT that the Christian life and its pursuit of holiness is clearly lived out in the familial setting, instituted and sustained by God, whereby the members mutually sanctify, edify, and serve one another, building the Body up in the power of the Holy Spirit and for the glory

---

10. Hendriksen, *Ephesians*, 248.
11. Packer, *Holiness*, 29.

of God.[12] The Spirit's role in maintaining unity is also significant. Ephesians 4:3 exhorts the Christians to make every effort to keep the unity of the Spirit "through the bond of peace." A pneumatic-christological understanding of the church acknowledges the role of the Spirit to bind the Body; the Spirit is the fiber of the sinews keeping the Body together. Kuiper affirms this in church practice as the congregation worships not as an "aggregate of individuals, but as a body. Those present sing the same songs, pray the same prayers, attend to the same Word, contribute to the same offering, receive the same benediction. And they perform all those activities under the control of the one Spirit."[13]

Covenantal Commitment to Diversity

The corporate imperative means that the diversity of the Body is to be fully celebrated and expressed in love and service to one another for the sake of the gospel, as Paul's famous body analogy teaches in 1 Cor 12. Paul presumes the Christ-church union as he exhorts the believers to unity in the Holy Spirit (1 Cor 12:13). Here the Apostle encourages a covenantal sharing in one another's lives, a love and care for all the members of the Body that affirms the reality that the believer in Christ is covenantally one with his or her brothers and sisters in Christ. Here Paul leaves no room for apathy and disregard for other members or superficial relationships. The believer, fully reconciled to God through union with Christ, is to live fully reconciled to others. Experiential union with Christ ensures that all human categories fall away and there is no distinction in gender or race, or in economical or marital status; the female, Gentile, slave, and widow are "all one in Christ" (Gal 3:28).

This appropriation of union with Christ in the cultivation of a unified Body that covenantally rejoices in its differences of age, class, race, and background, so proclaiming the gospel, is significantly the fulfillment of the second commandment to love one's neighbor.[14] The display of any prejudice in the covenantal Body of Christ is far from the picture Paul conveys, belittling corporate union and injuring Christian maturity and growth in Christ. The believer who breaks from the sinful and un-Christ-like tendency to commit to relationships that only serve their own interests, and

12. Rom 14:19; 1 Cor 14:3–4, 12, 26; 2 Cor 12:19; 13:10; Jude 1:20.
13. Kuiper, *Body*, 354.
14. Sittser, *Love*, 26.

instead selflessly welcomes and loves the stranger or cultural "untouchable," covenantally lives out their union with the incarnate Christ and his Bride.

Community and Connectedness in Contemporary Spirituality

In our introductory chapter we saw that new spiritualities are characterized by a desire for "connectedness" represented in the spirituality articulated by Catholic author Kathleen Fischer in *Reclaiming the Connections: A Contemporary Spirituality*. Her contemporary spirituality is one that reconnects the fragmentation of "individual and community, self and others, humanity and the earth, nation and nation, God and the world, prayer and action, work and holiness, body and spirit, imagination and reason,"[15] strongly advocating a spiritual life set in community. Schneiders underlines this historical shift in relational longing as she observes the contemporary yearning for the community context contrasted with the "overly individualistic understanding of spirituality encountered in many manuals from the eighteenth to the twentieth century."[16]

Feminist historian Allison Stokes draws attention to the rise of feminine spirituality groups in the nineteenth century that transcended denomination and even religious adherence. Whilst these women vented their frustration with the restrictions put on them in church life in light of the emerging feminist project, the initial grounds for fellowship was their shared womanhood and the spiritual camaraderie and solidarity, felt to be lacking in institutional religion.[17] Additional to their channeling of increasing "feminist consciousness," Stokes says, they "deepen[ed] spiritual connections" by means of shared leadership, full member participation, consensus-based decision making, open and personal communication, mind-body-soul integration, and acceptance, affirmation, and nurture of personal empowerment and creativity.[18]

The existence of feminist ritualistic activity, apparent in restoration of the individual in "feminist therapy"[19] conducted in community and spiritual ritual, challenges the church in its integration of women, appropriate and effective pastoral care for them, and the establishment of a corporate church life that relationally nourishes and supports them. The feminine de-

15. Fischer, *Connections*, vii.
16. Schneiders, "Christian Spirituality," 2.
17. Stokes, "Spirituality Groups," 272–73.
18. Ibid., 273.
19. Neu, "Women's Empowerment."

Complementarian Spirituality

sire for "interconnectedness" is further obvious in the growing popularity of the Goddess, Wiccan, and sex-spirituality movements, and their feminist forms, which seek spiritual encounters of oneness with the universe or creation, exemplified in the mysticism of Alice Walker's *The Color Purple* as the female character engages in a cosmic orgasm with the universe.[20]

The valuing of community in these spiritualities and theologies, however, comes at the cost of orthodoxy. The anthropocentric approach, found in the rise of "relational theology" in liberation, feminist, black, and environmental thought, stresses spiritual holism through reconciliation with humankind on a horizontal level, defining sin predominantly as an assault against fellow humanity and rejecting an Augustinian framework.[21] On the other hand, the traditional biblical view on human relations, in line with Reformed thought, is based on Christ's commandment to "love your neighbor as yourself" (Matt 22:39) and does not necessitate the reinterpretation of sin or any other doctrine to arrive at a Christian humanitarianism.[22]

Corporate Feminine Reformed Life

A corporate spirituality of the church can meet this deep need for spiritual connectedness in the fragmentation of modern life. Here the Reformed tradition offers a pertinent response to contemporary spiritualities in its native sixteenth-century implementation of corporate life, to which we must return. "In the view of the reformers, the church is a community of faith within which God has provided the means to make their pilgrimage successful. *Within the church, believers enjoy spiritual union with Christ and with one another.*"[23] Thus, the Christian's experiential enjoyment and appropriation of union with Christ can be found in the context of the Body knit together. "Union with Christ then is communal as well as individual because it inducts converts into the church, where Christians are bound together by the Holy Spirit in a fellowship of caring and sharing."[24] The unity and the relationship that stems from this doctrine and its Reformed

---

20. Jones, *Christianity*, 31.

21. Raiter, *Stirrings*, 36–38, 44, 76; Fischer, *Connections*, vi; Zappone, *Wholeness*, 63; Plaskow and Christ, *Weaving the Visions*.

22. As Marjorie Hewitt Suchocki articulates, representative of Relational Theology, "sin is first and foremost a rebellion against creation," for "to call all sin a rebellion against God too easily translates into a social formula for keeping marginalized and oppressed peoples in places of poverty and/or powerlessness." Suchocki, *Original Sin*, 16–17.

23. McGoldrick, "Calvin's Spirituality," 54.

24. Ibid..

appreciation can fulfill the immense longing in the new spiritualities for the relational both with God and others.[25]

In relation to the feminist spiritualities outlined above, the Reformed church in its traditional and increasingly unique complementarian stance has the opportunity to cultivate a church practice that celebrates the distinct spiritual needs and gifting of women as they minister to each other and the Body as a whole. The need remains for the Reformed church to respond accordingly to the challenges put to it by secular and religious feminism by renewing church practice consistent with its complementarianism.[26] Instead of avoiding gender-related issues in the church, or relegating "women's ministry" to the sidelines, the Reformed church must encourage women as they contribute to the theological, pastoral, and spiritual life of the Body.[27] "The church needs the theological contributions of each individual woman in the lives of other members of the Body, and the church needs the collective participation of women in the spiritual life of the church if it is to remain strong."[28] In the acknowledgement that women can minister biblically and effectively to one another (Titus 2:3–5) this ministry should be viewed as indispensible to the life of the Body and not executed separately or peripherally. If the spiritual service and care of women does not remain integral to the Body, women will go elsewhere for a spiritual affirmation that meets their own expression and experiences, and the Body will be in disarray. If the Reformed tradition can responsibly promote and foster biblical feminine spirituality, then Reformed women will be both safeguarded from wandering to other traditions and mature spiritually as they biblically commit to the Body's edification. In turn, the Body too will benefit. Carolyn Custis James reminds us that this is a basic Christian duty. "The truth is that the vast majority of Christians will never serve as pastors or hold offices within the church. Yet New Testament writers believed *every* Christian shared significant responsibility for the spiritual welfare of the church."[29]

Picking up from the Ephesians 5 text, we will consider the three bridal virtues of submission, love, and purity of the wife towards her husband, and then apply these attributes to the church's corporate spirituality in relation

25. Raiter, *Stirrings*, 76.
26. James, "Women and the Church."
27. Cf. James, *Life*, 213–14.
28. Ibid., 203.
29. Ibid., 204.

Complementarian Spirituality

to union with Christ. This will then climax in an exploration of the *unio mystica* in the corporate sacrament of the Eucharist.

THE BRIDE'S SUBMISSION TO HER LOVING HUSBAND

In Pauline teaching the wife is commanded to submit to her own husband as she submits to her spiritual head, Christ. Peter also exhorts this godly practice: "Likewise, wives, be subject to your own husbands, so that even if some do not obey the word, they may be won without a word by the conduct of their wives. . . . For this is how the holy women who hoped in God used to adorn themselves, by submitting to their own husbands, as Sarah obeyed Abraham, calling him lord" (1 Pet 3:1, 5). However, we should always consider submission in light of it complementing authority, an authority given with the duty of sacrificial love. These household codes teach the mutual responsibilities of *both* the husband and wife for a harmonious union, therefore one code should not be isolated from another. The wife's voluntary submission to her husband affirms his authority in leadership and love. We consider authority *with* love and not merely the duty of "authority" or "headship" as other complementarian outlines. In this male-female order established in the *taxis* of the triune Godhead who "is love" (1 John 4:7–8) and dwells perichoretically in perfect love, love should not be marginalized. When authority *and* love *and* submission are seen together, these biblical codes make perfect sense.

This is also true for the parallelism found in the Christ-church union. "Christ leads, governs, protects, provides and lays down his life for the church" and "the church is the model of submission, in her willing, loving affirmation of the leadership of Christ."[30]

Significant to this authority/love-submission dynamic in the Christ-church union is the complementarian thought that this is the pattern of marriage per se:

> Paul saw that *when God designed the original marriage He already had Christ and the church in mind*. This is one of God's great purposes in marriage: to picture the relationship between Christ and His redeemed people forever! But if this is so, then the order Paul is speaking of here (submission and love) is not accidental or temporary or culturally determined: it is part of the *essence of*

---

30. James, *God's Design*, 71–72.

marriage, part of God's original plan for a perfect, sinless, harmonious marriage.³¹

The root of this harmony found in the coexistence of authority/love and submission in the maintenance of full equality is the *intra*-Trinitarian order as God the Son is in "dignified submission"³² to the Father, and the Holy Spirit proceeds from the Father and the Son:

> The order is non-reversible, but there is also complete equality of status, dignity and worth. Thus the creation of man and woman, two sexes equal but complementary, mirrors something very wonderful within the Holy Trinity. Both authority and submission are seen within the Godhead as beautiful and glorious . . . To dislike patterns of authority and submission (whether in the family or church or society) implies that we dislike a pattern that is intrinsic to the beauty and glory of God himself.³³

This relational dynamic intrinsic to the Trinity is seen in 1 Corinthians 11:3. "But I want you to understand that the head of every man is Christ, the head of a wife is her husband, and the head of Christ is God." Paul then later refers to the creation order in Genesis as one of "glory," "For a man ought not to cover his head, since he is the image and glory of God, but woman is the glory of man" (1 Cor 11:7). As the Trinitarian *taxis* works out in mutual glorification, the husband-wife relationship is similar. Jones elaborates, "just as the woman glorifies the man and is glorified by the man, so Jesus glorifies the Father, and is glorified by the Father. The Son glorifies the Father in submission to Him; the man glorifies Christ in submission to Him; and a wife glorifies her husband in submission to him."³⁴ Furthermore, just as Christ's submission is dignified, Paul calls for feminine submission that is joyful, as Harold Heohner says of the text that there is nothing to infer that the church's submission is forced.³⁵ Christopher Ash underlines, "morally honourable and [with a] Spirit-given willingness," the wife voluntarily surrenders herself under the care and protection of her loving spouse.³⁶

---

31. Knight, "Husbands and Wives," 176; Ash, *Marriage*, 321; Foh, *Biblical Feminism*, 178–79.

32. Ash, *Marriage*, 314.

33. James, *God's Design*, 55.

34. Jones, *Christianity*, 174; cf. Ash, *Marriage*, 288.

35. Hoehner, *Ephesians*, 731.

36. Ash, *Marriage*, 319.

Thus, the submission of the wife and authority of the husband in the marriage union does not involve inequality. Indeed, as in Trinitarian relations, how can equality be a concern when the husband and wife are "one flesh"? It remains for complementarian discourse to present a higher esteem for the profound oneness of marital union so egalitarian debate can distinguish less opportunity for the independency of passive female subservience and male domination.

The profound intimacy of marital oneness eradicates questions not only of equality but also spiritual standing. Both are equally made in the image of God and the wife is a spiritual "heir" equal to her husband (1 Pet 3:7), for there is neither male nor female in Christ.

However, because the Christ-church union is the union of Redeemer-redeemed, Creator-creatures, and King-subjects, there is not this same spiritual equality in the *unio mystica*. Of course, Christ's divine supremacy and pre-eminence pre-exists and possesses the church. Yet Scripture does point to a *type* of spiritual equality present in the doctrine of adoption: "The Spirit himself bears witness with our spirit that we are children of God, and if children, then heirs—heirs of God and *fellow heirs with Christ*" (Rom 8:14–17). As the Bride of Christ cleaves to her kingly Savior in union, she enters into a marriage that is "as lasting as blood ties,"[37] reckoning her a co-heir with her husband in the family of God.

Obedience: How the Church Submits to Christ

In the same way that Paul teaches that the wife must bring honor to her husband, as she is his "glory,"[38] the church also is the "glory" of Christ, bearing his image and name (2 Cor 8:23). Therefore, the church must voluntarily commit to the authority/love and submission pattern because "the realities of headship and submission in marriage have their counterparts in the church."[39] The submission of the church *in everything* is "voluntary, wholehearted, sincere, enthusiastic," thus displaying her covenantal union with Christ as she conforms to his loving plans and purposes for her.[40] For his Bride belongs doubly to him, firstly because he is sovereign over all creation, and secondly because he purchased her with his blood. In such wifely submission to his headship, the church also actively demonstrates

---

37. Cf. Ash, *Marriage*, 266.
38. Ash, *Marriage*, 293.
39. Piper, "Complementarity," 53.
40. Hendriksen, *Ephesians*, 250.

her holiness. For biblical submission is a holy act or pure conduct, able to win over the unbelieving husband (1 Pet 3:1). Just as the wife displays the priceless "imperishable beauty of a gentle and quiet spirit, in her feminine submission, which in God's eyes is very precious" (1 Pet 3:4), so the church cleaves to her Head, calling him "master" or "lord," as Sarah did Abraham, trusting in her Spouse completely and not fearing "anything that is frightening" (v. 6). Any harboring of fear belittles the all-sufficiency of her divine Husband and her intimate covenantal union with him.

An initial outworking of the spousal submission of the church is obedience. The church must submit to and obey Christ or she has no part with him. "If you keep my commandments, you will abide in my love, just as I have kept my Father's commandments and abide in his love" (John 15:10). Obedience is integral to Christian spirituality because submissive love for the Head is crucial for the life of the Body of Christ. Raiter asserts that Pauline spirituality pertains more to the pursuit of righteousness and holiness than devotional or pietistic acts.[41] Obedience and submission are, however, neglected subjects in contemporary Christian spirituality, yet sin remains the most powerful opposing force to a lively Christian life. Peter Adam concurs that "the great barrier to true spirituality is not the lack of technique in spiritual aptitude, but sin."[42] We shall see that the "taproot," as Packer terms it, of holiness is union with Christ and the freedom from sin and love for God that results from it.[43] A Reformed spirituality set upon the *unio mystica* builds upon the marital authority/love-submission dynamic in its intercourse with the Savior. "There is no such thing as a saving *faith* in Christ where there is no real *love* for Him, and by 'real love' we mean a love which is evidenced by *obedience*."[44]

Submit to One Another

If the church is the Body of Christ then submission to Christ involves submission to his Body and submission to his Body includes submission to Christ. So intimate is the *unio mystica* between Christ and his church that ministry to one becomes ministry to the other (Matt 25:35–40). Conversely, persecution of one involves persecution of the other (John 15:18; Acts 9:4–5).

41. Raiter, *Stirrings*, 203.
42. Adam, *Biblical Spirituality*, 39.
43. Packer, *Holiness*, 172.
44. Pink, *Christianity*, 21.

Complementarian Spirituality

The church therefore has a duty of submission to its members. Paul captures this before his household codes in Ephesian 5 when he instructs, "be subject to one another out of reverence for Christ" (Eph 5:21 NRSV). It is from this transitional verse, which serves as a "hinge" for the preceding and following verses, that Paul develops the specific marital application of this wider Christian grace.[45] George Knight insists further that this proceeds from the exhortation of verse 18 to "be filled with the Spirit," "thus conclud[ing] the list of things that should characterize Spirit-filled living by the redeemed."[46] Harold W. Hoehner emphasizes that this is imperative as "only believers filled by the Spirit are able to please the Lord by fulfilling their duties and are able to live blameless lives in close and continual contact" with others, thus affirming Paul's foundational tenet of the Body's unity *in* and *by* the Spirit.[47]

So as the wife "in Christ" is exhorted to submit to her husband as the church does to Christ, the church as the Body must follow this directive in a "voluntary yielding to others" in love.[48] Clearly, Paul is stressing the need for "mutual subjection" in order to maintain a harmonious and healthy Body. Gerald Sittser explains that in this section of household duties, including later instructions to parents, children, masters, and slaves, the apostle is advocating a radical ethic of servanthood like that of Christ. He encourages that in the freedom of the Christ-union those in authority "subject themselves to their subordinates" and those who "occupy subordinate positions in the social order" as "free moral agents" voluntarily make themselves subject.[49]

This NT ethic of voluntarily yielding oneself to authority is especially pertinent in the case of church leadership, as the writer of the book of Hebrews indicates: "obey your leaders and submit to them, for they are keeping watch over your souls, as those who will have to give an account" (13:17 ESV). We shall develop this further below, but suffice to say at this point that the Body's compliance to its human leadership as that instituted by her Head, Christ Jesus, has huge ramifications for the unified life of the church. In his discussion on the meaning of "femininity," Piper writes, "at the heart

---

45. Hoehner, *Ephesians*, 729; Knight, "Husbands and Wives," 166–68; Ash, *Marriage*, 307–8.
46. Knight, "Husbands and Wives," 166.
47. Hoehner, *Ephesians*, 729, 733.
48. Knight, "Husbands and Wives," 166.
49. Sittser, *Love*, 42–43, 45.

of mature femininity is the freeing disposition *to affirm, receive and nurture strength and leadership*" in relationship to "worthy" men.[50] Here we note the wife's selfless submission as she looks to her husband, encompassing a "demeanor that honors him as leader even when she dissents."[51] This feminine affirmation, reception, and nurturing of strength and leadership should be the disposition of the local Body as it dwells under familial authority. As the Bride leans on the authority of her covenantal Head, clothing herself with a "gentle and quiet spirit," the church too must be "gentle" (*praus*). That is, the Body cannot live divisively and each of its members should "not [be] insistent on one's own rights or not pushy, not selfishly assertive, [and] not demanding one's own way."[52] Corporate union with Christ means the holy cultivation of oneness, for no body or "city or house divided against itself will stand" (Matt 12:25), executed in a selfless submission that honors Christ as Head. Local church submission that reflects the scriptural spousal mandate of the church and the Christian wife will dress the Body in a Christ-like disposition of selfless humility that will save it from unnecessary church politics and division as it submits to its Head in the power of the Spirit.

THE BRIDE'S LOVING RESPECT FOR HER HUSBAND

This brings us on to an essential prerequisite for submission, which Paul acknowledges in Epheisans 5:33. Submission is the required behavior for wives in Christ towards their husbands but one motivation for the practice of submission is respect.

> Wives are asked to render their submission in a way that is most like that of the submission of the church to Christ, that is, a truly respectful submission because it is rendered voluntarily from the heart. A wife's respecting [of] her husband and his headship therefore implies that her submission involves not only what she does but also her attitude in doing it. As with the husband, so with the wife, it is the heart's attitude of grateful acceptance of the role God assigns to each and the determination to fulfill the particular role with all the graciousness God gives.[53]

---

50. Piper, "Complementarity," 46.
51. Grudem, "Wives," 196.
52. Ibid. 197.
53. Knight, "Husbands and Wives," 175.

In sum, biblical submission stems from an attitude of honor towards the one in authority. The wife respects and appreciates her husband because he establishes her and builds her up, having her good at the center of his purposes. She honors him because he took it upon himself to extend his arm out to her in unconditional covenantal love, to provide for her, to take responsibility for her. Hoehner writes, "the church benefits from the headship of Christ and so also should the wife's submission enhance her well-being."[54] The Christ-church–husband-wife parallelism calls for the wife to "recognize that, in his capacity as her head, her husband is so closely united to her and so deeply concerned about her welfare that his relation to her is patterned after the sacrificial interest of Christ in his church, which he purchased with his own blood."[55] Thus, the wife's response is to be one of respect and honor to her husband's commitment to her. Such is apparent in the Christ-church relationship as the Bride honors her Head with all humility because of his lavish graciousness and covenantal love towards her. The Bride of Christ submits to her Head by the Spirit with a reverence and awe far too profound for the marriage union, as she witnesses his work of purification and edification in her. This building up of the Body is the objective underpinning to the pastoral exhortations to the church in Pauline text. The Bride's love and honor for the Bridegroom causes her to enjoy the unity of her members in a love that builds her up to holiness (Eph 4:15–16).

Significantly then, submission must be married with a loving respect; otherwise its voluntary nature is lost. We consider love together with the biblical concepts of respect, honor, and submission because they are outworkings of love. This becomes apparent in the need to "train the young women to love their husbands," as well as submit to them (Titus 2:4–5), and Paul's admonishment to the Body to submit to church leaders (1 Thess 5:12–13). Loving respect for one's husband confirms a peaceable union in the marriage as it does in the unified church. A union that is not peaceable not only has little enjoyment of fellowship but little unity. Part of the privileged membership into the Body of Christ is that its members "outdo one another in showing honor" (Rom 12:10) and so pay respect to Christ himself. Hence, we see the imperative for the exercise of mutual submission in the Body of Christ in loving respect for Christ's Body.

---

54. Hoehner, *Ephesians*, 745.
55. Hendriksen, *Ephesians*, 248.

Above All Put On Love

Love, however, does remain the most prominent NT commandment to the church. Love is to be the banner over the church and all that it does, which is why Paul urges the church in Corinth to "pursue love" and "let all that you do be done in love" (1 Cor 14:1; 16:14). In his letter to Colossae he writes, "and above all these put on love, which binds everything together in perfect harmony" (Col 3:14). True union cannot exist without love, as there is no harmony or accord. The life of the Bride of Christ united by the Spirit must be one primarily spent in love as Christ's sacrificial love for his Body demands imitation. If believers do not love their brothers and sisters in Christ then Scripture promises devastatingly that they have no membership in the Body and can have nothing to do with it or God.[56] As love galvanizes the union and communion between the husband and wife, love also binds the church together in union. Hate for the Body is hate for Christ but love for Christ's Body is love for him and appropriation of spiritual union with him.

There can be no enjoyment of a corporate spirituality of the church without the commitment to pursue Christian covenantal love. Clowney declares that this Christian spirituality will exhibit the gospel to the world. "Christian witness that is limited to private religious experience cannot challenge secularism. Christians in community must again show the world not merely family values, but the bond of the love of Christ."[57]

Edifying and Serving the Body

From Ephesians 5:29 we have seen that the husband ought to care for his wife as Christ "cherishes" and "nourishes" or "feeds" (*ektrephein*) his own Body. This confirms the ministry of Christ to edify and build up his Bride in him. David Peterson asserts, "edification is first and foremost the responsibility of Christ as the 'head.'"[58] We have noted that it is to this end that Christ sent his Spirit. Furthermore, Muddiman perceives an "oblique allusion" to the Lord's Supper in this verse, since Christ's institution of the Lord's Supper is a ready means of such spiritual nourishment whereby the church Body feeds upon Christ by the Holy Spirit.[59]

---

56. 1 Cor 13:1–3; 1 John 3:10, 14, 17; 4:8, 20–21.
57. Clowney, *Church*, 16.
58. Peterson, *Engaging*, 287.
59. Muddiman, *Ephesians*, 268.

Complementarian Spirituality

Peterson also says that through the mutual service or ministry of its members, according to Christ's specific gifting to each, the Bride receives Christ's care. Thus, believers meet "together to draw on the resources of Christ and to take our part in the edification of his Church."[60] So one important fruit of shared union with Christ is the mutual ability to serve and edify one another. "A significant part of the Lord's ministry to us comes through others in whom He lives. And He intends for us to experience much of this comforting, encouraging, instructing, reproving, guiding, and sustaining ministry through fellowship."[61] Just as any human tends his or her own body by feeding, cleaning, and making it stronger, so too the church Body must seek the mutual edification of its members in the power of the Holy Spirit so the Bride can grow up in her Holy Spouse.

Bloesch recognizes these features of church love and edification to be instrumental to the glorification of Christ in the church family and in the world:

> The church of God will take institutional form, but it is not primarily an institution. It is fundamentally a movement of the Spirit directed to the praise of Christ. It is a catalyst that binds believers together in a fellowship of love (*koinonia*). It contributes to the edification of the saints, but it also empowers the saints for service in the world. In this respect a gospel spirituality will be both churchly and worldly.[62]

This view, however, should not overlook the initial corporate pattern of worship found in the family unit. As Beeke describes from Puritan spirituality, daily family worship is a necessary and "powerful tool" in Reformed spirituality that permeates into wider church life.[63] It is from the initial corporate base of the family unit that we progress to corporate church life and worship. This then alters the contemporary notion of local church services as "worship services." As our discourse explores, the coming together of the Bride in a local church context is for the purpose of *corporate* worship in order to participate in mutual edification.[64] This is in accordance with the exhortation to, "let all things be done for building up" and "strive to excel in building up the church" (1 Cor 14:12, 26). Therefore, church programs

---

60. Peterson, *Engaging*, 287.
61. Whitney, *Simplify*, 190.
62. Bloesch, *Spirituality*, 140.
63. Beeke, "Puritan Family," 340.
64. Peterson, *Engaging*, 219.

are not for an experience of worship for the individual but a feeding of the Body of Christ. Church life exists for the mutual edification of the saints as their union in Christ is cultivated and enjoyed in family corporate worship. This means that all the features of our local church services should expressly build up the Body and the omission of any items that do not fulfill this objective.

The Reformed belief that all those united to Christ are "bound" "by profession" to active service in the Body, stewarding one's gifts appropriately as endowed by the Holy Spirit, is well expressed in the Westminster Confession of Faith.[65] Thus, it is incumbent upon each believer to identify their own gifts and graces in the Spirit and to use them readily.[66]

Crucial to our discussion on feminine Reformed spirituality is the use of gifts by Reformed women in line with a complementarian stance. Yet in many conservative Reformed churches, an intentional use of women in church practice that extends beyond the tea-making stereotype needs to be readdressed.[67] Evidence for the reluctance of Reformed church leaders to utilize female members in fundamental church ministries will be unpacked in the next chapter; at this point however, with Jay Adams we observe that there is a leash placed upon women in Reformed church life that is unbiblical and spiritually stifling for the Body and Reformed feminine spirituality.[68] However, the contemporary movement in women's ministries, throughout Christian traditions, together with the biblical vision of women actively ministering to women in Titus 2:3–5, suggests that women have a distinct and unique role in pastoral care and teaching of other women. Duncan and Hunt, who seek to be "self-conscious" in ministry to Christian women, forcefully emphasize this. "We need to help Christian women appreciate the manifold areas of service that are open to them in the church and to equip them distinctively as women to fulfill their ministry. But this will never happen if our approach to discipleship in the church is androgynous—that is, if it *refuses to take into account the gender distinctives of the disciple.*"[69]

If the Reformed complementarian perspective on gender is the identification and celebration of gender differences, then the traditional model

---

65. WCF 26.1–2.
66. Clowney, *Church*, 64.
67. Johnston, "Where Are We Today?"
68. Adams, *Pastoral Life*, 102.
69. Duncan and Hunt, *Women's Ministry*, 38, 41.

Complementarian Spirituality

of the male pastor undertaking *all* biblical teaching and pastoral care for both genders needs to be re-examined. This study will suggest other methods to complement this normative approach in chapter 6. The Reformed minister must prioritize encouragement of the biblical mandate for all church members to engage in the spiritual edification of the Body. This is to be accomplished, as John Piper recommends; "by prayer and study and humble obedience to discover the pattern of ministry involvement for men *and women that taps the gifts of every Christian* and honors the God-given order of leadership by spiritual men."[70]

It has been suggested that in the Titus 2 text Paul is purposefully exhorting Titus to delegate responsibility of the younger women in the church family to the older women. "Paul does not tell Titus to teach the young women. This non-instruction probably reflects Paul's concern that a young woman perceive her husband as the male who is her primary spiritual instructor." In addition, the apostle has Titus's own safety in mind. "Paul also apparently desires to establish a pattern of instruction in the church that does not lead to sexual temptation."[71]

Many contemporary Reformed female writers have discussed the Titus 2 model for the care and discipleship of Christian women, that is, "to teach what is good, and so train the young women to love their husbands and children, to be self-controlled, pure, working at home, kind, and submissive to their own husbands" (vv. 3–5).[72] Within the apostle's rather comprehensive syllabus for his own protégé to pass onto the mature women, we find a clear biblical precedence for the integration of women to women ministry for the edification of the Body as a whole, as Paul looks to "affirm the importance of community contribution for mature Christians. The older women are not to hoard their knowledge but rather should pass it on to younger women who need the advice of those with greater experience."[73] These will be developed further below, but now it is sufficient to say that the biblical directive of mutual member edification and service as vital to the life of the Body, insists that conservative church practices free women out

---

70. Piper, "Complementarity," 53 (emphasis mine).

71. Hughes and Chapell, *1 & 2 Timothy*, 328–29, cited in Duncan and Hunt, *Women's Ministry*, 124.

72. Cf. Martha Peace's *Becoming a Titus 2 Woman* and Carolyn Mahaney's *Feminine Appeal* for two notable examples.

73. Hughes and Chapell, *Titus*, 328–29, cited in Duncan and Hunt, *Women's Ministry*, 124.

THE BRIDE'S PURITY

In our Ephesians 5 passage, the Bride's purity is of utmost importance to the divine Husband because he sacrificed himself to the horrors of Calvary in order for her purification to take place. Muddiman describes this glory of the church to be the lacking of physical blemishes or disfiguration, metaphorically conveying moral perfection.[74] In his love for the church, Christ gave himself up so "that he might sanctify her, having cleansed her by the washing of water with the word, so that he might present the church to himself in splendor, without spot or wrinkle or any such thing, that she might be holy and without blemish" (Eph 5:26–27). It is so essential that the righteous Bridegroom take a virgin wife, pure and holy, that Paul underlines this "threefold" throughout these two short verses. He "sanctifies her" in "cleansing" and "washing," and then "presents" her to himself in "splendor," "without spot or wrinkle," so finally she is "holy and without blemish."

As we observed above, Christ's sending of his Spirit is crucial to his purpose of cleansing his people. If Christ does not purge the church absolutely of sin then his work of salvation remains incomplete. Just as justification, in Reformed thought, is integral to the soteric matrix that makes the believer one with Christ, so too is sanctification.[75] That is, Christ's security of the church's justification and sanctification are distinct yet indispensible to one another as they together flow from union with Christ. This triangulation of these three fundamental elements of soteriology, outlined in chapter 2, encompasses the fullness of salvation by means of *total* union with Christ and the imparting of all his benefits.[76] Like a groom who pays a dowry for the virginity of the woman he wants to marry, Christ has bought back the church's purity by his blood.

The Gospel of John further affirms Jesus Christ as the Bridegroom cleansing his blood-Bride in its account of the Savior washing his disciples' feet in the upper room, where Jesus answers Peter, "'If I do not wash you, you have no share with me'" (13:8). Unless Christ washes and purifies his people he can have no part in them. There can be no union with the spotless Lamb of God unless he cleanses us from all unrighteousness by the

---

74. Muddiman, *Ephesians*, 266.
75. Carpenter, "Calvin and Trent," 371.
76. Cf. Gaffin, "Justification," 269.

power of the Holy Spirit. Union with Christ and sanctification are therefore intrinsic to one another. Edward Donnelly begs the question, "Why are we to become like Christ? Because we are already in him."[77]

Hoehner and Kuiper believe that in this passage Paul is probably alluding to the ceremonial bath that a Jewish bride underwent in preparation for her marriage ceremony, but Muddiman disagrees with this, maintaining a cultic allusion.[78] This bath symbolically washed away under defilement, affirming her virginal purity.[79] Further to this is his insinuation of the sacrament of baptism as the outward symbol of the inward work of sanctification in the believer in order to attain membership into Christ's Body, and the necessary accompaniment of the Word in accomplishing this. Essentially, it is the spoken word that is vital here. Hoehner states that Christ acts as the Jewish Bridegroom who speaks the word of betrothal over his Bride-to-be to set her apart for himself. Then a year later, she participates in a prenuptial bath for her preparation, "symbolizing the cleansing that would set her apart," yet it was the spoken word that was efficacious not the bathing.[80] Certainly, in Reformed belief the Word of God is the primary instrument used by the Holy Spirit for the cleansing of Christ's Bride. This means that in Reformed churches the corporate life must revolve around the authority of the Word and the Body's submission to it as the Holy Spirit rides upon the holy Word.

At this point, our analogy of the husband-wife relationship does little justice to the force of Christ's nuptial and eschatological work to conform his Bride to himself. Nonetheless, Hendriksen declares it the duty of the husband to assist her progress in sanctification.[81] It is essential to our discourse to note the faithfulness of Christ in the sending of his Spirit, who is the cleansing power or fire with which he baptizes his people. The Bride needs the Spirit to keep her and move her towards her Head.

Equally paramount is the eschatological reality of the Bride's complete purity found in biblical prophecy (Rev 7:9–17; 19). However, the Bride's union with Christ and his purchase of her virginity has inevitable ramifications for her own responsible living. Their covenantal union demands she live a life of faithfulness to her deserving spouse.

77. Donnelly, *Life*, 39.
78. Muddiman, *Ephesians*, 265.
79. Hoehner, *Ephesians*, 753–57; Kuiper, *Body*, 364.
80. Heohner, *Ephesians*, 756.
81. Hendriksen, *Ephesians*, 254.

The Church the Bride of Christ

In his letter to the Corinthians, Paul addresses the fact that when those in Christ indulge in sexual immorality they join Christ to a prostitute. This is owing to the intimacy of the *unio mystica* where believers are "one spirit" with Christ (1 Cor 6:15–17). Thus, the sinful act of sexual immorality is infidelity to Christ as the introduction of a third person breaches the covenantal union. Of this adultery Smedes surmises, "flesh-union with a prostitute violates spirit-union with Christ."[82] Yet in the text, Paul is emphasizing this as unthinkable! Union with Christ makes such sin "inconceivable."[83] "How striking that the inspired apostle, dealing with earthly, shameful physicality, finds the *motivation for avoiding sin in the mysterious union between Jesus and his people*. Christ himself is involved somehow when you or I sin. We are joined to him so closely that we take him with us into disobedience."[84] The doctrine of union with Christ means a change of reality for the believer. No longer does a person belong to him/herself (1 Cor 6:19–20). He or she belongs to Christ and his covenant Body. Believers in Christ have the profound privilege to live according to their identity as a member of the spotless Bride of Christ. Appropriation of one's union with Christ and its promise of purity in the last day, furnishes the believer for holy living. "Sin will not reign as king in the life of the Christian who by virtue of his union in Christ's death to sin self-consciously knows and seriously regards himself as dead to sin and alive to God in Christ Jesus."[85]

The presence of sin in Christ's covenant Body is a hideous reality and has to be subject to serious treatment. Any spirituality anchored on union with Christ demands the mortification of sin by incorporating the spiritual practices of repentance and confession. In the life of the Body, this means these practices must take corporate form. Because the Spirit's power is so readily available to the church, the Body has no right to be idle in striving for godliness.[86]

Corporate Sanctification

As we have explored a Reformed feminine spirituality of the church founded on the doctrine of union with Christ, we have unpacked features of corporate living in the spousal response to Jesus Christ and his gift of salvation.

82. Smedes *Union*, 162.
83. Donnelly, *Life*, 38.
84. Ibid., 27.
85. Reymond, *Systematic*, 739.
86. Pink, *Christianity*, 143

Complementarian Spirituality

In our deliberation of the Bride's purity, we now come to consideration of the pursuit of holiness in the corporate sphere. Christian holiness, a work authored by God, not man,[87] in its contemporaneous understanding is explicitly individualistic and rarely placed into the context of the Body. Yet members of the church cannot truly submit, love, respect, serve, and edify the Body if they have no concern for its holiness, for all these factors are closely interrelated. In addition, because sin in the Body is its greatest divisive force, the maintenance of unity requires the careful eradication of sin and a united struggle for purity. A Christian spirituality aware of its union with Christ must seek the mortification of sin in Christ's Bride by investing in mutual accountability, as Paul writes, "bearing with one another's burdens" so the law of Christ can be kept (Gal 6:1–2). Such care for one's brothers and sisters in Christ, and Christ's Bride at large, lies at the heart of Reformed spirituality. In the words of Calvin, "every Christian should have his Church enclosed within his heart, and be affected with its maladies, as if they were his own—sympathize with its sorrows, and bewail its sins."[88]

The Lord's Supper

Those in Christ have a duty to use the God-given means of grace at their disposal for "ever-increasing" sanctification.[89] Therefore, the fostering of spousal faithfulness to Christ includes the prizing of corporate practice given to the Body to drive it towards holy living and enjoyment of Christ. Necessary to this is the recentralizing of the sacraments in the life and constitutional perception of the Body, in accordance with Scripture. This means that the Reformed tradition must counteract the relegation of the sacraments caused by the widespread influence of eighteenth-century revivalist and Evangelical thought.[90] Our interest in this study lies with the corporate Christ-feast of Communion. Letham declares that in its demoted appreciation the Lord's Supper enjoys little regard or spiritual significance, conceived in many churches as an "optional extra" or a "pleasant and cozy meal" added to the end of a service.[91] This reveals the deficiency of a Reformed theological position of the meal in its function of *koinōnia*, the "sharing together" of the Body, and the power of the Spirit enabling

---

87. Berkhof, *Systematic*, 534.
88. Calvin, *Calvin's Wisdom*, 56, cited in Duncan and Hunt, *Women's Ministry*, 45.
89. Berkhof, *Systematic*, 534.
90. Letham, *Supper*, 2.
91. Ibid., 1.

spiritual feeding upon Christ for the enlargement of faith in the believer. Contemporary downgrading of the Eucharist has in part cheated Christians of an enlivening and fruitful spirituality nurtured by the work of the Holy Spirit. Consequently, contemporary Reformed spirituality possesses a largely inadequate respect for this Christ-given institution, rendering the meal for many contemporary Reformed Christians, theologically and experientially, to be an individualistic act of Zwinglian memorialism. Renewing the Bride's appetite for this Christ-feast and treasuring it above many of its more trivial activities will galvanize a biblical and Christ-exulting corporate life.

Confession and Repentance

A spirituality that centralizes the corporate feeding of the Bride in the Lord's Supper will also take into account the accompanying spiritual disciplines of confession and repentance. As Eleanor Kreider notes, "pastorally, the themes of repentance, forgiveness, and restoration are vital to the life of the church. Although a penitential tone does not dominate, the communion service is a natural place for the themes of restoration to be spelled out."[92]

The biblical discipline of confession to one another, assumed by the New Testament writers to be vital and rewarding to the Christian life (Jas 5:16) and effective in the mortification of sin, is rarely encouraged in Reformed church life. Yet how necessary in the life of the Body: "Confession makes us sinners before one another, breaks us of our self-righteousness and enables us to become a fellowship of sinners. Thus we become the church that is founded on Christ's righteousness, not our own."[93] The humble confession of one member will also encourage further confession and repentance in the Body and heal any rising schism or rivalry.[94] This is an outworking of submission to the Body, whether the wrongs confessed have been personal to the Body or not. Shared or corporate confession then entails the corollary of repentance, which Packer expresses as a dire need in contemporary Evangelical and Reformed spirituality:

> Repentance nowadays rarely gets mentioned in evangelism, nurture, and pastoral care, even among evangelicals and Christian traditionalists. The preoccupations of stirring congregational excitement, sustaining believers through crises, finding and honing

---

92. Kreider, *Given for You*, 107.
93. Sittser, *Love*, 80.
94. Ibid., 80–82.

gifts and skills, providing interest-based programs, and counseling people with relational problems, have displaced it. As a result, the churches, themselves, orthodox and heterodox together, lack spiritual reality, and their members are all too often superficial people with no hunger for the deep things of God.[95]

The Christ-union stipulates in the believer a submissive heart to Christ and the Body, and by the power of the Bond of union enables liberation of sin in the Spirit-led acts of confession and repentance. As the church lives in spousal union with its Savior, obedience to Christ and submission to his Headship will draw the church from its sinful tendencies into bridal purity. "Submission in Scripture is at root the willingness of the penitent believer to submit to God. Rebellion is the essence of sin; submission is at the heart of repentance and faith."[96]

THE EUCHARISTIC UNION OF THE BRIDE AND GROOM BY THE SPIRIT

One of the ultimate ways that Jesus Christ, the perfect Bridegroom, nourishes and feeds his beloved Spouse is through the Word accompaniment of his life-giving flesh and blood. In the Eucharist meal, he, "the bread of God," becomes her "bread of life" (John 6:33, 35), and in her feeding upon him she is soterically joined to him; "whoever feeds on my flesh and drinks my blood abides in me, and I in him" (v. 56). In Christ's institution of the Eucharist meal, he is the persona of the godly husband who self-sacrificially seeks the spiritual growth and maturity of his wife. Yet distinct from any husband, he is both the means and the goal, for she feeds *on* him to grow up *in* him (Eph 4:15; Col 2:19).[97] Akin to every bridegroom, Christ's ultimate longing and purpose in all things is attaining uninhibited union and communion with his Bride in Glory. As the husband and wife enjoy and appropriate their union to the uttermost in close communion and fellowship, the Lord's Supper is the earthly fellowship and communion between Christ and the church, by the power of the Holy Spirit, looking to the coming pinnacle of redemption—the glorious marriage supper of the Lamb. The Trinitarian context of all this is significant; that is, as the *unio cum Christo* is Trinitarian so is the Eucharist. It is a meal whereby the believer communes with

---

95. Packer, *Holiness*, 144.
96. Ash, *Marriage*, 334.
97. Ibid., 324.

The Church the Bride of Christ

the *entire Godhead*; "the faithful feed on Christ in faith by the Holy Spirit, and thus in union with Christ the Son we share in his access to the Father." Letham continues in his challenge that such a Trinitarian perception is "worlds apart from an act of mental recollection of the human Jesus."[98]

It is the suggestion of this work that a Reformed experience of "the full reality of holy life in an unholy and needy world, by means of a fresh and constant awareness of our union with Christ in and through the Holy Spirit,"[99] is available in the renewal of church participation in the Lord's Supper. In other words, reasserting the weighty role of the Eucharist *agape* feast in a corporate church life as outlined throughout this discourse will recover a lively biblical Reformed spirituality anchored in union with Christ, richly consistent with its Reformation heritage.

> The eucharist community which joyfully celebrates its identity and its liberation through the lifeblood of Christ poured out will grow in deep inner commitment to each other and to Christ. This depth is the maturity which holds the community from wavering or collapsing when under pressure, a fruit quite different from that of superficial or over-personalized understandings of eucharist.[100]

Eucharist participation "sustains" the corporate life of the Body, just as baptism initiates it,[101] declaring the church to be a unified body, moreover, *Christ's* Body: "The cup of blessing that we bless, is it not a participation in the blood of Christ? The bread that we break, is it not a participation in the body of Christ? Because there is one bread, we who are many are one body, for we all partake of the one bread" (1 Cor 10:16–17). Consequently, in Pauline thought, the Eucharist meal is a fervent expression of the united covenantal Body of Christ. It is a celebratory badge of covenantal belonging. Therefore, practice of the Supper should be outward and not individualistic: "The experience of the bread does not summon individual minds to commune with their private thoughts of a passion just for them. We are not invited by the sacrament to a trembling imagination within insulated souls. We eat together; and as we eat the bread we are recreated anew in the *corporate* reality that Christ created by His death."[102]

---

98. Letham, *Trinity*, 423.
99. Kelly, *Systematic*, 310 (emphasis mine).
100. Kreider, *Given for You*, 114.
101. Bloesch, *Church*, 160.
102. Smedes, *Union*, 179.

Complementarian Spirituality

In the communion service then, members of the Body should acknowledge one another and pray for one another and the unity of the church family. This means that hearts, minds, and eyes should focus on the local visible representation of Christ's invisible Bride. Allowing one's eyes to drift over the Body and marvel at its diversity and union in and with Christ will move the heart to love, respect, and serve the church members. Furthermore, in this the Reformed eucharistic community will reflect the NT *agape* feast in celebration of one another as brothers and sisters in Christ, the sharing of one another's lives, and the meeting of specific spiritual and material needs in the family.

In some Reformed circles there is an undue reservation caused by our conservativism, which can create an excessive sobriety begging for the expression of warm affection towards one another. As Berkouwer rightly reminds us of the joyous security of the Christ-church union: "There is no tension between the joy-motif of the Supper and its content, the remembrance of Christ's death. For the Messianic joy is completely based on the death of Christ."[103] The contemporary church can so readily forget its hope of glory by union with Christ (Col 1:27), but a godly reemphasis of the meal should point the church to the fact that "the Lord's Supper and the Lamb's Supper are two sides of the same reality."[104]

Feeding on Christ by Faith in the Spirit

The "wedding ring" of faith and actual participation in the elements by eating and drinking are both "necessary" and "inseparable" in feeding on Christ's spiritual presence: "Faith does not exist apart from the Supper, but neither does the Supper apart from faith, for faith is indispensible."[105] Thus, the corporate commitment to participation in the Lord's Supper should fill the Body with an anticipatory faith in the divine Spirit who imparts it, seeking his power of blessing the believer with the presence of Christ.

However, the elements should only remind the church of continual union and fellowship with Christ owing to the continual work of the Spirit of Christ, manifest in the presence of faith. The Eucharist feeding on Christ is not an isolated "Christ encounter" but spiritual nourishment by means of thanksgiving (Luke 22:17, 19; 1 Cor 11:24), remembrance, proclamation, self-examination, and participation in Christ (1 Cor 10:16; 11:24–27). The

---

103. Berkouwer, *Sacraments*, 197.
104. Letham, *Supper*, 63.
105. Ibid., 13, 29.

meal confirms to Christ's people that salvation is through the possessing of Christ alone, and not only his benefits. In the words of Calvin, the visible signs enable us to not "contemplate him outside ourselves from afar" but acknowledge that "he deigns to make us one with him."[106] The elements transport the Body to Calvary to witness the broken and bleeding Savior, whilst affirming Christ's human body as the image and primary instrument of salvation and not the cross. Thus, the bread should be broken in front of the Body to give a visible sign of Christ's broken body; similarly, the blood is to be poured, to display the shedding of Christ's blood for the forgiveness of sin. The Lord's Supper is a time for the church to behold Calvary and in light of it deal with sin, cleansing out the "old leaven" so that life as a new unleavened lump might be realized. For we are in union with Christ the Passover Lamb who was sacrificed (1 Cor 5:7).

Pneumatic-Eucharistic Sanctification

Robert Letham declares that the "inseparable companion" to union with Christ is repentance.[107] Indeed, our discourse has stressed that the doctrine of union with Christ in Reformed theology is a soteriological, ecclesiastical, and transformative doctrine. Sanctification through union with Christ is a corporate reality, as Murray states "this progression has respect, not only to the individual, but also to the church in its unity and solidarity as the body of Christ. In reality the growth of the individual does not take place except in the fellowship of the church as the fellowship of the Spirit."[108]

In the Eucharist meal, the "Wonderful Counselor of the church,"[109] serving as the Bond of union, enlarges faith and sanctifies the Body. Thus, it is crucial that there is an *intentional* partaking through the Spirit. Because the purification of Christ's Bride is subject to the Holy Spirit's use of the purifying Word, the minister should emphasize before teaching, the role of the preached word for the preparation of the Body for Eucharistic confession and repentance. For the Word of God is the Spirit's instrument to show the church its sin. The Body, in faith, must anticipate this work, praying for full spiritual nourishment and strengthening, increase of faith, and conviction of sin. When this is emphasized, the Eucharist becomes the

---

106. 3.11.10.
107. Letham, *Christ*, 81.
108. Murray, *Systematic*, 299.
109. Tripp, *Instruments*, 51.

foremost opportunity to respond to the preached Word by confession and repentance by feeding on the Savior.

This will enable believers to not only deal with sin biblically and responsibly, but also build upon any understanding of union with Christ. In feeding upon Christ by faith in the Lord's Supper, believers proclaim Christ's resurrection (1 Cor 11:26) thereby announcing life in him, and sharing in his death; "crucified with Christ, it is no longer I who live but Christ who lives in me" (Gal 2:20). It is this eucharistic declaration of death to sin and life to God that leads the church in confession and repentance.

Corporate Confession and Repentance

Paul's instruction to the church in Corinth for self-examination before taking the bread and the wine emphasizes the need to properly discern Christ in the meal and not partake just to satisfy one's physical or religious hunger or thirst. "Whoever, therefore, eats the bread or drinks the cup of the Lord in an unworthy manner will be guilty concerning the body and blood of the Lord. Let a person examine himself, then, and so eat of the bread and drink of the cup" (1 Cor 11:27–29). In union with Christ, the Body benefits from the convicting power of the Spirit to lead it in the identification of unrecognized or unrepented sin. Careful participation in the Lord's Supper minimizes the lazy dismissal of sin by promoting a spiritual reflection upon it, its mortification, and forgiveness in Christ.

> Free-church Christians often move too quickly, too lightly, to appropriate God's forgiving mercy. Sensitivity to our sin and regular confession of it are necessary components of mature Christian faith. Communion services can help to shape a healthy and realistic awareness of sin, both corporate and personal, and also to provide a setting in which we receive and rejoice in God's gracious forgiveness.[110]

Once identified, the process of confession and repentance can begin. In this, offering time after the exposition of the Word and prayer for mutual (that is, one to one or in small groups) or public (to the whole Body) confession will promote a seriousness in relation to sin. This, however, takes some care on the part of the church leader as judgment of one another, which has no place in the Body (Jas 4:11–12), must be discouraged. Instead, the corporate life of the church looks to fulfill the NT obligation to exhort one another to holiness (Heb 3:13–14).

110. Kreider, *Given for You*, 108.

Indeed, the corporate structure outlined above, to submit, love, respect and serve the Body is necessary for the implementation of mutual and public confession and repentance. Yet leading a brother or sister in Christ in confession and repentance is the height of mutual care within the Body. "As Christ's ambassadors, we seek to lead people to speak humble, specific words of confession to the Lord. We also need to encourage them to identify people who have been affected by their sins and seek their forgiveness."[111]

Significantly, James's biblical commandment to confess sin to fellow believers in the Body is married together with intercession for one another. The apostolic writer seems to paint a picture of corporate Christian life that shares in one another's lives, in joy, sorrow, and sin. If the Reformed church demonstrated a greater degree of love and consideration for one another then Christian experience would be richer as the Body mutually leads itself to Christ, disregarding notions by non-believing outsiders of a self-seeking sterile community. As Paul David Tripp clarifies, "The church is not a theological classroom. It is a conversion, confession, repentance, reconciliation, forgiveness, and sanctification center, where flawed people place their trust in Christ, gather to know him and love him better, and learn to love others as he has designed."[112]

In the modern day, Christ's teaching to be rightly reconciled with one's brother or sister before offering a sacrifice (Matt 5:24) has been recontextualized to restoration of church relationships prior to participation in the Lord's Supper, aligned with the Pauline call for self-examination and consideration for one another (1 Cor 11:18–27). This, together with the use of a corporate prayer or liturgy, now predominantly used in Anglican circles but thoroughly Reformed, as seen in the *Westminster Directory for Public Worship*, should be emphasized further in Reformed church practice and developed so that the Eucharist becomes the foremost opportunity for the Body to respond corporately to the preached Word in confession and repentance, feeding on Christ in faith.

Careful contemporary use of the *Directory* would, Ray Lanning declares, vastly improve Reformed corporate worship.[113] Alternatively, the Anglican penitential liturgy for the Holy Communion is a helpful form of corporate confession and repentance, consistent with Reformed thought as it confesses the Body to have corporately "sinned in thought, word and

---

111. Tripp, *Instruments*, 229.
112. Ibid., 116.
113. Lanning, "Foundations."

deed," emphasizing the need to love one's neighbor and walk humbly with "our God." Similarly, the practice of thanksgiving after communion, such as this Anglican prayer that acknowledges union with Christ throughout it and the necessary prior opening of the Word, will also benefit confession and repentance in response to union with Christ:

> We thank you, Lord,
> That you have fed us in this sacrament,
> United us with Christ,
> And given us a foretaste of the heavenly banquet
> Prepared for all peoples.
> Amen

> Faithful God,
> In baptism you have adopted us as your children
> Made us members of the body of Christ
> and chosen us as inheritors of your kingdom:
> we thank you that in this Eucharist
> you renew your promise within us,
> empower us by your Spirit to witness and to serve,
> and send us out as disciples of your Son,
> Jesus Christ our Lord.
> Amen.

> You have opened to us the Scriptures, O Christ,
> And you have made yourself known
> In the breaking of the bread.
> Abide with us, we pray,
> That, blessed by your royal presence,
> We may walk with you
> All the days of our life,
> And at its end behold you
> In the glory of the eternal Trinity,
> One God for ever and ever.
> Amen.

The Church the Bride of Christ

If a more biblical text is preferred then a pertinent confessional and penitential prayer can be found in the book of Daniel:

> O Lord, the great and awesome God, who keeps covenant and steadfast love with those who love him and keep his commandments, we have sinned and done wrong and acted wickedly and rebelled, turning aside from your commandments and rules. To you, O Lord, belongs righteousness, but to us open shame. To the Lord our God belong mercy and forgiveness, for we have rebelled against him and have not obeyed the voice of the LORD our God by walking in his ways. O our God, incline your ear and hear. Open your eyes and see our desolations, and the church that is called by your name. For we do not present our pleas before you because of our righteousness, but because of your great mercy. O Lord, hear; O Lord, forgive. O Lord, pay attention and act. Delay not, for your own sake, O our God, because your church and your people are called by your name. (Dan 9:4–5, 7, 9–10, 18–19).

Such confession then leads to repentance, which will inevitably assist in the mortification of sin, "for the acts of repentance are hatred of sin, sorrow for it, determination to forsake it, and earnest and constant endeavor after its death."[114] Packer purports the need in contemporary church life for specific repentance. "Vague repentance is nothing, or at least next to nothing."[115] In consideration of this, corporate preparation for the Eucharist meal gives the church a rare opportunities to dwell upon the root of ungodly living in considering all possible hindrances to holiness, as outlined in the NT: idolatry, rebellion or lawlessness, adultery, fornication, lust, impurity, greed, lack of self-control, selfish ambition, impatience, pride, hate, prejudice, enmity, strife, jealousy, grumbling, slander, crude joking, foolish talk, evil desire, malice, rivalries, dissensions, divisions, envy, drunkenness, anger, laziness, unbelief, religiosity, discontentment.[116] Equally, public prayers or liturgy that brings specific areas to mind can help identify sin in one's personal life.

This does not have to be a frequent activity, nor does it have to be executed at every Communion service. Nonetheless, repentance is a necessary characteristic of the life of Christ's Bride. Repentance must mark Reformed and Evangelical spirituality. Authentic Christian living, in touch with the Bible and above all the Holy Trinity, must have a profound and

---

114. Pink, *Christianity*, 39.
115. Packer, *Holiness*, 140.
116. Gal 5:19–21; Eph 4:31; 5:4; Col 3: 5; 2 Thess 2:3; 1 Tim 6:4–6; 2 Tim 3:2.

broken awareness of the sinful state of the church. "A genuine mourning over sin makes for fruitful spiritual soil, and no grace can flourish in any life that has not been and is not being, humbled by sin."[117]

CONCLUSION

Before moving on to our next chapter in applying our discussion to pastoral implications within the Reformed tradition, we offer a brief interim conclusion.

Our feminine approach to union with Christ led us to consider the *unio mystica* in the milieu of marital union between Christ and his church. "Before Christ, marriage's real purpose was veiled. But now God's design is revealed. He planned marriage to be a stunning visual aid. The relationship between man and wife was originally designed as an illustration of the eternal, faithful, self-giving love of Jesus Christ for his bride, the church."[118] Therefore, we have outlined a distinctly corporate Reformed spirituality that celebrates God's purposes in Christ's Bride. This has appropriately contextualized the ministry of the Holy Spirit in the Body of Christ, confirming with Ferguson that "the model we employ for structuring the Spirit's ministry should be that of union with Christ."[119] In response to the biblically corporate and pneumatic-christological nature of Reformed union with Christ, a contemporary Christian experience that is rewarding, spiritually satisfying, and rightly channeling the ongoing work of the Spirit in the Christian is to be found in a covenantal commitment to the church as the Bride of Christ.

Thus, the doctrine of union with Christ unites Christian spirituality, in its soteriological, transformative or pastoral, and ecclesiological relevance. The permanency and totality of the mutual possessing in the Christ-church union holistically shapes family, work, relationships, corporate worship, leisure, and all aspects of human life. It does not and cannot promote a fragmented, disconnected view of spirituality.

---

117. Hamilton, "Experiential Calvinism," 33.
118. James, *God's Design*, 70.
119. Ferguson, *Holy Spirit*, 100; cf. 144.

6

Women in the Reformed Tradition

THIS STUDY HAS BEEN concerned with identifying Reformed spirituality in its contemporary form, specifically using a feminine approach. However, this project has not yet contributed its own unique appreciation of a Reformed feminine spirituality. Many would deny the existence of any feminine mode owing to assumed patriarchy in Reformation thought. Critical of the spiritual benefits of the Reformation for women, Lyndal Roper states, "not even a distinctive feminine mode of religious experience, such as we see in the Catholic saints and Marian cults, or in the extreme hyperpiety of saintly widows, lived on in early mainstream evangelicalism."[1] She continues, "far from endorsing independent spiritual lives for women, the institutionalized Reformation was most successful when it most insisted on a vision of women's incorporation within the household under the leadership of their husbands." Many feminists and critics would consider this still the case in Reformation spirituality.

However, does the Reformed complementarian stance impede any vision for a Reformed feminine spirituality? Is not the authority-submission model of marital union outlined in our previous chapters suggestive of a biblical foundation and shaping of a feminine spirituality? It seems Roper and feminist systems of thought critical of the complementarian pattern have wrongly identified biblical gender roles with spiritual equality and personal spiritual expression. There need be no logical entailment that the Reformed view of male leadership, in the home or in the church, prohibits or inhibits a rich biblical feminine spirituality.

Self-critical observations made in this chapter suggest that contemporary Reformed church practice contributes to such misinterpretation of the complementarian pattern. Until Reformed women enjoy a standing in the

1. Roper, *Holy Household*, 2.

tradition in line with complementarian belief, confusion both inside the Reformed community and outside of it will continue. In a backlash from feminism and Christian egalitarianism, the Reformed tradition has severely underestimated the significance of feminine contribution in the spiritual, theological, pastoral, and practical spheres. What is left is a historical tradition that confesses a fruitful complementarian theology, founded by the sixteenth-century reformers, but largely overlooks its application in church life and practice. Although recent conservative Evangelical discourse has benefited the tradition in maintaining a biblical view of gender and gender distinctions in light of feminist reinterpretation, many churches that are distinctively Reformed in confession and traditional (or conservative) in practice are in need of further reform in the area of women's service and ministry.

WHERE WE ARE HEADING:
SPIRITUALITY AND PASTORAL THEOLOGY

In our exploration of a feminine approach to the *unio mystica* in the previous two chapters, we employed marital union and the Christ-church husband-wife parallelism in our articulation because marital or "Christ as spiritual husband" language has certain prevalence in feminine works and thought. In this chapter and the following, this feminine theme comes to a head in the presentation of an initial sample or tracing of a Reformed feminine spirituality, which might prove to be valuable to further academic discourse in this subject and germane to women in Reformed churches and the wider Evangelical community. It is unreasonable to propose that Christian spirituality is uniform wherever it is found. Just as expressions of Reformed spirituality are palpable in the many different theological schools (e.g., United Reformed Church or American and Dutch Presbyterianism), rendering Reformed *spiritualities* a fairer term, so also spiritual expression differs in the two genders. This will particularly be the case if construed in a complementarian framework that acknowledges the "sameness" and "difference" in God's creation of male and female. In other words, the well-received assumption that ministries to men and women will have different qualities is symptomatic of variety in male and female spirituality.[2]

This delineating of a distinctively *feminine* spirituality is necessary for the practice of a corporate Reformed life, and is therefore profitable for

---

2. Prime, *Women in the Church*, 26.

Women in the Reformed Tradition

Reformed spirituality as a whole. Christian spirituality, as we have seen, is essentially a response to salvation in Christ. A feminine appreciation is "distinct but not separate from the masculine experience. The two experiences are complementary. Each states and calls forth in the other essential elements of response to Christ."[3] Carolyn Custis James concurs, "sadly, in the church today, important ministries are overlooked or done poorly because the feminine perspective is missing."[4] The male-centeredness of the Reformed tradition means that the tradition is spiritually and practically weak and malnourished.[5] Reformed pastor Derek Prime states, "there are insights and sensitivities women possess that are special to them, and which are invaluable to the well-being of the body of Christ."[6]

We will consider this in further detail below, but for now suffice to say that if the different pastoral needs and spiritual expressions of the male and female disciple of Christ are recognized, then it is probable that conceptual and practical complementarian spirituality will enhance Reformed spirituality in its entirety. In addition, further consideration of the uniqueness of feminine experience, needs, and gifting will help knock down the "stumbling block" of the tradition's inconsistency used by critics. This will generate sympathy for the complementarian belief, which currently is so grossly stereotyped and misunderstood.

The aim of this chapter then is to suggest ways in which our preceding discussions may be relevant to pastoral church life, especially to women. This will sharpen the corporate spirituality we have explored, whilst discussing the pastoral implications of the Christ-church union pertinent to contemporary women.

Methodologically, we will draw upon pastoral theology in order to achieve this.

The *Blackwell Reader in Pastoral and Practical Theology* describes pastoral and practical theology conjoined as the "place where contemporary experience and the resources of the religious tradition meet in a critical dialogue that is mutually and practically transforming."[7] Stephen Pattison and James Woodward focus on pastoral theology solely as the term "to describe the theological activity that undergirds and accompanies pastoral

3. Ring, "Feminine Spirituality," 148–49.
4. James, *Life*, 217.
5. James, *God's Design*, 87.
6. Prime, *Women in the Church*, 99.
7. Woodward and Pattison, *Pastoral and Practical Theology*, xiii.

care," "ensuring the individual and corporate wellbeing and flourishing of the 'Christian' flock."[8] A distinctively Reformed pastoral theology "exists alongside historical and systematic theology, distinguished yet inseparable from them, with a particular responsibility for explaining the actual relationships between the Word of God and the lives of God's people."[9]

In one sense, this chapter is the bringing together of spirituality and pastoral theology. As we saw earlier in the work, Packer declares this to be necessary: "Competence in the field of spirituality is always important as a basis for pastoral care and direction, whereby penitents are pointed along the path of growth in Christ. . . . *Pastors need insight into spirituality in order to teach and advise for the furthering of spiritual health.*"[10] Since our aim is to suggest ways in which this research may be relevant to pastoral church life, it attempts to be of assistance to pastors and church workers in meeting the spiritual needs of the women in their congregations and providing appropriate care for them.

Owing to the aim and direction of this chapter, however, this discussion will be concise and work under a degree of generalization. Therefore, at this point clarification must be given that every Reformed church is different and in some British and American Reformed churches, women enjoy a higher degree of theological, spiritual, pastoral, and ministerial concern than in others.

WOMEN IN THE REFORMED TRADITION: SELF-CRITICAL OBSERVATIONS

In the conservatism and reserve of many confessional Reformed churches, overwhelmed by current controversies pertaining to the role of women in the church, there is an enormous need for the reappraisal of the *positive* aspects of biblical feminine service and spiritual responsibility to the Body.[11] The poverty of feminine contribution in many Reformed congregations infers a spiritual inequality between the genders in church life. Sharon James surveys the situation amongst conservative Evangelical British churches in a publication belonging to the partnership group *Affinity* wherein she represents the women's team of the FIEC (Fellowship of Independent Evangelical Churches).

8. Pattison and Woodward, "Pastoral and Practical Theology," 2.
9. Arnold," "Pastoral Care," 271.
10. Packer, "Evangelical," 232 (emphasis mine).
11. Catherwood, "Women."

> There are variations of how this [complementarianism] works out in practice. In some, more conservative churches, there is little emphasis on women's ministries. From the outside it may look as though women are only really encouraged to assist in such areas of hospitality, childcare, and maybe Sunday School teaching. In such churches there may be such a strong emphasis on headship and submission within marriage that abuse is not effectively confronted.[12]

James's article, voicing the concerns of many complementarian women within the FIEC, observes the "insensitivity" of many conservative Bible-believing churches to "the needs and situation of many of the women in the congregation," highlighting that such churches operate largely on a male basis wherein the women are not only inaudible but spiritually silent too.[13]

Importantly, this neglect of the feminine is distinct from—although not without irony—the *cultural* feminization of the church. For seemingly it is possible that feminization of church culture can coexist with a restrictive, unbiblical over-reserve regarding the role of women in the church. Prime agrees that church practice is too male focused. "Women's gifts have been, and are, frequently neglected. Some women feel insecure, devastated and robbed of their ministry."[14] He admits that many conservative male leaders have recognized this need but succumbed to the temptation of inactivity out of the fear of being misunderstood. Consequently, there is much room for development in an intentional *use* of women, that is, Reformed male leadership must take seriously the integration of women's ministries and women *to* the ministry as vital to the corporate life of the Body. Yet in many Reformed churches "the topic of a woman's spiritual responsibility to the wider church seems to be missing from our ecclesiastical thinking."[15] Elizabeth Catherwood, daughter of Dr. Martyn Lloyd-Jones, and J. Ligon Duncan are strong in their criticism of this, observing the swing of the pendulum from the feminist cause to overly conservative church culture:

> Fear of increasing female emancipation has led many men— "conservative fellows of the fundamentalist sort"—to make certain that *their* women are kept in their place. Biblical verses are wretched from their context, married women are allowed to

12. James, "Women and the Church."
13. Ibid.
14. Prime, *Women in the Church*, 8, 97.
15. James, *Life*, 204.

> possess nothing of their own (that was preached not long ago from an evangelical pulpit!), and total obedience is demanded from the women in the church. Such overreaction can only do immense harm to the cause of the gospel and bring unnecessary suffering to the women concerned.[16]

> Some church leaders are so afraid of women assuming unbiblical roles in the church that they fail to equip them for the roles to which they have been indisputably called in the home and church. On the other hand, in the name of not squandering women's gifts and abilities, Christian women are often encouraged to take up unbiblical roles in the life of the church, even in Bible-believing congregations.[17]

This is not only the fault of Reformed male leadership, however, for women too are guilty of being male centered—sometimes more so—and overlooking their capable counterparts for leadership and teaching.[18] This might be, in part, owing to the generally higher degree of leadership experience gained in the workplace by men, rendering them proficient managers. In short, women are used to male leadership. Nevertheless, *semper reformanda* includes the reform of church culture, ensuring that the tradition does not become unduly traditional and stagnate.

"Myopic concentration" on the wife's submission has produced unbiblical practice and confusion pertaining to gender roles, so causing a tendency to hamper feminine church service.[19] Carolyn Custis James critically describes the experience of many women in Reformed churches to be restricted to ministering only to physical needs or privately to other women and children. In the spiritual shaping of the corporate Body, the Reformed woman is of little benefit, particularly if her circumstances "break" the traditional mould because she has commitments in the workplace or is a single parent.[20] The Reformed belief in the priesthood of all believers means that church leadership should spend time and effort encouraging all its members, including *all* women, into a variety of church ministry,

---

16. Catherwood, "Women," 121.
17. Duncan and Hunt, *Women's Ministry*, 22.
18. Prime, *Women in the Church*, 113.
19. Foh, *Biblical Feminism*, 184, 247.
20. James, *Life*, 202, 204.

instead of ignoring the satirical assumption that female church ministry is limited to the kitchen, as Mark Johnston elucidates:[21]

> Women who have very obvious intellectual and spiritual gifts, who have perhaps been active in missionary work, or in para-church organizations, have struggled with restrictive and even repressive regimes in local evangelical congregations. Situations where the role of the women in practice is little more than tea-maker or cleaner. In some cases where these "evangelical" practices have been questioned by such women, the response they have received has been sufficiently shallow and ungracious to make them wonder even more about what the Bible really says about the worth and usefulness they have as women.[22]

Possibly the situation is worse than it seems at first since pastoral incidents witness to male preference in conservative church life. This is evident in cases of disbelief by church leadership in alleged domestic violence by Christian husbands, whereby the allegation is ignored or the woman is sent back into the abusive situation with the instruction to be more submissive.[23]

This chapter intimates that this ministerial neglect is in part down to a lack of appreciation for the uniqueness of female Christian living and need for a pastoral care sensitive to feminine experience and spiritual perspective. The complementarian belief of "same but different" demands a consistency that permeates across church life by means of pastoral strategies and preaching schedules as well as in use of ministry personnel, thus exercising an intentional ministry *to* women. In her work, *Preaching That Speaks to Women*, Alice Mathews asks how pastors can encourage a spiritual formation in women anchored in Scripture, changing habits of the heart, soul, and mind without awareness of her spirituality and unique epistemology.[24] Equally, Sharon James observes that Reformed preaching has a propensity to stereotype the female pastorally as well as underemphasize her. "All too many male preachers stick to sermon illustrations [or application] that

---

21. Catherwood, "Women," 120.
22. Johnston, "Where Are We Today?," 14.
23. James, "Women and the Church"; James, *Life*, 53. One such case is known personally to the author and another identical case was relayed by a Reformed pastor in an email communication on March 6, 2010.
24. Mathews, *Preaching*, 94–95.

Complementarian Spirituality

assume that the women in their congregations are married with children. The majority may be single, or divorced, or career women, or single mothers."[25]

Of further significance to this discourse is Reformed pastoral practice, which has long operated on the traditional model of the sole pastor undertaking all pastoral care of the flock. The current study looks to challenge Reformed pastors and leaders to readdress this method and question whether this is biblical, wise, or even most spiritually effective for the Body at large. The biblical paradigm of discipleship outlined in Titus 2 sets in place a corporate dependency by the Spirit that prizes the spiritual gifting of the individual and their use for spiritual growth. Certainly, Paul's vision here is not the pastor or elder's redundancy in pastoral care but full strategic use of the Body in mutual edification.

A rigorous structuring of a Titus 2 discipleship program into Reformed church life is the biblical solution to both intentional *use* of women and intentional ministry *to* women. Reformed pastor and counselor Jay Adams believes that neglect of the Titus 2 model especially in female-to-female discipleship is a serious deficiency. "Up until now, women (as well as *male pastors*) have neglected this all-important task. It is high time for conservative pastors to see both the need and the opportunities that this whole untapped area affords."[26] Additionally, proper use of women in the Body will avoid the disadvantages of an overstretched women's worker or an overstretched church budget where low finances cannot realistically afford one. The Titus 2 model is just one feature of a biblical corporate spirituality, which upon implementation can test the contemporary trend in staff appointments, ascertaining whether they are a sign of a healthy rather than unhealthy church Body. Paul David Tripp affirms this:

> Christ has given his church leaders, not to bear the full ministry load of the body of Christ, but to equip each member to join in God's work of personal transformation. Remember: no local church could hire enough staff to meet all the ministry needs of a given week! In the biblical model, much more informal, personal ministry goes on than formal ministry. The times of formal, public ministry are meant to train God's people for the personal ministry that is the lifestyle of the body of Christ.[27]

25. James, "Women and the Church."
26. Adams, *Pastoral Life*, 102.
27. Tripp, *Instruments*, 19–20.

In conclusion, a thoroughly biblical and Reformed view of the Body wherein the older men pray for and nurture biblical living and values in the next generation of men, and the older women commit to the same for their spiritual daughters, will reinforce the church with the mechanics given by the Apostle for spiritual growth and harmony.

How a Reformed Feminine Spirituality Can Benefit Reformed Spirituality

The eighteenth-century rise of Evangelicalism meant "a piety of emotion and sudden conversion collided with a [Reformed] piety of doctrine, nurture, and order."[28] Evangelical notions have since gained ground in Reformed churches in the West, which, together with the recent popularity of Charismatic expressions, has made the Reformed nervous about contemporary approaches to spirituality. It is necessary for the Reformed community to gain confidence in the area of spirituality so it can develop its own contemporary expression and grasp the importance of spirituality in contemporary culture.

This work's proposed vision for a Reformed feminine spirituality, devoid of the excessive individualism and sentimentality of Evangelical piety, could foster further contemporary contribution in Reformed Christian experience. It is feasible that the experiential and practical features of this feminine approach might help quench the dry orthodoxy of the Reformed tradition currently shaped by male thinkers. One might ask, therefore, whether a channel for Reformed spiritual renewal might lie in a dynamic and fruitful feminine experience coming from within its own ranks. This is a question we will consider further in chapter 7.

In addition, the definition of a unique Reformed feminine spirituality may strengthen the profile of complementarian thought as it positively shapes the spheres of family, church, and society. As mentioned above, this could improve dialogue between the tradition and its critics. In addition, this impartation of a feminine voice to a male-dominated tradition will enrich and complement Reformed spirituality as a whole, if married together with a change in church practice. "In the church—as elsewhere—men and women need each other, and God intends them to be complementary in their gifts and personalities"[29] as well as in their perspectives and contributions. "In the family the wife is very much to be her husband's helper.

---

28. Lanning, "Foundations," 241.
29. Prime, *Women in the Church*, 29.

Men's abilities are often either greatly enhanced by the help and wisdom of their wives, or greatly hindered by the lack of it. In the same way, though leadership in the church is to be male, that leadership needs help."[30] Thus, the Reformed embrace of a uniquely feminine spirituality will specifically display the Christ-church husband-wife parallelism in the beauty of biblical complementarity and the Reformed esteem for marriage.

This implies, nonetheless, that any neglect of women in the Reformed tradition belittles the Christ-church union and the creation ordinance of marriage. If the biblical complementarian pattern is not prevalent in Reformed thought and practice then the tradition is in major conflict with itself. "When women are not included in the conversation, there are blind spots in the church's ministry—overlooked needs and issues, places where our theology is underdeveloped and detached. In Christ's body, every member needs all the others—not simply to be there but to contribute."[31] This brings us to the want for academic contribution from the female Reformed community in the disciplines of theology and spirituality.

Reformed Feminine Scholarship

The author's personal research highlighted the substantial need for theological contributions from conservative Evangelical and Reformed women after a literature survey was unable to identify any feminine *academic* theological works, and observed little theological interaction in the many popular works written by women.

The advantages of a Reformed feminine contribution to Reformed spirituality given above are also apparent and transferable to Reformed scholarship in the disciplines of spirituality and theology. As this study has done, Reformed women need to be contributing contemporary articulations of Reformed doctrine and its praxiological outworking in spirituality, in the key areas of soteriology, Trinitarianism, ecclesiology, missiology, and pastoral studies. The current reality that formal theological study is a pursuit solely undertaken by male scholars is of course a serious weakness to the thought of the Reformed tradition and its place in academia. Yet theological scholarship is not an area in which Reformed women are encouraged to enter, as conservative church culture wrongly impresses upon its adherents the surmise that theology is a male arena.[32]

30. Benton, "Husband and Wife," 170.
31. James, *Life*, 59.
32. Cf. James, *Life*, 24, 46–47.

For the sake of the factors above, it is suggested that Reformed church leadership and scholars take it upon themselves to undo the inattention of women in church scholarship by actively encouraging women in their congregations who are suitably gifted in this area. Initially this might be addressed in the Reformed pulpit by means of church leaders keenly stimulating women out of their apparent theological sloth and into formal study. Furthermore, biblical preaching that corrects the obvious confusion regarding complementarian application in Reformed life might encourage *informal* feminine interest in theology as well. Such advantages of increased feminine theological appreciation on an informal level will be inestimable, first benefiting the home, and then the church Body and subsequently society. Reformed ministerial *use* of women will automatically coax them into further interest in theology and spirituality, as an improved and deeper understanding is required for their acts of service. For example, the implementation of a Titus 2 model by church leaders will stretch women and encourage them to build upon their theological knowledge as they deem it imperative and valuable to other members of the corporate Body.

MINISTERIAL USE OF THE REFORMED FEMALE COMMUNITY

Reformed feminine spirituality is innately corporate and relational; an expression that coexists harmoniously with the personal and private life. It is a spirituality of commitment to the covenantal Body regardless of degree of spiritual maturity because it is "other-preferring" in its celebration of shared union with Christ and portion in the Bride of Christ. Hence, it seeks to work in agreement with the rest of the Body by utilizing specific gifts and skills in service. If there is no or limited channeling of these gifts and skills then the spiritual life is incomplete and growth is stunted, bearing negatively upon the corporate and private spheres.

In this section, we will look particularly at women-to-women teaching and pastoral care as well as provide an overview of the types of ministries that Reformed women can undertake. However, before we do so we must highlight evidence of improvements in Reformed use of women in order to be fair to our subject.

There have been recent positive developments in the last two or three decades, particularly in less traditional Evangelical churches, where the integration of contemporary thought and practice is perhaps more readily received. The employment of women in full-time or part-time roles, particularly in conservative Evangelical churches or in Reformed charismatic

Complementarian Spirituality

and contemporary Calvinistic groups (such as the Sovereign Grace community), is becoming an increasing trend. The huge ongoing debate regarding female ordination and the position of women in the church has stimulated many British and American Reformed churches to readdress the biblical notions of female ministry, settling on the roles designated "women's pastor," "women's worker" or "director of women's ministries."[33] In such churches, the voluntary capacity has also opened up, enabling many women to exercise their skills in a variety of ways.

Robert Letham describes the myriad of female ministry positions in the American Orthodox Presbyterian Church (OPC), where he ministered as senior minister for many years. Here women had a wide range of ministries other than the somewhat stereotypical ones of hospitality, church catering, and nursery. Of particular significance was the active diaconal ministry undertaken by women. Although the OPC do not ordain women as elders or ministers, and equally the title "deacon" is not given, Letham states this team to be diaconal in everything but name—involved in ministry to the sick, elderly, and those in a range of material needs. The formal diaconate liaised with the team, serving in a more financial and executive manner. Additionally, women in the church undertook a range of teaching and managing ministries by heading up discipleship conferences for women and evangelistic outreach ministries aimed at women in which women taught. Key secretarial and managerial roles, formal Christian counseling, and leadership over church building projects are other examples pertinent to this case study. In the significant area of the Sunday school, this was led by many of the women who exercised their teaching gifting under the oversight from the church leaders, with material approved by the denominational committee on Christian education.

Susan Foh confirms a similar breadth of female service:

> Women can be Sunday School superintendents, Sunday School teachers on all levels, administrative officers, church paper editors, treasurers, writers (magazine articles, Sunday School literature, tracts, systematic theologies, hymns, commentaries, etc.), counselors, choir directors, committee chairpersons. Women's gifts and talents should be employed in the church and they can be without opening ordination to the ministry to them.[34]

---

33. Cf. Johnston, "Where Are We Today?," 15.
34. Foh, *Biblical Feminism*, 254.

It is incumbent upon Reformed churches to encourage a church life that practically works out the belief that men and women are complementary and necessary to each other. There is a duty upon Reformed church leaders to be self-critical of past practice, as well as creative in finding new avenues of service. Sharon James agrees: "1 Timothy 2:12 indicates that the functions of governing and authoritative Bible teaching should be restricted to men. All other roles should be open to women. There is no New Testament limit on female participation in (for example) evangelism, or ministries of mercy (diaconal ministries)."[35] The fact that some women are informally fulfilling the diaconal role in the church, and that women possess diaconal or administrative roles in the home and society in general, indicates the need to readdress the conservative pattern of shying away from the formal female deacon. This reticence is made further apparent in noting the practice of some conservative Presbyterian denominations in South Korea to ordain women for an exclusive pastoral role to women. It is suggested that the tradition in the UK and US can be bolder in structuring complementarian church leadership.

On a different but similar vein, one may ask, why are women *sometimes* excluded from the welcoming teams of conservative churches? Surely it is more appropriate to have both sexes included in the ministry of greeting rather than just men, which can potentially make female visitors and attendees feel uncomfortable. Placing women as well as men on the welcome team is decisively strategic because it is the first and last place of contact. Here women are in a natural position to integrate fringe female attendees by providing relevant introductions and to promote and ensure the involvement of every woman in a discipleship or pastoral relationship. This is particularly essential in large churches, where people are easily lost or unrecognizable. Consequently, placing both men and women on the door can include the offering of appropriate hospitality, ensuring visitors and irregulars do not pass through the mechanics of the church without any personal contact.

Teaching

Many might question the need for the teaching of women additional to that of the pulpit. Prime is adamant, however, that it complements the public teaching of the word given by church pastors.[36] Duncan and Hunt agree:

35. James, "Women and the Church."
36. Prime, *Women in the Church*, 112.

"without in any way discounting the regular pulpit ministry of the church, we should recognize that there are certain matters more aptly addressed and applied in the context of a specific discipleship of women, whether in large groups, in small groups, or in situations of confidentiality, as *women minister to women*."[37] Owing to the cultural pressures of the time and significant influence of popular feminist thought, and the fact that Sunday pulpit ministry is taught by men, Reformed feminine spirituality can benefit from women-to-women teaching of biblical text and doctrine, application to spiritual life, and Reformed feminine response to contemporary secular issues. As Duncan and Hunt acknowledge, there are features of feminine life and experience that are more suitably handled by women in a single-sex environment. This is also part of the Titus 2 model as the spiritually mature woman trains the younger in "what is good" (vv. 3–5). The seven virtues of loving one's husband and children, being self-controlled, pure, hard working at home, kind, and submissive to one's husband or family head are all aspects of feminine spirituality—in both marriage and singleness—that should be central to women-to-women teaching. Nevertheless, this requires the equipping of Reformed women to fulfill this task theologically and practically. In relation to the former, together with the call for Reformed feminine scholarship, this means that Reformed women need to be trained thoroughly and keenly admitted to conservative theological seminaries. Church pastors should support and liaise with women with a call in this area, facilitating and resourcing a women's ministry that will complement their own preaching schedules.

Essentially, this requires a change of view regarding biblical complementarian womanhood, with the appreciation that a Reformed feminine spirituality can be one of intelligent biblical and theological teaching to women (and children). Catherwood writes, "many strong, articulate, energetic women are frequently depressed by being told that they are *unbiblically* unfeminine. Or they are told that they may not teach, because men have clearer minds and are therefore more suitable for proclaiming the truth."[38] Catherwood reminds us that Priscilla is a pertinent biblical precedence of a well-informed spiritual woman who privately instructed the less theologically competent Apollos (Acts 18:26).[39] Thus, "if a woman believes that God has given her the gift of teaching, and this is ratified by

---

37. Duncan and Hunt, *Women's Ministry*, 39.
38. Catherwood, "Women," 122.
39. Ibid., 124, 127.

the church, there is ample scope for her to exercise this gift, both in the local congregation and outside it, in women's meetings of all kinds."[40] Seeing that the biblical womanhood of Priscilla included teaching the truths of redemption in Christ, Reformed feminine spirituality must encompass biblically informed declaration for the edification of those in Christ, where the Spirit of Christ has so equipped.

Pastoral Care: The Titus 2 Model

In his commentary on Titus, Gordon Fee claims that the Greek compound word *kalodidaskalous* ("teach what is good") in 2:3 probably does not mean formal instruction but "informal teaching by word and example" in relation to being a godly wife.[41] Philip H. Towner, however, unpacks the text more comprehensively: "while there is no reason to doubt that this role would include modeling or mentoring in areas ranging from domestic responsibilities to personal godliness (vv. 4–5), Paul nevertheless entrusts to these older women a very significant educative responsibility within the context of the *oikos*."[42] Guthrie summarizes, "Christian matrons are to assist younger women in the discipline of family love, not of course as interfering busybodies, but as humble advisors on problems of married life."[43] Interestingly, Towner views Paul's use of the verb *sōphronizō* in verse 4 to be indicative of a corrective teaching, that is, "a figurative, sobering 'slap in the face,'" in light of Cretan and Roman immorality or, as Raymond Collins sees it, "immodesty."[44] Nevertheless, whether such instruction is one of urgent correction or one of gentle guidance in counseling, Paul's principle is clear. The corporate duty of older Christians to take spiritual responsibility for younger Christians is basic to the godliness of the church. Carol Cornish, in the useful treatise on women to women counseling, states that while the Bible does not outline "a distinct process called 'counseling,' it does couch counseling-type issues within discussions about ministry and discipling and body life within the church. Thus it seems reasonable to conclude that these principles from Titus still apply today in terms of who should disciple/counsel whom."[45] The biblical counseling or pastoral care

40. Ibid., 126.
41. Fee, *Titus*, 186.
42. Towner, *Titus*, 724.
43. Guthrie, *Pastoral Epistles*, 205.
44. Towner, *Titus*, 725–26; Collins, *Titus*, 343.
45. Cornish, "Why Women Should Counsel Women," 88.

Complementarian Spirituality

of women by women is a vast resource that is advocated by Scripture but largely unexploited in Reformed circles.

The Titus 2 paradigm ensures a pastoral ministry that intentionally centers on issues and experience (e.g., domestic violence, infertility, abortion, self-esteem, and motherhood), approaches, language, and solutions germane to women. The role of women in undertaking this pastoral care creates a freedom for deep relationships, judicious to the relational need in contemporary feminine spirituality and the development of a Reformed feminine spirituality. It is a biblical mandate that verifies our corporate "churchly" spirituality anchored in union with Christ, as articulated in our previous chapter, enabling mutual edification and sanctification in both parties.

To define it simply, the Titus 2 model is the implementation of single-sex church relationships that provide biblical counseling for growth in Christian discipleship. Just as Paul Tautges purports, biblical counseling is simply the fulfillment of the Great Commission in making disciples:[46]

> Biblical counseling is an intensely focused and personal aspect of the discipleship process, whereby the more mature believer (counselor) comes alongside the less mature believer (counselee) for three main purposes: first, to help that person to consistently apply Scriptural theology to his or her life in order to experience victory over sin through obedience to Christ; second, by warning that person, in love, of the consequences of sinful actions; and third, by leading that person to make consistent progress in the ongoing process of biblical change in order that he or she too may become a spiritually reproductive disciple-maker.[47]

Derek Prime says that the "particular responsibility" of this pastoral care of women by women is "ideal and advisable" so as to save men from the temptation and snare of emotional and sexual involvement.[48] Importantly, this is not in conflict with wider New Testament teaching when one discerns the essential differences between "pastoral care" and "pastoral rule."[49] In other words, the pastor's unique spiritual authority is not lost since others engage in this care under his oversight. Prime claims that "providing we see the difference between rule and care, and teach and demonstrate the

---

46. Tautges, *Counsel*, 25.
47. Ibid., 21–22.
48. Prime, *Women in the Church*, 91.
49. Ibid., 91, 95.

difference, no reasonable objections to women's ministry can be raised."[50] Where there are struggles of homosexuality, however, a team model might be more appropriate.

To be sure, this paradigm of authentic biblical counseling creates a strong interrelational structure of discipleship that can benefit the local church immensely. It ensures the "kind of fellowship [that] transcends all superficial distinctions, such as age or marital status, and instead promotes spiritual growth through cross-generational, same-gender mentoring."[51] It creates unity in the Body, as younger generations and older generation commit to long-term relationships and fellowship. This will lessen the apparent ageism in our Reformed congregations evident in social mixing, where the younger are largely disinterested in the older generations and the older generations somewhat intimidated by the younger. Nevertheless, the Titus 2 model does not necessarily infer huge age gaps. Of course, spiritual maturity is the real qualification for the counselor or mentor, as a result allowing a suitable younger Christian who is spiritually mature to mentor an older woman who is younger in the faith. In this there are mutual benefits. Through loving instruction and the mature Christian example modeled to them, the mentee grows in godliness and Christian understanding. Similarly, the mentor experiences spiritual growth as she serves her sister in Christ and the Body in this way. Equally, as mentioned above, her responsibility and usefulness in the work of spiritual discipleship gives her reason to sharpen her own spiritual life and theological thinking.

As the demographics of society continue to change, younger Christian wives and mothers are less likely to have their own mothers, whether Christian or not, living nearby. This model is also a context for basic yet essential works of service, as the experience of older Christian women in the areas of childrearing and domestic management can be passed on. The mentor might provide voluntary child-care for the single-parent mother, undertake domestic assistance, or give financially or materially. Whatever the modes of ministry, the Titus 2 model is inherently corporate and pastorally strategic. In the complementarian framework, it affirms the central role of marriage and the family and their influence upon church life and society.[52] Jay Adams exhorts pastors with his belief that this model of female

---

50. Ibid., 99.
51. Tautges, *Counsel*, 153.
52. Cf. Catherwood, "Women," 131.

discipleship, together with preaching and teaching, will assist in counteracting contemporary attacks upon marriage and the family unit.[53]

In concern for undue overemphasis upon one-to-one discipleship and subsequent imbalance in the life of the Body, this study proposes that the implementation of a Titus 2 discipleship model balances the corporate with the practical and pastoral requirements for one-to-one care. Derek Tidball is critical of recent trends of counseling in church practice. "The contemporary emphasis on individual counseling may owe more to an absence of corporate teaching and a lack of agreed doctrinal consensus in our churches than to an exact role model within the NT."[54] Reformed church implementation of this biblical model must consider it as serving the wider church Body and not replace corporate principles and expressions.

PASTORAL IMPLICATIONS OF A REFORMED FEMININE SPIRITUALITY OF MARITAL UNION

The theological restatement of the Christ-union in contemporary Reformed spirituality, fundamental to this project, demands that our concern of pastoral care also operate within this doctrinal category. Rigorous theological interaction should not cease at the point of pastoral care, for the employment of other psychological, clinical, or social-scientific methods, but must pervade throughout all Reformed church ministries.[55] This conviction is imperative to the essential "Christian" nature of pastoral care, as purported by Andrew Purves in his work *Reconstructing Pastoral Theology: A Christological Foundation*. The thought of T. F. Torrance and his centralization of union with Christ is evident in Purves' approach as he pays particular attention to the doctrine in his outline of a christological pastoral theology of the "pastoring God."[56] He writes, "the whole of Christian faith and life, everything in discipleship and ministry, is the explication of Jesus Christ and faith in him, which means a sharing in his *life*."[57] This section on the pastoral implications of our articulation of a "marital spirituality" affirms this premise. Since the *unio mystica* served as the basis for our spirituality and our projections for a Reformed spiritual renewal, then it must also be the category of our discussion on the pastoral care of Reformed women.

53. Adams, *Pastoral Life*, 101.
54. Tidball, "Practical and Pastoral Theology," 46.
55. Purves, *Pastoral*, xvi.
56. Ibid., 4; cf. Lee, *Living in Union*.
57. Purves, *Pastoral*, 153.

Furthermore, it is imperative that pastoral care of women addresses feminine spirituality as its corollary, looking to impart an improved relational and experiential spiritual life as well as pastoral healing, nurture, and support.

Within the limits of this chapter, an extensive report of all applicable pastoral implications cannot be presented. For this reason, the discourse below is somewhat indicative as it highlights the pastoral issues most pertinent to our discourse.

Unhappy and Broken Marriages

The preceding articulation of a Reformed corporate spirituality of the church as the Spouse or Bride of Christ raises the issue of many unhappy or broken marriages. Contemporary Reformed women are certainly not immune to marriages of conflict, whether both partners are Christian or not, and the parallelism of union between Christ and church and husband and wife might be a source of further pain in the light of such circumstances.

Edmund Clowney is right to observe that "Paul invests so much in this analogy, making marriage so solemn and marvelous that it is easy to see why he would preserve the relationship of husbands and wives in the ordering of the church as the family of God."[58] Yet what of the marriage where preservation is too late? The Reformed woman who seeks to appropriate and understand her union with Christ in a covenantal spirituality of the corporate Bride might find such a spousal response confusing and unstable in the light of past divorce or separation. Equally, a corporate spirituality that considers the familial nature of the church as family can be equally troublesome in the experience of a family breakup.

J. Elwyn Davies highlights the need for pastoral sensitivity in relation to such situations and the Christ-church marriage parallel:

> It is no secret that there can be considerable unhappiness even in Christian homes. In many instances this is due not so much to ignorance or willful sin, but to an inbred prejudice, a fear that to comply with the terms of the divinely prescribed relationship would result in something which husband or wife may have had reason to fear or resent in early childhood. . . . [This] is extremely tragic.[59]

---

58. Clowney, *Church*, 225.
59. Davies, "Marriage," 44.

Davies' observation helpfully underlines the responsibility for pastors to discern each marriage individually, considering the unique, sometimes hidden, personal implications therein. In order to encourage mutual perseverance in the relationship, the pastor should focus on the growth of each individual in Christ as well as work towards full reconciliation and marital renewal. If marriage counseling is to be given then this is ideally done in a team situation, with the pastor and his wife or a mature believer. In addition, intelligent weekly preaching must seek continually to reflect the apostle in exhorting reverence and respect for one another, and repentance where this is not the case. Adams affirms that the most pertinent need in the church Body is the "preservation and care of families and marriage," which represents up to 80 percent of the pastor's pastoral problems.[60]

A Titus 2 model of ongoing pastoral care (as opposed to acute crisis counseling) can continually focus on the biblical requirement of love and voluntary submission as godly feminine behavior, and subsequently might act in a preventative manner. Only in this single-sex scheme can a woman benefit from constant care, support, and biblical instruction without placing unreasonable demands on the pastor's time or emotions.

Women with the daily grind of a difficult marriage need to be taught their responsibility of biblical God-honoring behavior so that the "word of God is not reviled" (Titus 2:5) and, whether their husband is Christian or not, "that they may be won without a word" (1 Pet 3: 1). The harboring of bitterness, self-righteousness, cynicism, hate, depression, anger, and self-pity are never legitimate responses, as the forbearance of Christian love "keeps no records of wrongs" (1 Cor 13:6), even if separation is necessary. Long-term biblical counseling can sustain a woman through such difficulties, helping her see the purposes of a sovereign and loving God as she is led to completely trust and depend on him in the power of the Holy Spirit. Cornish offers valuable content for discipleship of women in unequal marriages where the husband is not a believer. It is in part pertinent to the spiritual experience of women in unhappy Christian marriages too.

> It is freeing when a woman realizes she doesn't have to be concerned with changing her husband. . . . It's a trap to believe God doesn't have her in exactly the best circumstances for her growth in Christlikeness. Let your counselee know that changing her circumstances would not make her better able to serve God. She

---

60. Adams, *Pastoral Life*, 100–101.

can serve the Lord best right where she is, even married to an unbeliever.[61]

This personal counseling can explore the practice of a Reformed spirituality unique to each woman and her circumstances, yet consistently acquainted with the central reality of union with Christ. For example, in private prayer she presents her trials to her loyal Intercessor and his faithful mediation by means of union (Rom 8:24). In corporate worship her faith is renewed and strengthened by the sacraments of baptism and the Lord's Supper, which witness and confirm her union with Christ. She does not quench the Holy Spirit but welcomes his sanctification and is mindful of his joining her to her Lord, which is a daily source of assurance to her.

Unequal Marriages

Although the union of a Christian woman with a non-believing husband may not reflect the spousal responses of Christ and the church to the same degree as a marriage between two Christians, the biblical parallel still stands. "While it is clearly an advantage to the Christian to have this sublime example of how a husband should love his wife, it does not make the responsibility of the non-Christian husband to love his wife any the less, for the union between non-Christians is no less real than that between Christians."[62] In short, it is the marriage institution that reflects the *unio mystica*, not specific marriages. Therefore, the Christian wife married to an unbelieving husband takes her domestic responsibilities seriously to the glory of God to the same degree as if she were married to a believer.

In some ways, a corporate Reformed spirituality anchored on marital union that highlights the all-sufficiency of Christ as the ultimate Bridegroom might be of most benefit to women in unhappy, broken, abusive, and unequal marriages. Their need for support and relationship, keenly felt in feminine experience, involves a higher degree of local church family commitment. In relation to ministry use, spiritually mature women with these backgrounds are valuable personnel to the church in the prevalence of marital struggle. Importantly, the ministerial employment of a woman who has been divorced or separated does not mean that the church leadership is endorsing divorce, although wisdom in each case is necessary.[63]

---

61. Cornish, "Counseling Women," 205–231.
62. Davies, "Marriage," 40.
63. Tyson, "Counseling Divorced Women."

Complementarian Spirituality

Single-Parent Motherhood

It is incumbent that Reformed complementarian discourse and the corporate spirituality of the church take into account families made up of single parents due to bereavement, divorce, or the conversion of an unmarried mother. The Reformed esteem for marriage and the immediate family unit must not possess any prejudice against those who do not fit into the typical family pattern. Church leadership should particularly consider the position of such members in the social and ministerial life of the church. "When we take into consideration the high incidence of broken homes, the 'latchkey children' phenomenon, the proliferation of single-parent families, and the singularly unfulfilling marital relationships which seem to be on the increase everywhere, what is left of family life Britain today falls far short, to say the least, of what God ordained for mankind."[64] Hence, the preaching and teaching of complementarianism in Reformed churches, as it highlights the initial role of women in the home, must delicately recognize the impossibility of full-time home life in the economic pressures of a single-parent home. Too much complementarian material hastily advocates the ideal of full-time homeworker, wife *and* mother, without much examination of other circumstances. The complementarian stance must accommodate the Reformed feminine spirituality of the single-parent mother forced to put her children in full-time day care, or the Reformed wife who serves God in a career because of infertility or owing to high house prices—apt in the British context. In addition, there is the ministry of surrogate parenting. "[T]he existence of single parents represents a real challenge for our churches, and one which we have failed to meet. We must be alert to the difficulties of the children, and, assuming it is the father who is absent, the church must be ready to offer fathering."[65] Because the family unit, in line with Puritan thought, is the starting point for corporate Reformed life, the Body must be radically self-sacrificial in order to meet the needs of its female members and fill the gaps, providing a support that minimizes the negative effects of broken family life.

Infertility and Abortion

In light of our exploration into the subject of union, with one corollary of union being the production of fruit, we will briefly develop the issues

---

64. Davies, "Marriage," 29.
65. Shaw, "Bible and the Family," 24.

of infertility and abortion, which are germane to contemporary feminine experience.

With G. C. Meilaender Jr., this study insists that marital union is in no way compromised or incomplete in the occurrence of childlessness. This becomes apparent when one acknowledges that companionship, not reproduction, is God's ultimate purpose in marriage; for sexual union is not improper for those beyond childbearing years and marriage not banned for those who cannot physically engage in intercourse. "Such couples still take up the task of forging a lifelong bond . . . and they must still seek ways for their union—as a union—to turn outwards. They conform, therefore, to the Christian understanding of marriage."[66] Therefore, in the case of Christian infertility the "turning outwards" means the union produces fruit of another spiritual kind. This may mean reflecting the grace and mercy of the Father's love in the form of adoption or fostering.

Pastorally, however, a marriage that experiences the continual loss of infertility or repetitive miscarriage can be a union under great strain. The Christian woman can suffer daily bereavement by what she feels to be a lack of fruit and divine blessing in her marriage. In addition, if the wife knows her husband to be the cause of their infertility she might have to battle with the temptation to commit adultery in order to conceive. Equally, she might wrestle with progressive medical fertility techniques and the issue of Christian ethics therein. The continuing care found in feminine Christian relationships and biblical counseling can encourage these women to acknowledge the sovereignty of God in their circumstances, the enduring acceptance of God in the *unio mystica*, and the everlasting spiritual fruit of this eternal union. As in singleness and widowhood, women who struggle with infertility and miscarriage find comfort in the eschatological promises of the divine marriage between Christ and the church and the unending outward effects of this union in salvation.

In addition, abortion or the termination of the fruit of union, whether in marriage or not, can be a great hurdle to new life in Christ. Any personal association of one's body with the past sin of abortion must be avoided in the grace of the Christ-union. The woman's body in union with her Savior belongs to him and is no longer the vehicle of this sin. In reality, "Christ is not far off" but possesses the woman's physicality and redeems it fully as his own. Hence, it is a vessel of worship and praise. Women who carry bodily guilt and shame because of a past abortion or fornication, or even in the

---

66. Meilaender, "Sexuality," 74.

potentially self-abasing struggle of infertility, must look to the covenantal belonging and intimate, even "spatial" reconciliation of soteriological union with Christ.

Singleness

A Reformed feminine spirituality spent in singleness can wholly display the persona of the church, since Christ is the first husband. In response to our exploration of the feminine spousal response of the church in spirituality, we are to be reminded that in the new heavens and new earth there is no marriage and therefore singleness is the eternal eschatological state of all believers. Marriage is the earthly pale finite reflection of the Christ-church union and any marital perception of union with Christ should not esteem and normalize marriage to the degree that the eternal unmarried state of believers is forgotten. Furthermore, and relevant to the point above, in the new creation there is no sexual intercourse or cause for reproduction as the life of Christ's Bride physically endures by means of life in Christ.[67] Thus, marriage and childbearing are states restricted to earth. The temporal nature of these human states should prevent us from over-standardizing them and defining Reformed feminine spirituality in relation to them. True biblical spirituality is based on Christ, not female life roles or experience, especially those deemed "normative." The state of singleness, like those of widowhood and infertility, does not hinder a spirituality of biblical womanhood in any way:

> Devotion to Christ in our own lives may be expressed either in faithful marriage or in the single state. There were women who ministered to our Lord's needs, and those who contended at Paul's side in the cause of the gospel, and it seems more than likely that a number of these would have been single women. . . Singleness for the sake of the kingdom looks forward to the full realisation of God's purposes at the resurrection, when there will be neither marrying nor giving in marriage, and when the creation pattern will fade.[68]

In conclusion, contemporary Reformed discourse must present a holistic complementarian picture that encompasses these situations and God's use of such circumstances for his glory.

---

67. Foh, *Biblical Feminism*, 180.
68. Shaw, "Bible and the Family," 22–23.

Single women are unique personnel to the church. The tradition must rid itself of the tendency to send single women out into overseas ministry but not receive them as equally valuable full-time church workers at home. Conservative complementarian churches that prize marriage might also perceive single women as atypical members of the Body. Church leadership should counteract this and encourage a ministerial use of single women on the basis of spiritual gifting, not marital status, supporting them through specific pastoral issues relating to singleness.[69]

Singleness does remain a problem that many believers wrestle with in the church as they look for a godly partner who shares their confessional stance. Disappointment in this area and periods of loneliness have caused some Christian singles to enter into relationships and later marriage with unbelievers, contributing to some of the pastoral issues above.

Owing to the Reformed esteem for marriage and its biblical role of modeling the Christ-church union, informing a rich spirituality explored in this work, there is perhaps an opportunity for the church to actively engage in minimizing the geographical and social limits that impede judicious Christian dating. An inter-church Reformed network or an introductory Reformed website might serve the community advantageously in this area.

Isolated Reformed Feminine Spirituality

Due to illness, disability, or geographical location, some Reformed female believers are unable to participate in regular corporate worship. However, a Reformed feminine spirituality is not defective because of necessary solitude and the inability to commune with the saints. The writer of Hebrews is clear that some believers were *intentionally* neglecting the Body of Christ (10:25). Reformed spirituality is far from limited to the corporate sphere, for it possesses a rich private expression that we have not been able to explore in this study. In the case of isolation, a personal spirituality should be cultivated; the spiritual reality of union with Christ is a great comfort in times of loneliness, as Christ's uninterrupted society is experientially available for the believer.

Moreover, in the inactivity that comes with illness or disability, the centralization of *sola gratia* in Reformed feminine spirituality is fitting as nothing is required of the believer in order to share in and enjoy saving union with Jesus. "It is pastorally destructive to suggest that the presence of God is some other/extra/later experience a believer should seek. In Christ,

---

69. Catherwood, "Women," 130.

Complementarian Spirituality

all his children have been blessed with every spiritual blessing which he longs to give them, and these blessings are appropriated by faith in the crucified and risen Saviour."[70] A spirituality spent in Christ is complete as it reflects the sufficiency of Christ. Our corporate spirituality of mutual edification and service pertains to God's *gracious* use and equipping of members for acts of service to the Body and is not *de rigueur* for the Spirit's blessing upon the spiritual life.

Nevertheless, in the infrequent opportunity for the enjoyment of fellowship, it is the duty of the pastor or elder, together with female members, to visit the isolated female believer and nourish her spirituality by means of community and participation in the Lord's Supper. In addition, a Titus 2 discipleship ministry is remarkably applicable to this pastoral situation.

The growing number of online resources conveniently available to Reformed believers, including the numerous sermon portals and archives of popular American and British speakers, has given the community an open access to Reformed biblical exposition and teaching unimaginable in the past. This poses a danger to believers who do not have genuine reasons to be absent from corporate worship. The freedom of benefiting from one's favorite international speaker on a regular basis can potentially create a devaluing of local church commitment and attendance, comparable to a virtual or "electronic" church experience. The Reformed community, particularly younger student generations, ought to exercise caution and use these resources in a manner that does not replace the local Body.

CONCLUSION

It is the author's hope that presenting these pastoral implications of a spirituality anchored upon "marital union" will enrich and strength its articulation. There is great wealth in Paul's parallel between Christ and the church and husband and wife. When placed into its correct biblical context of the church community, and not restricted to the individual believer, these pastoral dilemmas are perhaps in some way "lightened," as the believer's true status and calling into a "chosen race, a royal priesthood, a holy nation, a people for his own possession" (1 Pet 2:9), is more clearly understood.

May the self-critical observations of some church operations and the practical inconsistencies of our complementarian belief, outlined above, move us to prayerfulness, repentance, and excitement as we look towards reform and reaping the rewards therein.

70. Raiter, *Stirrings*, 188.

7

A Reformed Feminine Spirituality

IN THIS CONCLUDING CHAPTER, our focus on the *unio cum Christo* in the Reformed tradition and concern for the tradition's contemporary spirituality will be pulled together in the presentation of a personal Reformed feminine spirituality and experiential enjoyment of union with Christ. Herein, the indispensable function of emotions in Christian spirituality will be touched upon in relation to the *mystik* elements of the Christ-union in order to propose a biblical spiritual expression in concord with past Reformed particularly Puritan perspectives. The accentuation on the spirituality of the individual believer here will give some balance to our largely corporate emphasis. This innovative Reformed feminine contribution will then narrow its focus specifically on elements innate to contemporary feminist and the "new spiritualities" movement. This is largely provocative in order to stimulate further academic commentary and examination, as well as seeking to profit Reformed women on a level pertinent to contemporary culture. Four interrelated key features will be examined: holism (as opposed to recent criticism that traditional Christian spiritualities create fragmentation), the place of the body and creation (themes prevalent in feminist and eco-feminist thought), societal influence (in its corporate emphasis), and self-reflexivity. We will concisely investigate these areas in relation to the doctrine of union with Christ and their relevance to personal and corporate spirituality.

This initial outline of a Reformed feminine spirituality is the apex of our unique feminine approach in its consideration of female spiritual experiences, perceptions, language, and expectations.

Complementarian Spirituality

A REFORMED FEMININE CONTRIBUTION

The "overriding theme" of Evangelical spirituality is "personal relationship to Jesus Christ."[1] Though rooted in the Reformation, the wide spread of Evangelicalism since its birth in the eighteenth century has overemphasized individual faith in spirituality, creating an imbalance of the personalistic with the corporate. This has determined the spirituality of many Reformed believers, particularly as many in the Reformed arena do consider themselves as both "Reformed" and "Evangelical." This became clear from the author's literature survey (not included in this work out of sympathy for the reader) when noting that many of the Reformed feminine works reviewed included little corporate or "churchly" discussion, not least any reference to corporate union with Christ. One might suggest that feminine spiritual writings have a proclivity for individual and personal expression, which is perhaps unexpected in the strong desire for the relational in feminine forms. Yet, seemingly, these two contradictory characteristics can coexist. In addition, it is a possibility that the male-centeredness of conservative church life may partially account for the lack of churchly feminine articulations, as women fail to find corporate life sufficiently spiritually satisfying.

On the other hand, some features of Evangelical spirituality have produced a converse response in Reformed spirituality. The proliferation of the Charismatic movement in Evangelicalism and charismatic forms of worship and "experience," epitomized in the Toronto Blessing, seen as highly affective and sentimental, has made the Reformed community wary. Hence, in its close and somewhat "overlapping" relationship with Evangelicalism, Reformed spirituality has been largely selective in what it has taken on. However, this study suggests that a thoroughly Reformed contemporary spiritual expression is ripe for development. In acknowledging the mutual shaping of the corporate and private spheres of spiritual life, it is proposed that a lively personal enjoyment of union with Christ characteristic of the feminine mode, together with our corporate spirituality of the church as Bride, might balance out these issues of individualism and spiritual dryness in Reformed spirituality, bringing about a biblical equilibrium.

Now, we will attempt a contribution of a unique Reformed feminine spirituality. In part, this initial tracing methodologically involves taking explicitly feminine aspects from secular, feminist, and wider Christian spirituality and integrating them into a Reformed theological framework. Therefore, it is incumbent upon our discourse to sketch briefly the

---

1. Randall, *Friend We Have*, 15.

contemporary understanding of "feminine spirituality" or "the feminine nuance" in spirituality to ground our Reformed exploration.

Feminine Spirituality

There has been an increasing reluctance amongst recent scholars to define the terms "feminine spirituality" due to the prominence of cultural stereotypes placed upon what is "masculine" and "feminine." This is exemplified in the fact that *The Westminster Dictionary of Christian Spirituality*, published in 1983 and edited by Gordon S. Wakefield, offers a bold yet somewhat helpful characterization of the term "feminine spirituality," whereas the 2005 new edition under the headship of Philip Sheldrake replaces this definition with "Women and Spirituality." In the latter, Joann Wolski Conn indirectly accounts for this in her discrediting of the term "feminine." "Until recently, female was usually equated with 'feminine', meaning such things as intuitive, emotional, receptive, motherly, more closely related to nature and matter than to culture and spirit. . . . Today, when these meanings are no longer universally accepted, female gender identity is ambiguous for many and even problematic."[2]

Consequently, feminine spirituality has therefore largely been "characterized" instead of strictly defined in a manner inclusive of both genders. This inclusivity is apparent in Bernard McGinn's writing of feminine spiritual expression in mysticism. He writes, "the fact that some, or even many, women may tend to use language in a certain way, or to adopt distinctive kinds of symbols, or to construct their gender identity and its relation to God according to particular patterns, does not necessarily mean that all women will do so, or that no men can."[3] In a similar care not to subscribe to gender essentialism, this project seeks to consider delicately a feminine mode that is conversant with other expressions. In acknowledging *unique distinctive feminine "nuances" in spiritual articulations, this work supposes these characteristics as applicable to both genders yet strongly apparent and most natural to the feminine.* As McGinn attributes the "flowering" of mysticism in the late medieval era with new freedom for monastic men and women to exchange in spiritual dialogue, so also the identification of a feminine nuance in Reformed spirituality might cause the tradition's spirituality to flourish, being of benefit to both men and women.[4]

2. Wolski Conn, "Women and Spirituality."
3. McGinn, "Changing Shape," 201–2.
4. Ibid.," 201; McGinn, *Flowering of Mysticism*.

Complementarian Spirituality

In a preliminary characterization of "feminine spirituality," then, the strong emotive drive and desire for intimacy in spiritual life is noteworthy: "One can say that feminine spirituality *as appropriated by male and female* is characterized by receptivity, affective response, waiting or attentiveness and the acceptance of pain as intrinsic to the bringing forth of life."[5] The significance of the feminine capacity to give life (whether physical or spiritual) as the fruit of union (again whether physical or spiritual) is evident. Additionally, the acceptance of pain, observed by Ring, may account for the openness of feminine works to explicitly deal with the issue of suffering.

The nuance of feminine spirituality may be expressed to be quintessentially "embodied spirituality," since it is aware of the body and makes full use of it physically and emotively. Historically, Christian feminine spirituality has effectively grasped hold of the person of Christ in the symbolism, language, and form of union, apparent in the sexual imagery of the *Mysticismus* uttered by Catherine of Siena and Teresa of Avila and the bridal mysticism of Mechthild of Magdeburg.[6] Criticism of the latter describes an overlooking of the corporate or communal life as the individual soul is perceived as the bride of Christ, though Ulrike Wiethaus defends that Mechthild "understands individual existence primarily as an extension of communal and cosmological patterns."[7] Popular feminine forms of Evangelical spirituality representing a "Dear Jesus" sentiment are simplistic contemporary forms comparable to this romanticized perception of Christ, similar to the Reformed and Evangelical feminine notions observed in our survey. Sandra Gustafson asserts that contemporary Evangelical language is familiar with that associated with feminized spirituality, wherein the individual soul is seen as Christ's Bride "couched in terms of swooning or ravishment," and even as Christ's mother in "giving birth to Christ" in the believing soul.[8] Akin to this latter point is the trend in feminine spiritualities (broad Christian, goddess, feminist, and again the female *Mysticismus*) to liberate or discover the divine *within* one's self. This is contrary to a Reformed view of the divine as "other" which is integral to biblical union with Christ.

A notable contemporary rendering of feminine spirituality is given in Amanda Porterfield's *Feminine Spirituality in America: From Sarah Edwards*

---

5. Ring, "Feminine Spirituality," 149 (emphasis added).
6. Ibid.
7. Wiethaus, "Mechthild of Magdeburg," 104.
8. Gustafson, "Edwards and 'Feminine' Speech," 189.

to Martha Graham. Porterfield idealizes Puritan feminine expression in the holism of "beauty, pleasure and sexuality," personified in the life of Sarah Edwards but lost in the late eighteenth-century "softening" of Calvinism in the rise of Evangelicalism.[9] Seen to be iconic of feminine spirituality, Sarah Pierrepont Edwards' "embodied spirituality" characterizes a bride-conscious motif wherein the Puritans "compared the life of a saint to the preparations of a bride and to the sustained bride-consciousness of a devoted wife."[10] Significant to Porterfield's understanding of feminine spirituality is her incorporation of the arts of novels, poetry, and dance. Catherine Albanese describes this to be a perennial characteristic of feminine spirituality in Porterfield's thinking, "substantively, there is the explicit identification of beauty and the continued scrutiny of the religious imagination more than the religious reason."[11] This infers that feminine spirituality is aesthetically driven. Furthermore, the fixation of the affections upon Christ in the feminine nuance suggests that the use of union or marital language in feminine spirituality is connected with the enjoyment of beauty in one's spouse, affirmed in the indispensable interaction of beauty with the emotions. However, this strong subjectivity does not at all mean that feminine spirituality is without objectivity, as stereotypes purport. Albanese does not do a disservice to Porterfield's rendering of an aesthetic feminine spirituality to be devoid of truth. "In a tradition of feminine embodied spirituality which celebrates wholeness, beauty is necessary, but so is truth (and theology)."[12]

In summary, feminine spirituality finds its source in female experience and is characterized by particular nuances in language, perceptions, and expectations and desire. This brief synopsis portrays that a fundamental feature relevant to our discourse is the feminization of the soul and perception of Christ as spouse. Emotions, beauty, and love, as we have briefly seen, are key interrelated experiential features.

This project looks to propose an appreciation of a personal Reformed feminine spirituality in the form of experiential enjoyment of union with Christ. Our understanding of a "Reformed feminine spirituality" is a spiritual life natural to female experience, possessing inclusive nuances to men and women characterized above, yet found in a Reformed theological

---

9. Albanese, Review of *Feminine Spirituality*; Porterfield, *Feminine Spirituality*, 51.
10. Porterfield, *Feminine Spirituality*, 8, 27.
11. Albanese, Review of *Feminine Spirituality*, 84.
12. Ibid., 84.

framework. By the term "experiential," from the Latin *experimentum* or *experior*, which Calvin used synonymously with "experimental," we mean "to try," "prove," or "test," or "to know by experience."[13] Our interest is with the integration of the soteric reality of union with Christ into biblical spiritual experience. For Gaffin reminds us that Pauline Christ-union entails the actual life experience of the individual believer, "therefore the union basic to this experience, of which this experience is an expression, is likewise experiential."[14]

We now turn to these elements in order to unpack a Reformed feminine spirituality and enjoyment of union with Christ.

Affections and Aesthetics in Spirituality

The role of the affections in feminine enjoyment of union with Christ is significant as this essentially spousal enjoyment finds its source and food in the beauty of Christ as Savior. This is particularly pertinent in the light of the contemporary Reformed suspicion of the emotions in religious life, calling for new contributions and appropriate handling of these issues. This project only observes the interface between the affections, personal delight, and aesthetic capacity in order to inform our initial tracing of a Reformed feminine spirituality and underline the current downgrading of an experiential Reformed spirituality. In the over-acceptance of Enlightenment rationalism and the Aristotelian dichotomy of emotions and reason, Reformed thought has little to offer on the ethics of emotions in the spiritual life, as the emotive is commonly associated with sensationalism or sentimentality and regarded to be dangerous to Reformed orthodoxy. The Reformed stress upon doctrine has given way to a cognitive-centered "spirituality of dogma," shying away from the affections as a vital display of authentic spirituality evident in the Bible.[15] The posture of human emotions is crucial for Reformed spirituality to be thoroughly biblical, loving the Lord your God with heart, soul, and might (Deut 6:5).

---

13. Beeke, "Word," 256.

14. Gaffin, *Resurrection*, 50.

15. The biblical text is full of emotive language and narrative; for example, the mourning and searching of Job, Elijah's despair, the "lament" Psalms and Lamentations, Habakkuk's perplexity, and the intensity of Jesus Christ's praying in Gethsemane. The author is grateful to Dr. D. Eryl Davies for these observations. On the last point, see Edwards, *Affections*, 40.

Robert Solomon, who has been influential in his writings on the subject, is sharply critical of the tendency evident in Western thinking overly to rationalize and stigmatize the emotions, a habit to which he associates Christian theology.[16] This Christian indigence is palpable in current academic discourse on the life of the emotions in religion, dominated by contributions from Aristotle, Spinoza, Hume, Darwin, and William James. Subsequently, religious contributions of Augustine, Aquinas, and, significant to our Reformed discussion, Jonathan Edwards, are rarely consulted.[17] The role and nature of the emotions has been under serious examination in recent philosophical and ethical discourse, proposing an existence of order in the emotional life that has always been overlooked in the presumption that the emotive is chaotic.[18] This questions the relegation of the emotions in orthodox religion as merely "animal energies or impulses" and the Aristotelian division of the cognitive life with the life of the appetites.[19] Feminist thought has also contributed, stating the role of the emotions as "embodied knowing."[20] Although academic debate on the epistemological nature of emotions continues, there is a growing consensus amongst scholars that emotions have a "cognitive dimension" involving "thought, judgment and evaluation" and can be subject to refinement or "education."[21] Martha Craven Nussbaum's *Upheavals of Thought: The Intelligence of Emotions* has been influential as she judges the emotions as forms of thought essentially evaluative and witnessing to the presence of value and importance in, and even self-dependency on, the object.[22] "Constructivist theory" is similar to that of Nussbaum as it also rejects the non-cognitive stance persuasively advocated by William James, regarding the emotions as "cultural artifacts" that display self-understanding as well as belief and judgment.[23] Thus, the emotions have been "reintroduced" into religious ethics. Instead of removing the emotions from religious life, as the Reformed tradition has essentially

---

16. Dixon, *Passions*, 2.
17. Ibid., 7.
18. Lauritzen, "Emotions," 307–24.
19. Nussbaum, *Upheavals*, 1; Cates, Review of *Upheavals*, 325–341.
20. Cates, Review of *Upheavals*, 326.
21. Cates, Review of *Upheavals*, 326–27; Lauritzen, "Emotions," 307.
22. Nussbaum, *Upheavals*, 22, 27–30.
23. Lauritzen, "Emotions," 308–9, 312.

done, Paul Lauritzen claims the emotions to be best placed in a religious vision in order for their moral transformation.[24]

The Nussbaum and constructivist stances regarding the emotions are comparable with that of Jonathan Edwards, who similarly maintains the emotions or affections to be intricate to human understanding, judgment, and will.[25] This is of course rudimentary to his renowned premise that "a great part of true religion lies in the affections."[26] Similar to the "education" of emotions that Lauritzen raises, Edwards maintains that the emotional life should be subject to "reasoned assessment"—undoubtedly a response to the over rationalism and sensationalism observed in the Great Awakening.[27]

In his high esteem for the emotions in the Christian life, Edwards appreciates their epistemological capacity, claiming that authentic spiritual experience cannot exist without "religious affections."[28] He writes, "the affections are no other than the more vigorous and sensible exercises of the inclination and will of the soul."[29] The affection produced by an object, whether pleasure or disdain, affirms the nature of personal cognitive judgment and act of the will towards the object.

> In every act of the will whatsoever, the soul either likes or dislikes, is either inclined or disinclined to what is in view: these are not essentially different from those affections of love and hatred. That likening or inclination of the soul to a thing, if it be in a high degree, and be vigorous and lively, is the very same thing with the affection of love; and that disliking and disinclining if in a great degree, is the very same with hatred. In every act of the will for or towards something not present, the soul is in some degree inclined to that thing; and that inclination, if in a considerable degree, is the very same with the affection of desire.[30]

In short, the affections "signal to us what is worth attending to at any particular point in time," not least in the ultimate enjoyment of the virtue and beauty of Christ.[31] Therefore, they connect closely to the aesthetic faculty, touched upon earlier from Porterfield's contribution. To Edwards aes-

24. Ibid., 318–21.
25. Edwards, *Affections*, 24–25.
26. Ibid., 24.
27. Lewis, "Springs of Motion."
28. Edwards, *Affections*, 48.
29. Ibid., 24
30. Ibid., 25–26.
31. Lewis, "Springs of Motion," 283.

A Reformed Feminine Spirituality

thetics is central to theology and ethics as he views beauty, or "excellence" that is perfection rather than "pleasantness," as an ontological and objective reality manifested to its uttermost in the Godhead.[32] He writes, "a love to divine things for the beauty and sweetness of their moral excellency, is the first beginning and spring of all holy affections."[33] Thus, beauty is not divorced from joy and benevolence because Edwards' beauty is not a passive virtue. Significantly for Christian spirituality, from the enjoyment of beauty comes praise and glorification of the object.

This is further apparent in the Westminster epigraph to Reformed spirituality, "The chief end of man is to glorify God and enjoy him forever," unmistakable in the contemporary writings of John Piper.[34] Roland Delattre sums up Edwards and the Reformed view of the beautifying glorification of God:

> The communication of God's glory is the end for which God created the world. The divine glory as communicated to intelligent willing creatures consists of God's (a) knowledge, (b) beauty, holiness, or love, and (c) joy, delight, or pleasure, according to the creature's capacities. What is thus communicated, Edwards insists, is not just something *from* God but something *of* God—a communication and participation in the life of God.[35]

The God-given faculties for the appreciation of perfection or beauty, and the subsequent invoking of desire and affection, are realized most fully and ultimately in spirituality in the glorification and enjoyment of God. "Our hunger for beauty is essentially a spiritual longing for an affirmative and nourishing connection with *the ground and source of our being*."[36] This tenor of delighting in God as the basis of a holistic experiential Christian life aligns Reformed spirituality with biblical spirituality, stabilizing the tradition's cerebralism. Although these themes are integral to a feminine nuance in spirituality, they are not exclusively so. It is necessary for both male and female believers to enjoy union with Christ by potentially integrating these themes into one's spiritual expression.

---

32. Delattre, "Aesthetics."

33. Edwards, *Affections*, 179. For critical evaluation of Edwards' position see, Dyrness, *Reformed Theology*, 278–87.

34. Piper, *Desiring*, 15, 33, 42–43.

35. Delattre, "Aesthetics," 282.

36. Ibid., 279 (emphasis added).

Equally, these themes are particularly momentous to a spirituality anchored in marital union with Christ. Because spirituality is essentially a human response to God in his natural and moral perfection, a spousal spirituality of union that appreciates Christ as the wholly sufficient Bridegroom is a devotional life aesthetically driven to all his saving merits. The marriage between Christ and the church is not a loveless marriage, and the personal response of the believer to Christ is biblically one of totality of heart, mind, and soul. We should not then withhold affections or place them under restriction, but intelligently assess them. Klaus Bockmuehl avows that loving God "with all your soul" is the spiritual employment of the emotions and desires, but "if we are to love God 'with all your mind' then this type of love, although passionate, clearly is not blind but circumspect and discerning in the pursuit of its aims."[37] Edwards writes of the spirituality of the authentic believer, "The true saint, when under great spiritual affections, from the fullness of his heart, is ready to be speaking much of God and His glorious perfections and works, and of the beauty and amiableness of Christ, and the glorious things of the gospel."[38] Although the over-rationality and sentimentality of Edwards' day caused him to write his treatise, Edwards endeavored to keep a biblical, balanced outlook on the crucial part that the human heart plays in spiritual life. Similarly, contemporary Reformed thought needs to be equally unmoved by external unbiblical modes of thought. There is need for further development into an Edwardsean use of the emotions in spirituality that is distinctively Reformed, possibly benefiting further from the academic discourse in the realm of religious ethics, to which we briefly looked. As Carson purports, the Reformed biblical tradition "should be rightly suspicious of forms of theology that place all the emphasis on coherent systems of thought that demand faith, allegiance, and obedience, but do not engage the affections."[39]

This project contends that the experiential yet mysterious or *mystik* nature of biblical union with Christ, as central to Reformed thought can encourage the tradition out of its overly reticent regard for the experiential. Certainly, one reason that our doctrine of interest has suffered inattention in Protestant thought is owing to its immense profundity and potent association with Catholic and Eastern Orthodox experiences of union and ascent to God. However, this should not discourage Christian enjoyment

---

37. Bockmuehl, "Great Commandment," 15.
38. Edwards, *Affections*, 178.
39. Carson, *Gagging*, 567.

of this central and foundational doctrine. Indeed the depths of this mystery should only accelerate enjoyment and revelry.

The core of Reformed feminine spirituality is the triune revelation in Christ, as outlined in the Bible. Fundamental to this is the "otherness" of the Godhead, which renders Reformed spirituality distinct from the secular feminine notion of a "goddess within." Conversely, the feminine believer obtains the "divine within" by means of a saving union that guarantees adoption and heavenly inheritance in Christ. In this, the Reformed female believer views herself and the divine Christ to be distinct entities but spiritually one. This is understood and appropriated in the context of the triune Persons and their mutual indwelling.

Authentic Reformed feminine spirituality sets both the mind and affections on Christ. In response to his gracious enjoining of himself to her by the Spirit, the Reformed female believer objectively commits herself fully to Christ, and his christological and soteriological beauty secures her subjective devotion to him as the lover and husband of her soul.

Her spiritual longing for intimacy with Christ is not any initiation on her part but is the fruit and evidence of Spirit-wrought enjoining to him, so the Reformed female believer possesses Christ fully in union and through this the whole Trinity. Thus, her spirituality is not characterized by attempts to ascend to union with God but instead she currently enjoys permanent and eternal union with Christ secured by God the Holy Spirit. The mystery of Christ has been made known to her through this union, "which is Christ in you, the hope of glory" (Col 1:27); thus her intimate fellowship and participation with and possession of Christ means there is no need for any esoteric revelation of him. She seeks to know Christ more but her covenantal state of oneness with him ensures the fullness of divine revelation. A Reformed feminine spirituality, then, in acknowledgement of the biblical profundity of this union, is a daily spiritual response to Christ, who is not far off but immanent and personal.

Related to this, a Reformed feminine spirituality exults in Christ as the visible expression of the Godhead. Christ is continually acknowledged to be her personal Way, Truth, and Life, and through him she enjoys communion with the entire Godhead. She cherishes the triune *perichoresis* alongside her union with Christ because by this she *knows* God and communes with the whole Godhead. Through this Spirit-wrought union she can now call upon the Father in the same way Christ does in the intimacy of "my Father." Indeed, all three Persons are personal to her and she enjoys and speaks of them, like Gregory Nazianzen, as "my Trinity."[40] Reformed spirituality that is Trinitarian worships the triune Persons distinctly and the believer is sensitive not to belittle one dear member and his gracious vocation. Her spiritual expression reflects this in her prayer, thanksgiving, worship, thought, and conversation as she considers each Person and his soteric and sanctifying vocation towards her. She approaches the Trinity in worship in a mode that reverses the Trinitarian outworking in salvation, "by the Holy Spirit through Christ to the Father."[41]

Contrary again to the feminine notions of an inner goddess, a Reformed feminine spirituality incorporates praxis regarding the presence of sin, its mortification, and increasing conformity to Christ. However, this is experienced in the Holy Spirit's keeping, taking the form of submission to Christ as head and heavenly husband. The Reformed woman is content in this authority/submission model, rejoicing in it because Christ's federal headship has saved her.

Significantly, where other feminine perspectives on spirituality have demonstrated a tendency to use sexual language and imagery in its desire for the divine, specifically in the feminine *Mysticismus* literature and contemporary goddess thought, Reformed feminine spirituality utilizes the biblical "marital" imagery, as explored in chapters 4–6. As a Reformed feminine spirituality *theologically* perceives Christ as the salvific Bridegroom, this theological cognitive element then instigates love, devotion, and delight in him in the heart of the believer, creating a thirst for communion with him. The soul's inclination for Christ is inseparable to its attraction and enjoyment of permanent and unconditional covenantal union with him.

Feminine Enjoyment of Union with Christ

Faith Cook demonstrates a Reformed feminine enjoyment of union with Christ in her hymns, for example in her words, "drink of Christ and share his life," "wrapped up in Him, my one desire."[42] However, Cook's embrace of Samuel Rutherford's letters, said to "throb" with the loveliness of Christ, demonstrates that both Cook and Rutherford prize the Christ-union, affirming that this feminine nuance is not exclusive.[43] Linda Dillow's work *Satisfy My Thirsty Soul* articulated similarly, "I yearned for a joy unspeak-

---

40. Letham, *Trinity*, 409.
41. Ibid., 414.
42. *Christian Hymns*
43. Cook, *Rutherford*, 18.

able, for a deeper union and oneness, for spiritual, bridal union."[44] Here the person of Christ is desired above all things and so the intimacy of union with him is sought. Cook and Dillow are contemporary representatives of the Reformed feminine experiential enjoyment of the *unio mystica* apparent in the spirituality of Calvinistic Baptist Anne Dutton (1692–1765), who refers, in bridal imagery, to the Christ as "Husband" or "Spouse," and is even described by Michael Sciretti as reflecting the Christian *Mysticismus*.[45]

Reformed feminine spirituality is one marked by possession of Christ and thirst for further experiential knowledge of this possession. Enjoyment of personal *unio cum Christo* perceives the centrality of this state as defining every aspect of one's daily life. The Reformed feminine believer seeks to be preoccupied with Christ in all that she does. She looks to honor him in work, home, relationships, in church or in leisure, and strives to be concerned ultimately for his welfare, namely, his glory and purposes. In her Christ-union she is married to the King and so in everything she esteems his kingdom and rule. The belief that Christ has graciously counted one worthy for eternal covenantal union is a source of great joy to the believer. She indeed views herself individually as wed to Christ but she never isolates herself from the Body, for one cannot separate or tear the members from the Bride.

Reformed feminine spirituality possesses Christ soteriologically and prizes this spiritually with desire and love for his person. In this manner, enjoyment of union with Christ is intrinsic to Reformed feminine spirituality. The believer contemplates her spiritual oneness with her Savior by meditating upon the beauty of Christ in his divine grace, his supremacy and sufficiency, his forgiveness and love, his servanthood and humility, his exaltation, victory, and lordship, and his glorious humanity as the means of union and communion with God. Union with Christ is not disassociated with his person; that is, the union is not enjoyed apart from Christ since enjoyment of the *unio mystica* is essentially enjoyment of Christ and the whole Trinity. In addition, the central posture of union with Christ to Reformed thought demands that it is worked into the consciousness of the believer by deliberation, prayer, Scripture reading, and daily mental reminders. Recognizing her own weakness, the Reformed female believer preaches the doctrine of *unio cum Christo* to herself for its daily and wide appropriation.

44. Dillow, *Satisfy*, 19.
45. Sciretti, "Anne Dutton."

Complementarian Spirituality

She jealously guards her enjoyment of her Christ-union and its enlivening of her Christian experience, and so she does not entertain anything that might hinder it. The believer's increasing knowledge of possession of Christ produces a disdain for sin and ungodliness. In frustration over habitual sin or in times of spiritual silence and depression, the believer looks to Christ for solace. She preaches to herself the glories of the incarnation and that the initiating, covenantal Godhead will fetch his Bride wherever she wanders in her sin. This covenantal faithfulness and loyalty to her galvanizes the same in her response to Christ. When sin is apparent in her life, she actively repents in prayer and humility to the Godhead and enjoys full reconciliation and assurance. Thus, the initiation of her Bridegroom fills the believer's life with grace and is also a humbling reality upon the believer. She can persevere knowing that he who called her will also sustain her.

The believer examines and curbs the undue projection of human superficiality, sentimentality, and excessive emotionalism upon her spiritual experience by continually grounding herself in the objective Word. In corporate musical worship she is particularly careful and reverent, as she ensures that her private enjoyment of Christ is consistent with that expressed in public contexts where there can be a tendency towards emotionalism.

Furthermore, a Reformed feminine spirituality looks to cultivate faith because this furthers enjoyment of the Christ-union. Therefore, the means of grace available to her—the sacraments, the preaching of the Word, private Scripture reading, and freedom in prayer—are all treasured disciplines. In this, the Spirit is recognized as the agent of faith and so in prayer she specifically asks the Father for the Spirit's outpouring in this. As God the Holy Spirit is the bond of her union with Christ, she seeks not to grieve him in anything (Eph 4:30), appealing to him for his purifying work in her.

Reformed feminine enjoyment of the Christ-union is also marked with wonder. The incomprehensible *mystik* of the *unio cum Christo* moves the believer to awe in the supernatural and eternal intimacy she has with Christ. She marvels particularly at the daily fellowship she enjoys by the power of the Holy Spirit with the exalted Christ, who is bodily at the right hand of the Father. In her wonder of this supernatural mystery, she participates wholeheartedly and with full liberty in the Lord's Supper, prayer, and worship. Consequently, in her repentance of even the most heinous sin she revels in complete acceptance, pleading her union with the heavenly Intercessor. This furnishes her spirituality with a certainty and assurance. In spiritual appropriation of her marital union with Christ, unlike Queen

A Reformed Feminine Spirituality

Esther, the feminine believer delights in unreserved access to the King, his scepter continually raised, as she wears pleasing royal garments that are his, marked with his blood.

A SAMPLE OF CONTEMPORARY CHARACTERISTICS

Now we will develop and focus our contribution of a Reformed feminine spirituality by contextualizing it into four characteristics. It is important to note that these features far from represent a comprehensive outline; they only attempt to introduce and stimulate further academic discourse in this area of Reformed thought.

First, we will briefly account for the selection of these particular features. The areas introduced are new to the current discussion and are not themes evident in Reformed or Evangelical feminine works. They are characteristic of contemporary and particularly feminine expressions of spirituality, as demonstrated, and some of them have already been touched upon in our discussions on contemporary spirituality. For example, in relation to the body, it has been said that "the bodily experience of a woman is intrinsic to understanding her response to the divine."[46] Furthermore, the fact that these features are themes apparent in particularly feminist discourses might enable academic dialogue between Reformed and feminist thought. As above, these are representative of a feminine nuance or female expression and perspective, but not exclusively so. Our consideration of holism in spirituality and society in particular are gender-neutral aspects that have been included because they are, respectively, necessary to the wider context or an area of neglect in Reformed female involvement. In an attempt to be of some value to the spiritual lives of Reformed women, these areas are particularly experiential in nature, so continuing our attempt to counteract the dry cerebralism and avoidance of subjective experience attributed to contemporary Reformed spirituality.

Significant to the four features to which we now look is their strong interrelationship. This becomes perceptible when observing their position in feminist spirituality and thought: "This new consciousness is the conviction that all beings are interconnected; each affects the other in the movement toward future life." It is an "interrelatedness of all reality," a "praxis [that] depends on the lived experience of mutually supportive relations between self, others, God and nature."[47] This interdependency is consis-

46. Ring, "Feminine Spirituality," 149.
47. Zappone, *Wholeness*, 12–13.

tent in our areas of interest: The holism of feminist spirituality reveals a regard for the physical realm and therefore the role of the feminine body; and as we shall see, this esteem for the body, its harmony, sexuality, and reproductive nature, relates strongly to feminist ecological concern and earth-based spirituality.[48] The emphasis upon horizontal responsibilities to the earth is further demonstrated in the fundamental corporate nature of feminist thought, noticeable in its stress upon activism and social policy, for "eco-justice is intrinsically linked to social justice."[49] Furthermore, in the spiritual desire for self-realization seen in liberated bodily self-identity and in spiritual holism and connection of self to all areas of life and experience, there is a reflective element to feminist spirituality, which is perhaps more expressive than critical. This interconnectedness means that the four features are not to be understood separately but as a unit. The development of our discourse reveals how they mutually inform each other.

Holism

The holism of new and feminist spiritualities is directly visible in the interrelationship of these features. In our brief outline of the new spirituality movement in chapter 1, we observed the contemporary desire for a sense of holism or a united life experience, a characteristic that was first found in feminist spirituality but is now spread throughout new spiritualities. Feminist Anne Carr writes, "Spirituality is holistic, encompassing all one's relationship to all of creation—to the self and to others, to society and nature, to work and leisure—in a fundamentally spiritual or religious orientation."[50] Put simply, spirituality to the postmodern is understood quintessentially as the defragmentation of life. It is the thread that unites all human contexts, roles, and experience.

Reformed feminine spirituality is unified by the Reformed mantra to honor or glorify God (*soli deo Gloria*). This resonates into every sphere of life, as the whole world is the theater of God's glory.[51] Reformed self-knowledge and identity is based upon this "chief end," giving it an umbrella sense of purpose and eternal significance in all its features. This spirituality is defined by a gospel worldview, leaning on the "systematic and coherent approach" of Reformed theological belief, "by which the totality of the

48. Tomm, "Philosophy of Self."
49. Lesniak, "Contemporary Spirituality," 11.
50. Carr, *Transforming Grace*, 201.
51. Cf. Cornick, *Letting God*, 111.

scriptural witness to the real and redemptive action of God through Christ" is *"focused upon and channeled into the everyday world."*[52] This redemption in Christ involves the transformation of how one perceives "self" and the world.

Just as union with Christ undergirds soteriology, it also undergirds the Christian life, for the enduring reality of union with Christ unites the seeming fragmentation of contemporary life. Wendy Horger Alsup highlights the fact that the mindset of many believing women regarding their spirituality is one of incidents or spiritual events, whereby they "intersect" with God. Conversely, she asserts an understanding and personal meditation upon the permanency of connection to Christ.[53] A Reformed feminine spirituality anchored on union with Christ recognizes the enduring reality of this union and has built this central doctrine into its consciousness.[54]

The Body, Nature, and Creation

Feminist awareness has contributed to the recovery of the body in contemporary spiritualities, as the appeal for holism rejects the traditional "disembodied" spirituality that perceives both matter (therefore the body) and the feminine to be problematic or unholy.[55] Feminine spirituality is mind-body-soul integration, placing prominence on the physical body as a vehicle to the divine, particularly apparent in the Goddess thought of leading academic Carol Christ. There is also a focus on the feminine body in its reproductive and maternal capacities as a life-giving instrument. Thus, third-wave feminism, unlike the anti-pornographical activism of the first and second wave, accepts sexual freedom as a spiritual feminine expression. Feminist and specifically lesbian spirituality values the erotic use of the body as power or energy towards spiritual fullness, satisfaction, and empowerment, as well as relational enjoyment with others.[56] Rebecca Jones observes that in this mind-body-soul holism women look to heal the scars of contemporary sexual freedoms. Yet in seeking unity and harmony, these women have ironically reaped disaccord:

---

52. McGrath, *Roots*, 8 (emphasis added).
53. Alsup, *Practical*, 96, 98.
54. Donnelly, *Life*, 11.
55. Lesniak, "Contemporary Spirituality," 12; Sheldrake, "Spirituality."
56. Lorde, "Uses of the Erotic," 208–13.

Complementarian Spirituality

> To resolve the guilt in which they live, women have sought inner peace. They look to yoga, exercise, diet, and alternative spiritualities. Some women have split their bodies from their souls by allowing themselves to be caught up in loveless sex or abortions. They seek to bring the two entities together in 'new' forms of spirituality that are no longer defined by organized religion and accepted moral codes, but by acts of individual or group reflection, meditation, and prayer.[57]

Feminist philosophical thought has sought an awareness of the body that can prevent "biological determinism," deemed evident in traditional modes of thought where feminine self-identity is based on motherhood and domesticity.[58] Claiming one's body as an "essential reality" to oneself is a revolutionary act against patriarchy, therefore encouraging bodily expression in feminist spirituality. "Using body-based images to reflect female power" and "spiritual images which directly impact on women's bodies contribute significantly to personal coherence," a philosophy greatly developed in Luce Irigaray's book on plural feminine identities, *This Sex Which Is Not One* (1977).[59]

Reformed feminine spirituality also encompasses mind, body, and soul, for the whole self finds its identity in Christ. Importantly, the Reformed woman knows that although her physical body is in union with her Lord and Savior, it was or is not the initiatory vehicle of union. Only the crucified and resurrected body of Christ is her means for reconciliation with God, and because of the sufficiency of his incarnate agency she has full standing with God and rests in this. A Reformed feminine spirituality does "not press forward into a deeper union with Christ but seek[s] to demonstrate a union already actualized" as it lives out its faith.[60]

The Reformed woman tends to her body with love and respect, using it in all purity, because the Bond who unites her to Christ indwells it. She acknowledges her body to be "fearfully" and "wonderfully" created in the image of God (Gen 1:27; Ps 139:14) and has been its spiritual expression for her physicality belongs to Christ. Using her body for a spirituality of sexual union would only be the gross deriding of her union with Christ. Therefore, in her spiritual union with Christ, all her appetites are subject to him, for

---

57. Jones, *Christianity*, 12–13.
58. Tomm, "Philosophy of Self," 247.
59. Ibid., 252.
60. Bloesch, *Spirituality*, 143.

she submits to his authority. Elizabeth George writes of the stewardship of the body, "the goal in the physical realm is discipline, the self-control that is a gift of God's grace. His Spirit in us gives us strength to resist temptation, to control our appetite rather than allowing it to control us, and to train our body into obedience."[61] This issue of purity is also channeled into dress and appearance. Because Christ possesses her body, the Reformed believer seeks to demonstrate these truths by presenting herself as one belonging to the sanctified and purified Bride. She therefore counterculturally dresses and adorns herself in the pure white linen of modesty.

A Reformed feminine spirituality, as it looks to glorify God in everything, appreciates the body as a God-given instrument for worship. Thus the believer wields her body for greater experiences of private worship, exemplified in the fact that kneeling, lying prostrate, or simply bowing of one's head in prayer is more cogent to the spiritual adoration and humility, as well as mental concentration, than slouching. Similarly, in private worship, the believer might find that other physical expressions of thanksgiving and joy stimulate a lively authentic spiritual life.

As discussed previously, a Reformed feminine spirituality in union has an expectant regard for the eschatological physical renewal promised in Christ. Highly esteemed and treasured in the discipline of purity and exercise of self-control, the earthly body is perceived as "a body in waiting" as it anticipates perfection and therefore unadulterated union with Christ in eternity. A Reformed feminine spirituality acknowledges the beautiful significance of its created bodily self and the essential physical outworking in the earthly realm. It does not maltreat the physical in an over-regard for the spiritual, because the ultimate heavenly state includes physicality. Since heaven "is not a place where a choir of disembodied spirits will gather for a perpetual concert; the groaning of creation will be answered finally in the unveiling of a glorious new creation in which God will be the focus of all things."[62] The imperfections of the earthly bodily life—in disease, weakness, infertility, sexual frustration, mental ill-health, and above all the struggle against sin—are subject to perseverance in the daily appropriation of union with the resurrection with Christ.

Closely related to the focus on the body in feminist and feminine spiritualities is the spiritual import of nature. This is different though not fully removed from the old pagan feminizing of nature as "Mother Earth."

---

61. George, *After God's Own Heart*, 206.
62. Pennings, "All of Life," 313.

Complementarian Spirituality

The critique of feminism on the dominance of the male upon the female is believed to echo the dominance of culture upon nature. Radford Ruether's work *New Women/New Earth* broke ground in connecting feminist spirituality and nature in the premise in associating the "ideological interweaving of the degradation of women with a disdain for ecology."[63] The human participation in nature is not hierarchical but one of spiritual solidarity.[64] Feminine non-fiction, such as Alice Walker's *The Color Purple* and Annie Dillard's *Pilgrim at Tinker Creek*, has been markedly instrumental in expressing this element.

> Feminist reflection is characterized by an ecological point of view, which is rooted in the understanding of persons as psycho-somatic unities ... [consequently] feminists have called for the development of a non-exploitative technology which is in harmony with nature ... respect[ing] the order of the universe that is the very possibility of human existence. The physical world nurtures us physically and spiritually, for its beauty has the effect of purifying us.[65]

Valerie Lesniak suggests that this new mantra of nature being inherently sacred has enabled a change in human perception of the earth: "as we learn more about the story of earth, our own spiritual story changes. We are more conscious of our own interdependency on the planet and the effects of our lifestyle upon the continuance of the planet for future generations."[66]

Whereas feminist and other current spiritualities consider human interaction with nature to be participatory and egalitarian, a Reformed theocentric perception of nature, which sees it to be essentially "creation," supposes humanity to have a biblical viceroy role with the earth. Any exploitative action or passive irresponsibility is owing to the sinful condition of humanity and lack of regard for the Creator. A Reformed feminine spirituality then cares and tends for the earth, in a way similar to her own physicality, awaiting its eschatological renewal. Her stewardship is a holy thing for which she is held divinely accountable. Cornick writes of Reformed aesthetics, "The beauty of creation is to be enjoyed and delighted in" directing "attention to the Giver, and thanksgiving to 'the author.'"[67] Her interaction with creation is also stimulatory since creation continually

---

63. Yates, "Spirituality and the American Feminist Experience," 62.
64. Clifford, "Feminist Spirituality."
65. Eaton, "Weil and Feminist Spirituality," 701.
66. Lesniak, "Contemporary Spirituality," 11.
67. Cornick, *Letting God*, 113.

declares the glory, sovereignty, and genius of God and thus excites her to worship and praise.

The Corporate Movement: Family–Church–Society

Feminism, of course, had its conception in the act of social protest, and its desire for social change is essentially a challenge of patriarchal structures. Notably, this feature renders feminist thought inherently corporate in its concern for public policy and "corporate actions that bear ethical significance."[68] Certainly, global society has gained a lot from feminist action in response to world poverty, slavery, philanthropy, human rights, and ecological concern and development. The spiritual dimension of feminist activism is palpable when activists place it into a spiritual setting of spiritual interconnection in relation to self, the giving a sense of holism and self-worth, to God and to the others she is helping.[69] The spiritual empowerment of feminist spirituality from patriarchy is also related to empowerment for societal reform.

If feminism is "revolutionary" in nature, then the Reformed tradition is "reforming" in nature. Of course, the mammoth area for reform, perhaps more than the home and the church, is that of society. "Reformed spirituality is about public space as well as liturgical space, about the 'theatre' of God's glory, the world."[70] Beeke and Phillip Arthur agree that contemporary Reformed Christians must "recover their Calvinistic vision" by stepping out into society and fulfilling corporate Reformed obligations there as well as in the local church.[71] Pennings agrees that "to discourage any form of civic involvement, however, is to depart from a rich Reformed heritage," yet in recent times Reformed leaders and Christians have dismissed any belief in civil service and activism to be a religious duty.[72] Reformed spirituality as a whole should not be partisan to the self-absorption, withdrawal, and narcissism long attributed to social conservatism.

The prominence that the Reformers placed upon the family unit "may be described as the heyday of patriarchal nuclear family, " as the exaltation of marriage rendered it the "foundation and nucleus of society and

---

68. Yates, "Spirituality and the American Feminist Experience," 60.
69. Faver, "To Run and Not Grow Weary."
70. Cornick, *Letting God*, 110.
71. Beeke, "Family," 344.
72. Pennings, "Political Ministers," 365

Complementarian Spirituality

the divine instrument for its stability and reform."[73] Thus, contemporary Christian marriages and families are to instruct and stabilize society. This means that the ministry skills that God has given to Reformed women are not just for themselves or their family, homes, and local Body, but also the Reformed corporate ethic moves from the church into society. This should be apparent in vocation, community service, and political activism. Ray Pennings states that a lack of corporate Reformed vision is evident in church life:

> Today it is common, even in Calvinistic churches, to hear questions of vocation addressed primarily in personal terms. Careers are viewed in the context of personal gifts and passions, as well as the rewards and opportunities those occupations provide. What is missing from such an analysis is the weight of the 'common good.' Calvin employs the 'body' language of the New Testament not only to speak of the church, *but also to describe the Christian obligation to neighbours and society at large.*[74]

Thus, a holistic Reformed feminine spirituality, as it makes the corporate movement from family to church and then to society in general, must be seeking a societal reform that reflects the justice of God and better serves the community in which one lives. This means that Reformed feminine spirituality, in its nature of as "other preferring," and particularly in its Trinitarian qualities, may self-sacrificially strive for reform in an area that does not necessarily serve oneself or the lives of one's children. An authentic corporate Reformed feminine spirituality possesses a thoroughly Calvinistic vision to glorify Christ and be the means of his common grace in the world. The corporate concern of seeking societal reform demonstrates a mature and rigorous personal spiritual life of worship to Christ as King.

Reformed women with the appropriate giftings have the duty to steward them in social action and see this as a spiritual act of obedience. Such women serve administratively and practically in a type of feminine diaconate ministry in the home and perhaps in the church, and this does not preclude society. As Lovelace observes that "some popular and fruitful Protestant models of spirituality have made little effort to include bridges between interior spiritual development and responsible engagement with

---

73. Ozment, *Family Life in Reformation Europe*, 2, 8–9.
74. Pennings, "Working," 355.

society and culture," a Reformed feminine spirituality appreciates the fruit of personal spiritual development in service to societal community.[75]

A Reformed feminine spirituality of social engagement appreciates that the state is under God's sovereign rule and her Christian duty is to serve as God's vicereine. Her role in the family and in the church encompasses this but she is not forbidden to venture into the public sphere. Indeed, her love for Christ and appreciation for his beauty produces a desire to see the latter reflected in the world. "The rapture of passion is converted into sustained work . . . whoever loves God, will take a passionate interest in the state of God's affairs in the whole world, and attempt to further their progress in every field."[76]

One extremely valuable feminine expression of a Trinitarian Reformed corporate ethic impacting contemporary society in the role of spiritual vicereine is that of American Reformed Carolyn McCulley, an authoress and active church worker who is founder of Citygate Films. Her "filmanthropy" company produces short films to document and report on issues neglected in mainstream media, particularly third-world poverty. Another very different example is a British Reformed woman known by the current author who now in retirement years serves voluntarily as a Magistrate in her local civil authority. The opening of public office to women in Britain and North America, and the little Christian representation or values in government, calls for Reformed women to formalize their role as vicereine in the political arena to the glory of God.

Reflexive

Feminist spirituality seeks self-awareness and identity in order to free oneself from oppressive structures. Through this reflective "vital, active energizing interior perception" the self is connected with all areas of life and experience.[77] This reflection is expressive or contemplative as well as critical of external powers upon the self.

> As a style of response, spirituality is individually patterned yet culturally shaped. Implicit metaphors, images, or stories drawn from our culture are embodied in a particular style; these can be made explicit through reflection, journal keeping and conversation with friends, or therapy. We each live a personal story . . . When our

---

75. Lovelace, *Dynamics*, 17.
76. Bockmuehl, "Great Commandment," 13.
77. Yates, "Spirituality," 60.

myths are made conscious, we can affirm or deny them, accept parts and reject others, as we grow in relationship to God, to others, to our world.[78]

A Reformed feminine spirituality, in the air of *semper reformanda*, is critically self-reflexive as it considers sinful habits and tendencies that inhibit holiness and areas of weakness or omission in order to constantly reform itself and mortify sin. The devotional life of adoration, joy, thanksgiving, and praise to God for salvation in Christ and the disciplines of bible study, prayer, intercession, fasting, Christian witness, tithing, repentance, and service to the Body are reflected upon, and where repentance is due the believer engages in it fully and wholeheartedly. The believer also considers her relationship with others and asks the Holy Spirit for assistance in love, submission, humility, grace, and forgiveness. A Reformed feminine spirituality makes good use of meditating and praying around the seven feminine virtues in Titus 2:4–5, particularly questioning whether she is sufficiently loving her husband, if she is married, and her children if she is a mother. Similarly, the fruits of the Spirit in Galatians 5:22–23 are another scriptural tool to focus this self-reflection. She is critical about her lifestyle in areas such as purity, thought life, finances, contentment, use of words and time, self-control, justice issues, responsibility to society, adhering to the law, and work ethics (whether in the home or in the workplace), questioning whether these spheres of her life are bringing glory God.

Watchful that it does not become overly self-abasing or insular, this reflection is executed in the freeing knowledge of sufficient grace (*sola gratia*) and for spiritual progress in Christ. This self-reflexive practice is expressed in writing in a personal journal or prayer diary, or online blogging, through personal meditation, and, in some degree, through intimate conversation with others.

In summary, this study has proposed that the distinctively feminine mode of personal Reformed spirituality above, anchored in corporate expression of the Body in chapter 5, might encourage Reformed spirituality to a higher interest in experiential expressions of Christian living, moving the tradition in its contemporary mode closer towards a biblical balance. Since "religion which God requires, and will accept, does not consist in weak, dull and lifeless wishes, raising us but a little above a state of indifference;

---

78. Carr, "Feminist Spirituality," 380.

A Reformed Feminine Spirituality

God, in His word, greatly insists upon it, that we be in good earnest, 'fervent in spirit,' and our hearts vigorously engaged in religion."[79]

CONCLUSION

In conclusion, this discourse has self-critically assessed the place of women in the Reformed tradition and suggested an intentional use of women in church life and a conscious integration of a pastoral practice that considers unique feminine experience. In the climate of today, "the crisis of womanhood is too critical for the church to be passive" and "scores of evangelical women are functional feminists, because the world's paradigm for womanhood is the only one they have heard. The church should lead the way in equipping God's people to think biblically about all of life, including a biblical perspective of gender roles and relationships."[80] Upon implementation, the Reformed church will affirm its complementarian framework as well as effectively model a corporate spirituality of the Body anchored in shared union with Christ.

In accordance with its rationale to contribute helpfully to the pastoral needs of Christian women in Reformed churches and stimulate an increased experiential enjoyment of Christ in personal spirituality, this work has also presented an innovative sample of contemporary Reformed feminine spirituality. However, Reformed female scholars need to take this further since the discourse above is largely introductory.

In noting the dearth of contemporary Reformed discourse on spirituality and the need for further vibrant experiential expressions in the tradition, we have attempted a contribution to a corporate and personal expression anchored on the doctrine of union with Christ that is distinctively Reformed and uniquely feminine. It is in this manner that this project has sought to respond to the lack of academic contributions from Reformed women and these other shortcomings, whilst presenting an innovative sample of a Reformed feminine spirituality that may stimulate further academic discourse.

In conclusion, the doctrine of union with Christ is the central basis of salvation and experiential enjoyment of Christ in the Christian life. Within the empirical realms of this doctrine, Reformed corporate and personal spirituality can find renewed life and growth as it is appropriated in the life of the believer. We conclude that a rewarding, vigorous Christian

79. Edwards, *Affections*, 27.
80. Duncan and Hunt, *Women's Ministry*, 42.

experience can be enjoyed by both men and women in the integration of a relational and responsible shared union with Christ in the Body, and, with a particular feminine nuance, a personal spiritual aesthetic towards the person of Christ as Spouse.

Additionally, this project concludes that within some strands of the Reformed tradition, conservative "man-centered" church practice needs to be readdressed in light of the diverse and distinctive female perspective and experience. Our self-critical assessment of the tradition verified the need to sharpen Reformed complementarian belief by taking into account the unique spiritual, pastoral, and ministerial input of women and subsequently widening modes of female leadership in the church, such as the role of deacon or even an ordained role for an exclusive women's ministry.

Areas for Development

There are many areas that this project has merely touched upon that lie open for development. Our research has highlighted an indigence of interaction by Reformed scholars with the subject of spirituality, especially in the employment of a doctrinal approach. As the academic discipline of spirituality gains ground, mirrored in popular movement in spirituality, Reformed scholars cannot afford to dismiss spirituality's contemporary import.

It is suggested that there is considerable need for further biblical and contemporary articulations of Reformed spirituality that make full use of features peculiar to the recent spirituality movement. Such Reformed perspectives that do not stray from Scripture but satisfy the postmodern believer will undermine frustrations that have led some to look to other spiritual traditions. In addition, Reformed articulations that apologetically dialogue with contemporary spiritualities, both secular and religious, will improve the profile of the tradition, moving it from its seemingly fringe and stigmatized position. This could strengthen Reformed spirituality and its place in contemporary society as well as in academia.

Our doctrinal outline highlighted the strong Trinitarianism of Reformed theology and the pneumatic-christological features of the *unio mystica*. Reformed thought has much to offer on a Trinitarian expression of the Christian life that has not yet been fully explored. Further, the biblical personhood and role of the Holy Spirit in Reformed spirituality is in need of attention in light of the Charismatic overemphasis. These doctrines can be developed directly towards the Christian life and their relationship to the practical matters of repentance, prayer, church life, and the sacraments, for example. The frequent observations in this project regarding the widespread influences of Evangelical spirituality might be subject to development, wherein a detailed analysis might detect certain areas where a Reformed appreciation is under threat.

Further development of this work may require thorough academic engagement with feminist spirituality. The Reformed tradition, with its distinctive complementarian stance and holistic Calvinistic worldview with its desire for reform, might gain insightfully from further dialogue with feminist expressions. Here, this study concludes that it is especially imperative to encourage Reformed women to take up academic theological pursuit in these areas, helping to give Reformed women more of a voice in the tradition.

In addition and related to this, we have only touched on female insights and expectations in spirituality and the issue of female pastoral care. There is opportunity to develop a Reformed practice of pastoral care that is specifically mindful of spirituality in its expression and practice. This might delve into the complementary features in the two genders and the implications therein for church ministry and practice.

Bibliography

Adam, Peter. *Hearing God's Words: Exploring Biblical Spirituality*. Downers Grove, IL: InterVarsity, 2004.
Adams, Jay E. *Shepherding God's Flock: The Pastoral Life*. 1974. Reprint, Grand Rapids: Baker, 1975.
Albanese, Catherine L. Review of *Feminine Spirituality in America: From Sarah Edwards to Martha Graham* by Amanda Porterfiled. *JR* 62:1 (1982) 83–84.
Albin, T. R. "Spirituality." In *NDT*, 656–58.
Alsup, Wendy Horger. *Practical Theology for Women*. Wheaton, IL: Crossway, 2008.
Anderson, Marvin W. "Peter Martyr, Reformed Theologian (1542–1562): His Letters to Heinrich Bullinger and John Calvin." *TSCJ* 4:1 (1973) 41–64.
Aquinas, Thomas. *Summa Theologica: A Concise Translation*. Edited by Timothy McDermott. Notre Dame, IN: Ave Maria, 1989.
Ash, Christopher. *Marriage: Sex in the Service of God*. Leicester: InterVarsity, 2003.
Athanasius. *On the Incarnation of the Word of God*, 8:54. Online: http://www.ccel.org/ccel/athanasius/incarnation.ix.html.
Augustine. *De Trinitate*, 4.14.19. In *NPNF*. Online: http://www.ccel.org/ccel/schaff/npnf103.iv.i.vi.xv.html.
Baker, J. P. "Union with Christ." In *NDT*, 697–99.
Barth, Karl. *Church Dogmatics*, II/2. Edited by T. F. Torrance and G. W. Bromiley. Edinburgh: T. & T. Clark, 1985.
———. *Church Dogmatics*, IV/3. Edited by T. F. Torrance and G. W. Bromiley. Edinburgh: T. & T. Clark, 1985.
Bavinck, Herman. *Reformed Dogmatics*, vol. 3: *Sin and Salvation in Christ*. Edited by John Bolt, translated by John Vriend. Grand Rapids: Baker Academic, 2006.
Baxter, Richard. "The Poor Man's Family Book." In *The Practical Works of Richard Baxter*, 4:230–31. Morgan, PA: Soli Deo Gloria, 1996.
Bebbington, David. *Evangelicalism in Modern Britain: A History from the 1730s to the 1980s*. Grand Rapids: Baker, 1989.
Beckwith, R. T. "Eucharist." In *NDT*, 236–38.
Beeke, Joel R. "Applying the Word." In *Living for God's Glory: An Introduction to Calvinism*, edited by Joel R. Beeke, 255–74. Orlando: Reformation Trust, 2008.
———. "The Puritan Family." In *Living for God's Glory: An Introduction to Calvinism*, edited by Joel R. Beeke, 333–48. Orlando: Reformation Trust, 2008.
———. *Puritan Reformed Spirituality*. Darlington, UK: Evangelical Press, 2006.
———. "Seeing God's Glory." In *Reformed Spirituality*, edited by Joseph A. Pipa and J. Andrew Wortman, 19–28. Taylors, SC: Southern Presbyterian, 2003.
Beeke, Joel R., and Sinclair B. Ferguson, editors. "Union with Christ and the Communion of the Saints." In *Reformed Confessions Harmonised with an Annotated Bibliography*

Bibliography

of *Reformed Doctrinal Works*, edited by Joel R. Beeke and Sinclair B. Ferguson, 196–97. Grand Rapids: Baker, 1999.

Benton, John. "Husband and Wife—and the Church." In *Men, Women, and Authority: Serving Together in the Church*, edited by Brian Edwards, 160–71. Leominster, UK: DayOne, 1996.

Berkhof, Louis. *Systematic Theology*. London: Banner of Truth, 1939.

Berkouwer, G. C. *The Sacraments*. Studies in Dogmatics 10. Grand Rapids: Eerdmans, 1969.

Beynon, Graham. *God's New Community: New Testament Patterns for Today's Church*. Leicester: InterVarsity, 2005.

Billings, J. Todd. *Calvin, Participation, and the Gift: The Activity of Believers in Union with Christ*. New York: Oxford University Press, 2007.

Bloesch, Donald G.

The Church: Sacraments, Worship, Ministry, Mission. Christian Foundations. Downers Grove, IL: InterVarsity, 2002.

———. *The Crisis of Piety*. Grand Rapids: Eerdmans, 1968.

———. *Spirituality Old and New: Recovering Authentic Spiritual Life*. Nottingham: Apollos, 2007.

Bockmuehl, Klaus. "The Great Commandment." In *With Heart, Mind & Strength: The Best of CRUX, 1978–1989*, edited by Donald M. Lewis and J. I. Packer, 1:9–26. Langley, BC: Credo, 1990.

Boice, James Montgomery. *Foundations of the Christian Faith*. Downers Grove, IL: InterVarsity, 1986.

Bonner, Gerald. "Deification, Divinization." In *Augustine through the Ages: An Encyclopaedia*, edited by Allan D. Fitzgerald, 265–66. Grand Rapids: Eerdmans, 1999.

Braaten, Carl E., and Robert W. Jenson. *Union with Christ: The New Finnish Interpretation of Luther*. Grand Rapids: Eerdmans, 1998.

Bray, G. L. "Deification." In *NDT*, 189–90.

Brestin, Dee, and Kathy Troccoli. *Falling in Love with Jesus: Abandoning Yourself to the Greatest Romance of Your Life*. Nashville: Word, 2000.

———. *Forever in Love with Jesus*. Nashville: Word, 2004.

———. *Living in Love with Jesus: Clothed in the Colors of His Love*. Nashville: Word, 2002.

Bruce, F. F. *The Epistle to the Ephesians*. London: Pickering & Inglis, 1961.

Calvin, John. *Calvin's Wisdom: An Anthology Arranged Alphabetically*. Edited by Graham Miller. Carlisle, PA: Banner of Truth, 1992.

———. *Institutes of the Christian Religion*. Edited by John T. McNeill, translated by Ford L. Battles. Louisville: Westminster John Knox, 2006.

———. *Treatises on the Sacraments*. Translated by Henry Beveridge. Fearn, Scotland: Christian Focus, 2002.

Carpenter, Craig B. "A Question of Union with Christ? Calvin and Trent on Justification." *WTJ* 64:2 (2002) 363–86.

Carr, Anne. E. "On Feminist Spirituality." In *Exploring Christian Spirituality: An Ecumenical Reader*, edited by Kenneth J. Collins, 379–86. Grand Rapids: Baker, 2000.

———. *Transforming Grace: Christian Tradition and Women's Experience*. New York: Continuum, 1996.

Carson, D. A. *The Gagging of God: Christianity Confronts Pluralism*. Leicester: Apollos, 1996.

Cates, Diana Fritz. Review of *Upheavals of Thought* by Martha C. Nussbaum. *JRE* 31:2 (2003) 325-41.
Catherwood, Elizabeth. "The Role of Women in the Local Church." In *Social Issues and the Church*, edited by Ian Shaw, 119-33. Bridgend: Evangelical Press of Wales, 1988.
Christian Hymns. 2nd ed. Bridgend: Evangelical Movement of Wales, 2004.
Clancy, Finbarr G. "Redemption." In *Augustine Through the Ages: An Encyclopaedia*, edited by Allan D. Fitzgerald, 702-4. Grand Rapids: Eerdmans, 1999.
Clark, R. Scott. "Election and Predestination: The Sovereign Expressions of God." In *A Theological Guide to Calvin's Institutes: Essays and Analysis*, edited by David W. Hall and Peter A. Lillback, 90-122. The Calvin 500 Series. Phillipsburg, NJ: P & R, 2008.
———. *Recovering the Reformed Confessions: Our Theology, Piety, and Practice*. Phillipsburg, NJ: P & R, 2008.
Clifford, Anne M. "Feminist Spirituality." In *NWDCS*, 298-301.
Clowney, Edmund P. *The Church*. Contours of Christian Theology. Downers Grove, IL: InterVarsity, 1995.
Collins, Raymond F. *1 & 2 Timothy and Titus: A Commentary*. NTL. Louisville: Westminster John Knox, 2002.
Cook, Faith. *Grace in Winter: Rutherford in Verse*. Edinburgh: Banner of Truth, 1989.
Cornick, David. *Letting God Be God: The Reformed Tradition*. London: Darton, Longman & Todd, 2008.
———. "Reformed Spirituality." In *NWDCS*, 533-35.
Cornish, Carol W. "Counseling Women Married to Unbelievers." In *Women Helping Women*, edited by Elyse Fitzpatrick and Carol W. Cornish, 205-231. Eugene, OR: Harvest House, 1997.
———. "Why Women Should Counsel Women." In *Women Helping Women*, edited by Elyse Fitzpatrick and Carol W. Cornish. 85-108. Eugene, OR: Harvest House, 1997.
Cousins, Ewart. "Foreword." In *Contemporary Spiritualities: Social and Religious Contexts*, edited by Clive and Jane Erricker, xi-xiii. London: Continuum, 2001.
Dabney, R. L. "Union to Christ." Online: http://www.mbrem123.com/life/dabunion.php.htm
Davies, J. Elwyn. "The Marriage Covenant." In *Christian Family Matters*, edited by Ian Shaw, 29-47. Bridgend: Evangelical Press of Wales, 1985.
Davies, Thomas J. *This Is My Body: The Presence of Christ in Reformation Thought*. Grand Rapids: Baker Academic, 2008.
Delattre, Roland A. "Aesthetics and Ethics: Jonathan Edwards and the Recovery of Aesthetics for Religious Ethics." *JRE* 31:2 (2003) 277-97.
Del Colle, Ralph. *Christ and the Spirit: Spirit-Christology in Trinitarian Perspective*. New York: Oxford University Press, 1994.
De Witt, John R. *What Is the Reformed Faith?* Edinburgh: Banner of Truth, 1981.
Dillow, Linda. *Satisfy My Thirsty Soul*. Colorado Springs, CO: NavPress, 2007.
Dinnen, Stewart. *Learning about Union with Christ*. Fearn, Scotland: Christian Focus, 2000.
Dixon, Thomas. *From Passions to Emotions: The Creation of a Secular Psychological Category*. New York: Cambridge University Press, 2003.
Donnelly, Edward. *Life in Christ*. Bridgend: Bryntirion, 2007.
Dossey, Barbara M. *Florence Nightingale: Mystic, Visionary and Healer*. Philadelphia: Springhouse, 1999.
Douty, Norman F. *Union with Christ*. Swengel, PA: Reiner, 1973.

Bibliography

Duncan, J. Ligon, and Susan Hunt. *Women's Ministry in the Local Church.* Wheaton, IL: Crossway, 2006.

Dyrness, William A. *Reformed Theology and Visual Culture: The Protestant Imagination from Calvin to Edwards.* New York: Cambridge University Press, 2004.

Eaton, Jeffery C. "Simone Weil and Feminist Spirituality." *JAAR* 54:4 (1986) 691–704.

Edwards, Jonathan. *The Religious Affections.* 1746. Reprint, Edinburgh: Banner of Truth, 1986.

Eskridge, Larry. "Defining Evangelicalism." 2006. Online: http://www2.wheaton.edu/isae/defining_evangelicalism.html

Evans, William B. *Imputation and Impartation: Union with Christ in American Reformed Theology.* Milton Keynes: Paternoster, 2008.

Faver, Catherine A. "To Run and Not Grow Weary: Spirituality and Women's Activism." *RRelRes* 42:1 (2000) 61–78.

Fee, Gordon D. *1 and 2 Timothy, Titus.* New International Biblical Commentary 13. Peabody, MA: Hendrickson, 1988.

———. *The Holy Spirit.* Contours of Christian Theology. Leicester, UK: InterVarsity, 1996.

Fischer, Kathleen. *Reclaiming the Connections: A Contemporary Spirituality.* Kansas City: Sheed & Ward, 1990.

Flavel, John. "Sermon 2 on John 17:23." In *The Works of John Flavel*, 2:33–49. London: Banner of Truth, 1968.

Foh, Susan T. *Women and the Word of God: A Response to Biblical Feminism.* Phillipsburg, NJ: P & R, 1979.

Gaffin, Richard B. "Justification and Union with Christ (3.11–18)." In *A Theological Guide to Calvin's Institutes*, edited by David W. Hall and Peter A. Lillback, 248–69. Phillipsburg, NJ: P & R, 2008.

———. *Resurrection and Redemption: A Study in Paul's Soteriology.* Phillipsburg, NJ: P & R, 1987.

Garcia, Mark A. *Life in Christ: Union with Christ and Twofold Grace in Calvin's Theology.* Milton Keynes: Paternoster, 2008.

Garlington, Don. "Imputation or Union with Christ?: A Response to John Piper." *RAR* 12:4 (2003) 45–102.

George, Elizabeth. *A Woman after God's Own Heart.* 2nd ed. Eugene, OR: Harvest House, 2006.

Gordon, A. J. *In Christ; or, The Believer's Union with His Lord.* Michigan Historical Reprint Series. Ann Arbor: University of Michigan Library, 2008.

Green, Michael, and R. Paul Stevens. *New Testament Spirituality.* Guildford, UK: Eagle, 1994.

Grudem, Wayne. *Systematic Theology: An Introduction to Biblical Doctrine.* Leicester: InterVarsity, 2004.

———. "Wives Like Sarah, and the Husbands Who Honor Them: 1 Peter 3:1–7." In *Recovering Biblical Manhood and Womanhood: A Response to Evangelical Feminism*, edited by John Piper and Wayne Grudem, 194–208. 2nd ed. Wheaton, IL: Crossway, 2006.

Gustafson, Sandra. "Jonathan Edwards and the Reconstruction of 'Feminine' Speech." *ALH* 6:2 (1994) 185–212.

Guthrie, Donald. *New Testament Theology.* Leicester: InterVarsity, 1981.

———. *The Pastoral Epistles: An Introduction and Commentary.* Tyndale New Testament Commentaries. Leicester: InterVarsity, 1990.

Hageman, Howard. "Reformed Spirituality." In *Exploring Christian Spirituality: An Ecumenical Reader*, edited by Kenneth J. Collins, 138–57. Grand Rapids: Baker, 2000.

Hamilton, Ian. "Experiential Calvinism." In *Reformed Spirituality*, edited by Joseph A. Pipa and J. Andrew Wortman, 29–41. Taylors, SC: Southern Presbyterian, 2003.

Heelas, Paul, and Linda Woodhead. *The Spiritual Revolution: Why Religion is Giving Way to Spirituality*. Religion and Spirituality in the Modern World. Oxford: Blackwell, 2005.

Helm, Paul. "Calvin, A. M. Toplady and the Bebbington Thesis." In *The Emergence of Evangelicalism: Exploring Historical Continuities*, edited by Michael A. G. Haykin and Kenneth J. Stewart, 199–220. Nottingham: Apollos, 2008.

Hendriksen, William. *New Testament Commentary: Ephesians*. London: Banner of Truth, 1972.

Hesselink, John. "Reformed View." In *Understanding Four Views on the Lord's Supper*, edited by Paul E. Engle and John H. Armstrong, 59–71. Counterpoints: Church Life. Grand Rapids: Zondervan, 2007.

Hodge, A. A. *Outlines of Theology*. London: T. Nelson, 1880.

———. "The Presence of Christ at the Lord's Supper." Online: http://www.graceonlinelibrary.org/church-ministry/lords-supper/the-presence-of-christ-at-the-lords-supper-by-a-a-hodge/.

Hodge, Charles. "Idea of the Church." *Biblical Repertory and Princeton Review* 25 (1853) 249–90, 339–89.

Hoehner, Harold W. *Ephesians: An Exegetical Commentary*. Grand Rapids: Baker Academic, 2002.

Hoeksema, Herman. *Reformed Dogmatics*. Grand Rapids: Reformed Free, 1966.

Hogan, Linda. *From Women's Experience to Feminist Theology*. Sheffield: Sheffield Academic, 1997.

Horton, Michael S. *Covenant and Salvation: Union with Christ*. Louisville: Westminster John Knox, 2007.

———. *In the Face of God*. Dallas: Word, 1996.

Hughes, R. Kent, and Bryan Chapell. *1 & 2 Timothy and Titus: To Guard the Deposit*. Wheaton, IL: Crossway, 2000.

———. "Union with Christ."1992. Online: http://www.monergism.com/thethreshold/articles/questions/horton/union.html

James, Carolyn Custis. *When Life and Beliefs Collide: How Knowing God Makes a Difference*. Grand Rapids: Zondervan, 2001.

James, Sharon. "Women and the Church." *Table Talk* 18 (2006). Online: http://www.affinity.org.uk/downloads/publications/TT18_autumn_2006.pdf .

Johnston, Mark. "Where Are We Today?" In *Men, Women and Authority: Serving Together in the Church*, edited by Brian Edwards, 4–19. Leominster, UK: DayOne, 1996.

Jones, Owain W. "Welsh Spirituality." In *WDCS*, 392–94.

Jones, Rebecca. *Does Christianity Squash Women?* Nashville: Broadman & Holman, 2005.

Jones, R. Tudur. "Union with Christ: The Existential Nerve of Puritan Piety." *TynBul* 41:2 (1990) 186–208.

Kay, Brian. *Trinitarian Spirituality: John Owen and the Doctrine of God in Western Devotion*. Milton Keynes: Paternoster, 2007.

Kelly, Douglas F. *Systematic Theology: Grounded in Holy Scripture and Understood in the Light of the Church*. Vol. 1. Fearn, Scotland: Mentor, 2008.

Bibliography

Kevan, Ernest F. *The Grace of Law: A Study in Puritan Theology*. Morgan, PA: Soli Deo Gloria, 1993.

Knight III, George W. "Husbands and Wives as Analogues of Christ and the Church: Ephesians 5:21–33 and Colossians 3:18–19." In *Recovering Biblical Manhood and Womanhood: A Response to Evangelical Feminism*, edited by John Piper and Wayne Grudem, 165–78. 2nd ed. Wheaton, IL: Crossway, 2006.

Kreider, Eleanor. *Given for You: A Fresh Look at Communion*. Leicester: InterVarsity, 1998.

Kruse, Colin G. *Paul, the Law and Justification*. Leicester: Apollos, 1996.

Kuiper, R. B. *The Glorious Body of Christ*. Grand Rapids: Eerdmans, 1966.

Lane, Anthony N. S. *John Calvin: Student of the Church Fathers*. Edinburgh: T. & T. Clark, 1999.

Lane, Belden C. "Calvinist Spirituality." In *NWDCS*, 162–64.

Lanning, Ray. "Foundations of Reformed Worship." In *Living for God's Glory: An Introduction to Calvinism*, edited by Joel R. Beeke, 231–44. Orlando: Reformation Trust, 2008.

Lauritzen, Paul. "Emotions and Religious Ethics." *JRE* 16:2 (1988) 307–24.

Lee, Kye Won. *Living in Union with Christ: The Practical Theology of Thomas F. Torrance*. Issues in Systematic Theology 5.11. Oxford: P. Lang: 2003.

Lesniak, Valerine. "Contemporary Spirituality." In *NWDCS*, 7–12.

Letham, Robert. *The Holy Trinity: In Scripture, History, Theology, and Worship*. Phillipsburg, NJ: P & R, 2004.

———. *The Lord's Supper: Eternal Word in Broken Bread*. Phillipsburg, NJ: P & R, 2001.

———. "Reformed Theology." In *NDT*, 569–72.

———. *Through Western Eyes: Eastern Orthodoxy: A Reformed Perspective*. Fearn, Scotland: Mentor, 2007.

———. *Union with Christ: In Scripture, History, and Theology*. Phillipsburg, NJ: P & R, 2011.

———. *The Westminster Assembly: Reading Its Theology in Historical Context*. Phillipsburg, NJ: P & R, 2009.

———. *The Work of Christ*. Contours of Christian Theology. Leicester: InterVarsity, 1993.

Lewis, Paul. "'The Springs of Motion': Jonathan Edwards on Emotions, Character, and Agency." *JRE* 22:2 (1994) 275–97.

Lorde, Audre. "Uses of the Erotic." In *Weaving the Visions: New Patterns in Feminist Spirituality*, edited by Judith Plaskow and Carol P. Christ, 208–13. San Francisco: Harper & Row, 1989.

Lossky, Vladimir. *The Mystical Theology of the Eastern Church*. Crestwood, NY: St. Vladimir's Seminary Press, 1976.

Lovelace, Richard F. *Dynamics of Spiritual Life: An Evangelical Theology of Renewal*. Downers Grove, IL: InterVarsity, 1972.

———. "Evangelical Spirituality." In *Exploring Christian Spirituality: An Ecumenical Reader*, edited by Kenneth J. Collins, 214–26. Grand Rapids: Baker, 2000.

Luo, Michael. "Evangelicals Debate the Meaning of 'Evangelical.'" *New York Times*, Week in Review, April 16, 2006. Online: http://www.nytimes.com/2006/04/16/weekinreview/16luo.html

Luther, Martin. "The Freedom of a Christian." In *Luther's Works*, edited by Jaroslav Pelikan and Helmut T. Lehmann, vol. 31, *Career of the Reformer* 1, 333–77. Philadelphia: Fortress, 1955–86.

Mahaney, Carolyn. *Feminine Appeal: Seven Virtues of a Godly Wife and Mother*. Wheaton, IL: Crossway, 2004.
Mallard, William. "Jesus Christ." In *Augustine Through the Ages: An Encyclopaedia*, edited by Allan D. Fitzgerald, 463-70. Grand Rapids: Eerdmans, 1999.
Mannermaa, Tuomo. "Why Is Luther So Fascinating?" In *Union with Christ: The New Finnish Interpretation of Luther*, edited by Carl E. Braaten and Robert W. Jenson, 1-20. Grand Rapids: Eerdmans, 1998.
Marquart, Kurt E. "Luther and Theosis." CTQ 64:3 (2000) 186-205.
Mathews, Alice. *Preaching that Speaks to Women*. Leicester: InterVarsity, 2003.
McGinn, Bernard. "The Changing Shape of Late Medieval Mysticism." CH 65:2 (1996) 197-219.
———. *The Flowering of Mysticism: Men and Women in the New Mysticism (1200-1350)*. Vol. 3 of *The Presence of God: A History of Western Christian Mysticism*. New York: Crossroad, 1998.
McGoldrick, James E. "Calvin's Spirituality." In *Reformed Spirituality*, edited by Joseph A. Pipa and J. Andrew Wortman, 43-60. Taylors, SC: Southern Presbyterian, 2003.
McGrath, Alister. *Christian Spirituality: An Introduction*. Oxford: Blackwell, 1999.
———. *Iustitua Dei: A History of the Christian Doctrine of Justification*. New York: Cambridge University Press, 1986.
———. *Roots that Refresh: A Celebration of Reformation Spirituality*. London: Hodder & Stoughton, 1991.
Meilaender, G. C. "Sexuality." In NDCEPT (1995) 71-78.
Metzger, Paul L. "Luther and the Finnish School: Mystical Union with Christ: An Alternative to Blood Transfusions and Legal Fictions." WTJ 65:2 (2003) 201-12.
Morgan, D. Densil. *The SPCK Introduction to Karl Barth*. London: SPCK, 2010.
Muddiman, John. *The Epistle to the Ephesians*. London: Continuum, 2001.
Muller, Richard A. *After Calvin: Studies in the Development of a Theological Tradition*. New York: Oxford University Press, 2003.
Murray, John. *Christian Baptism*. Phillipsburg, NJ: P & R, 1962.
———. *Redemption: Accomplished and Applied*. London: Banner of Truth, 1961.
———. *Systematic Theology*. Vol. 2 of *Collected Writings of John Murray*. Edinburgh: Banner of Truth, 1977.
———. "Systematic Theology: Second Article." WTJ 26:1 (1963) 33-46.
Mursell, George. *English Spirituality: From Earliest Times to 1700*. London: SPCK, 2008.
———. *English Spirituality: From 1700 to the Present Day*. London: SPCK, 2008.
Nava, Alexander. *The Mystical and Prophetic Thought of Simone Weil and Gustavo Gutiérrez*. Albany, NY: SUNY Press, 2001.
Neu, Diann L. "Women's Empowerment hrough Feminist Ritual." In *Women's Spirituality, Women's Lives*, edited by Judith Ochshorn and Ellen Cole, 185-200. New York: Haworth, 1995.
Nevin, John Williamson. *The Mystical Presence: A Vindication of the Reformed or Calvinistic Doctrine of the Holy Eucharist*. Eugene, OR: Wipf & Stock, 2000.
Niesel, Wilhelm. *Reformed Symbolics*. Edinburgh: Oliver & Boyd, 1962.
Nussbaum, Martha C. *Upheavals of Thought: The Intelligence of Emotions*. New York: Cambridge University Press, 2001.
Owen, J. *The Works of John Owen*. Vol. 2. Edited by W. H. Goold. London: Banner of Truth, 1965-98.

Bibliography

Ozment, Steven E. *When Fathers Ruled: Family Life in Reformation Europe*. Cambridge, MA: Harvard University Press, 1983.
Packer, J. I. "Evangelical Foundations for Spirituality." in *The J. I. Packer Collection*, 227–43. Leicester: InterVarsity, 1999.
———. *Knowing God*. London: Hodder & Stoughton, 1975.
———. *A Passion for Holiness*. Nottingham: Crossway, 1992.
———. *A Quest for Godliness: The Puritan Vision of the Christian Life*. Wheaton, IL: Crossway, 1990.
Partee, Charles. "Calvin's Central Dogma Again." *TSCJ* 18:2 (1987) 191–200.
Patzia, Arthur G. *Ephesians, Colossians, Philemon*. New International Biblical Commentary 10. Peabody, MA: Hendrikson, 1990.
Peace, Martha. *Becoming a Titus 2 Woman*. Bemidji, MN: Focus, 1997.
Pennings, Ray. "Political Ministers of God." In *Living for God's Glory: An Introduction to Calvinism*, edited by Joel R. Beeke, 361–73. Orlando: Reformation Trust, 2008.
———. "A Theology for All of Life." In *Living for God's Glory: An Introduction to Calvinism*, edited by Joel R. Beeke, 303–16. Orlando: Reformation Trust, 2008.
———. "Working for God's Glory." In *Living for God's Glory: An Introduction to Calvinism*, edited by Joel R. Beeke, 349–60. Orlando: Reformation Trust, 2008.
Percy, Martyn. *Clergy: The Origin of Species*. New York: Continuum, 2006.
Perrin, David B. *Studying Christian Spirituality*. New York: Routledge, 2007.
Peterson, David. *Engaging with God: A Biblical Theology of Worship*. Leicester: Apollos, 1992.
Peterson, Eugene. *Christ Plays in Ten Thousand Places: A Conversation in Spiritual Theology*. London: Hodder & Stoughton, 2005.
Pink, A. W. *Practical Christianity*. Grand Rapids: Baker, 1991.
———. *Spiritual Union and Communion*. Lafayette, IN: Sovereign Grace, 2002.
Pipa, Joseph A. "Glory and Beauty of God." In *Reformed Spirituality*, edited by Joseph A. Pipa and J. Andrew Wortman, 1–17. Taylors, SC: Southern Presbyterian, 2003.
Piper, John. *Counted Righteous in Christ: Should We Abandon the Imputation of Christ's Righteousness?* Wheaton, IL: Crossway, 2002.
———. *Desiring God: Meditations of a Christian Hedonist*. Leicester: InterVarsity, 1996.
———. *Finally Alive: What Happens When We Are Born Again*. Fearn, Scotland: Christian Focus, 2009.
———. "A Vision of Biblical Complementarity: Manhood and Womanhood Defined According to the Bible." In *Recovering Biblical Manhood and Womanhood: A Response to Evangelical Feminism*, edited by John Piper and Wayne Grudem, 31–59. 2nd ed. Wheaton: Crossway, 2006.
Plantinga Pauw, Amy, and Serene Jones. *Feminist and Womanist Essays in Reformed Dogmatics*. Columbia Series in Reformed Theology. Louisville: Westminster John Knox, 2006.
Plaskow, Judith, and Carol P. Christ. *Weaving the Visions: New Patterns in Feminist Spirituality*. N: Harper & Row, 1989.
Porterfield, Amanda. *Feminine Spirituality in America: From Sarah Edwards to Martha Graham*. Philadelphia: Temple University Press, 1980.
Prime, Derek. *Women in the Church: A Pastoral Approach*. Cambridge: Crossway, 1992.
Principe, Walter. "Towards Defining Spirituality." In *Exploring Christian Spirituality: An Ecumenical Reader*, edited by Kenneth J. Collins, 43–59. Grand Rapids: Bakers, 2000.

Purves, Andrew. "Pastoral Theology." In *Encyclopedia of the Reformed Faith*, edited by Donald K. McKim, 271–72. Louisville: Westminster John Knox, 1992.

———. *Reconstructing Pastoral Theology: A Christological Foundation*. Louisville: Westminster John Knox, 2004.

Raiter, Michael. *Stirrings of the Soul: Evangelicals and the New Spirituality*. Surrey: Good Book Company, 2003.

Randall, Ian. *What a Friend We Have in Jesus*. London: Darton, Longman & Todd, 2005.

Reid, J. K. S. *Our Life in Christ*. London: SCM, 1963.

Reymond, Robert L. *A New Systematic Theology*. Nashville: T. Nelson, 1998.

Ridderbos, Herman. *Paul: An Outline of His Theology*. Translated by John R. De Witt. Grand Rapids: Eerdmans, 1975.

Ring, Nancy C. "Feminine Spirituality." In *WDCS*, 148–50.

Roberts, Maurice. *Union and Communion with Christ*. Grand Rapids: Reformation Heritage, 2008.

Roper, Lyndal. *The Holy Household: Women and Morals in Reformation Augsburg*. 1989. Reprint, New York: Oxford University Press, 2001.

Runcorn, David. *Spirituality Workbook: A Guide for Explorers, Pilgrims and Seekers*. London: SPCK, 2006.

Russell, Norman. *The Doctrine of Deification in the Greek Patristic Tradition*. New York: Oxford University Press, 2006.

Schaff, Phillip. "Calvin and Heshusius." In *History of the Christian Church*, vol. 8. 3rd ed. New York: C. Scribner's, 1889–1904. Online: http://www.ccel.org/ccel/schaff/hcc8.iv.xv.xvii.html.

Schneiders, Sandra. "Christian Spirituality: Definition, Methods and Types." In *NWDCS*, 1–6.

Sciretti, Michael. "Anne Dutton as Spiritual Director." 2009. Online: http://www.baylor.edu/content/services/document.php/98763.pdf.

Scougal, Henry. *The Life of God in the Soul of Man*. 2nd ed. Fearn, Scotland: Christian Focus, 2002.

Shaw, Ian. "The Bible and the Family." In *Christian Family Matters*, edited by Ian Shaw, 17–28. Bridgend: Evangelical Press of Wales, 1985.

Sheldrake, Philip. "What Is Spirituality?" In *Exploring Christian Spirituality: An Ecumenical Reader*, edited by Kenneth J. Collins, 21–42. Grand Rapids: Baker, 2000.

Sittser, Gerald L. *Love One Another: Becoming the Church Jesus Longs For*. Nottingham: InterVarsity, 2008.

Smedes, Lewis B. *Union with Christ: A Biblical View of New Life in Jesus Christ*. 2nd ed. Grand Rapids: Eerdmans, 1983.

Stackhouse, John G. *Finally Feminist: A Pragmatic Christian Understanding of Gender*. Acadia Studies in Bible and Theology. Grand Rapids: Baker, 2005.

Stetzer, Ed. *Planting New Churches in a Postmodern Age*. Nashville: Broadman & Holman, 2003.

Stewart, James S. *A Man in Christ: The Vital Elements of St. Paul's Religion*. New York: Harper, 1972.

Stokes, Allison. "Spirituality Groups." In *Dictionary of Feminist Theologies*, edited by Letty M. Russell and J. Shannon Clarkson, 272–73. London: Mowbray, 1996.

Stott, John. *Evangelical Truth: A Personal Plea for Unity, Integrity and Faithfulness*. Leicester: InterVarsity, 1999.

Bibliography

Suchocki, Marjorie Hewitt. *The Fall to Violence: Original Sin in Relational Theology.* New York: Continuum, 1994.

Tacey, David. *The Spirituality Revolution: The Emergence of Contemporary Spirituality.* New York: Brunner-Routledge, 2004.

Tamburello, Dennis E. *Union with Christ: John Calvin and the Mysticism of St. Bernard.* Louisville: Westminster John Knox, 1994.

Tautges, Paul. *Counsel One Another: A Theology of Personal Discipleship.* Leominster, UK: DayOne, 2009.

Tidball, D. J. "Practical and Pastoral Theology." In *NDCEPT*, 42–48.

Tipton, Lane G. "Union with Christ and Justification." In *Justified in Christ: God's Plan for Us in Justification*, edited by Oliphint K. Scott, 23–49. Fearn, Scotland: Mentor, 2007.

Tomm, Winne. "A Religious Philosophy of Self." In *Gender, Genre and Religion: Feminist Reflections*, edited by Morny Joy and Eva K. Neumaier-Dargyay, 239–55. Waterloo, ON: Wilfrid Laurier University Press, 1995.

Torrance, Thomas F. *The School of Faith: The Catechisms of the Reformed Church.* London: James Clark, 1959.

Torrance, Thomas F., and Robert Bruce. *The Mystery of The Lord's Supper: Sermons on the Sacrament Preached in the Kirk of Edinburgh.* 2nd ed. Fearn, Scotland: Christian Focus, 2005.

Towner, Philip H. *The Letters to Timothy and Titus.* The New International Commentary on the New Testament. Grand Rapids: Eerdmans, 2006.

Tripp, Paul David. *Instruments in the Redeemer's Hands.* Phillipsburg, NJ: P & R, 2002.

Trueman, Carl R. "Is the Finnish Line a New Beginning?: A Critical Assessment of the Reading of Luther Offered by the Helsinki Circle." *WTJ* 65 (2003) 231–44.

Tyson, Diane A. "Counseling Divorced Women and Single Moms." In *Women Helping Women*, edited by Elyse Fitzpatrick and Carol W. Cornish, 311–37. Eugene, OR: Harvest House, 1997.

Underhill, Evelyn. *Mysticism: A Study in the Nature and Development of Spiritual Consciousness.* Mineola, NY: Dover, 2002.

Vos, Geerhardus. *Biblical Theology: Old and New Testaments.* Edinburgh: Banner of Truth, 1948.

Watson, Thomas. "The Mystical Union between Christ and the Saints." Online: http://www.reformedsermonarchives.com/wat5.htm.

Wells, David F. *Above All Earthly Pow'rs: Christ in a Postmodern World.* Grand Rapids: Eerdmans, 2005.

Wenger, Thomas L. "The New Perspective on Calvin: Responding to Recent Calvin Interpretations." *JETS* 50 (2007) 311–28.

Whitney, Donald S. *Simplify Your Spiritual Life.* Colorado Springs, CO: NavPress, 2003.

Wiethaus, Ulrike. "Mechthild of Magdeburg (c. 1210 – c.1282), The Flowing Light of the Godhead." In *Christian Spirituality: The Classics*, edited by Arthur Holder, 98–110. New York: Routledge: 2010.

Williams, A. N. *The Ground of Union: Deification in Aquinas and Palamas.* New York: Oxford University Press, 1999.

Williams, Rowan. *The Wound of Knowledge: Christian Spirituality from the New Testament to St. John of the Cross.* London: Darton, Longman & Todd, 1979.

Willis-Watkins, David. "The Unio Mystica and the Assurance of Faith According to John Calvin." In *Calvin: Erbe und Auftrag, Festschrift für W. H. Neuser*, edited by Willem van't Spijker. Kampen: Kok Pharos, 1991.

Wolski Conn, Joann. "Women and Spirituality." In *NWDCS* (2005) 647–49.
Woodward, James, and Stephen Pattison, editors. *The Blackwell Reader in Pastoral and Practical Theology*. Oxford: Blackwell, 2000.
Wright, David F. "Westminster: Reformed or Ecumenical?" In *Reformed Theology in Contemporary Perspective: Westminster: Yesterday, Today—and Tomorrow?*, edited by Lynn Quigley, 162–77. Edinburgh: Rutherford House, 2006.
Yates, G. G. "Spirituality and the American Feminist Experience." *Signs: Journal of Women in Culture and Society* 9:1 (1983) 59–72.
Yeago, David S. "Luther, Martin." In *The Dictionary of Historical Theology*, edited by Trevor A. Hart, 331–35. Grand Rapids: Eerdmans, 2000.
Young, Pamela Dickey. *Feminist Theology/Christian Theology: In Search of Method*. Minneapolis: Fortress, 1990.
Zappone, Katherine. *The Hope of Wholeness: A Spirituality for Feminists*. Mystic, CT: Twenty-Third Publications, 1995.

www.ingramcontent.com/pod-product-compliance
Lightning Source LLC
Chambersburg PA
CBHW060605230426
43670CB00011B/1975